"Nolo's home page is worth b
—WALL STREET JOURNAL

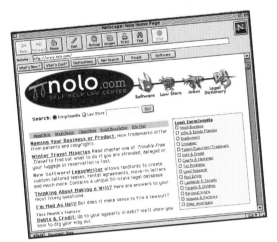

LEGAL INFORMATION
ONLINE ANYTIME
24 hours a day
www.nolo.com

AT THE NOLO PRESS SELF-HELP LAW CENTER ON THE WEB, YOU'LL FIND

- Nolo's comprehensive Legal Encyclopedia, with links to other online resources
- SharkTalk: Everybody's Legal Dictionary
- Auntie Nolo—if you've got questions, Auntie's got answers
- Update information on Nolo books and software
- The Law Store—over 250 self-help legal products including:

    Downloadable Software, Books, Form Kits and E-Guides

- Discounts and other good deals, plus our hilarious Shark Talk game
- Our ever-popular lawyer jokes
- NoloBriefs.com, our monthly email newsletter

Quality LAW BOOKS & SOFTWARE FOR NON-LAWYERS

Nolo Press legal books and software are consistently first-rate because:

- A dozen in-house Nolo legal editors, working with highly skilled authors, ensure that our products are accurate, up-to-date and easy to use.

- We know our books get better when we listen to what our customers tell us. (Yes, we really do want to hear from you—please fill out and return the card at the back of this book.)

- We are maniacal about updating every book and software program to keep up with changes in the law.

- Our commitment to a more democratic legal system informs all of our work.

KEEPING CURRENT

We update our books regularly to reflect changes in the law and in legal procedures. Use our **SPECIAL UPGRADE OFFER** to stay up-to-date. See the back of this book for details.

1ST EDITION

HOW TO CREATE A

BUY-SELL AGREEMENT

& CONTROL THE DESTINY OF

YOUR SMALL BUSINESS

BY ATTORNEYS ANTHONY MANCUSO & BETHANY K. LAURENCE

NOLO PRESS BERKELEY

Your Responsibility When Using a Self-Help Law Book

We've done our best to give you useful and accurate information in this book. But laws and procedures change frequently and are subject to differing interpretations. If you want legal advice backed by a guarantee, see a lawyer. If you use this book, it's your responsibility to make sure that the facts and general advice contained in it are applicable to your situation.

Keeping Up to Date

To keep its books up to date, Nolo Press issues new printings and new editions periodically. New printings reflect minor legal changes and technical corrections. New editions contain major legal changes, major text additions or major reorganizations. To find out if a later printing or edition of any Nolo book is available, call Nolo Press at 510-549-1976 or check our Website at www.nolo.com.

To stay current, follow the "Update" service at our Website at www.nolo.com. In another effort to help you use Nolo's latest materials, we offer a 25% discount off the purchase of the new edition of your Nolo book when you turn in the cover of an earlier edition. (See the "Special Upgrade Offer" in the back of the book.)

This book was last revised in: **April 1999.**

First Edition	APRIL 1999
Editor	RALPH WARNER
Illustrations	MARI STEIN
Book Design	TERRI HEARSH
Cover Design	TONI IHARA
Index	JANE MEYERHOFER
Proofreading	SHERYL ROSE AND JOE SADUSKY
Printing	BERTELSMANN INDUSTRY SERVICES, INC.

Mancuso, Anthony.
    How to create a buy-sell agreement and control the destiny of your
small business / by Anthony Mancuso & Bethany K. Laurence
        p.   cm.
    Includes index.
    ISBN 0-87337-464-9
    1. Small business--Law and legislation--United States--Popular
works. 2. Sale of business enterprises--Law and legislation--United
States--Popular works. I. Laurence, Bethany K., 1968-   .
II. Title.
KF1659.Z9M36 1998
346.73'0652--dc21

                                            98-19262
                                            CIP

Copyright © 1999 by Anthony Mancuso and Nolo Press. ALL RIGHTS RESERVED. PRINTED IN THE USA.

No part of this publication may be reproduced, stored in a retrieval system or transmitted in any form or by any means, electronic, mechanical, photocopying, recording or otherwise without the prior written permission of the publisher and the author.

Reproduction prohibitions do not apply to the forms contained in this product when reproduced for personal use.

For information on bulk purchases or corporate premium sales, please contact the Special Sales Department. For academic sales or textbook adoptions, ask for Academic Sales. Call 800-955-4775 or write to Nolo Press, Inc., 950 Parker Street, Berkeley, CA 94710.

Acknowledgments

Many people at Nolo Press contributed to this book: Our special thanks to Jake Warner, whose encouragement and guidance helped make this book a reality. Major thanks to Terri Hearsh for her patience and hard work in designing and laying out the book and to Toni Ihara for her colorful cover. Also, sincere thanks go to Mike Mansel for reviewing the funding and insurance chapter and to Walter Gibbons for lending a keen eye to the tax law chapter.

Dedication

To Jason, who became my husband somewhere in between the second and third drafts, without whose warm support and tireless tolerance I might not have finished this book, and to my mother and father, who continually encourage me to achieve whatever mark I set my sights upon.

—BKL

About the Authors

Tony Mancuso is a California attorney and the author of Nolo's best-selling corporate law series, including *How to Form Your Own Corporation* (California, Florida, Texas and New York book and computer editions). Tony's recent books include *The Corporate Minutes Book* and *Your Limited Liability Company: An Operating Manual*. Tony is a jazz guitarist and a licensed helicopter pilot.

Beth Laurence, a lawyer and Nolo editor, received her undergraduate degree from Boston University in 1990 and her law degree from University of California, Hastings in 1993. Beth is the editor of several Nolo books, including *Open Your California Business in 24 Hours, Nolo's California Quick Corp: Incorporating Your Business Without a Lawyer,* and *Your Limited Liability Company: An Operating Manual,* among other titles.

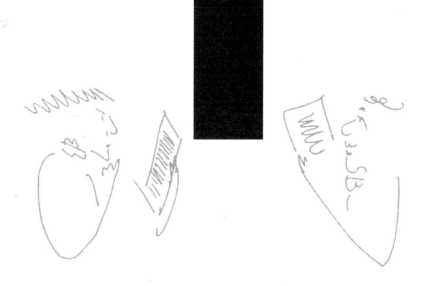

Table of Contents

10 Lawyers, Tax Specialists and Resources

Appendixes

A How to Use the Forms Disk

B Buy-Sell Worksheet

C Buy-Sell Agreement

CHAPTER

1

An Overview of Buy-Sell Agreements

The first days and months of a new business are heady times. As an owner, you have more than enough things to juggle—organizational papers, contracts and tax forms, to mention a few—never mind the actual work to be done. The last thing you have time for is worrying about what will happen when you or another owner retires, divorces, dies or just decides to move on. Unfortunately, it's a huge mistake to ignore the fact that sooner or later your business will lose old owners and gain new ones. And when ownership interests change hands, conflicts often arise that can upset the functioning of a small, closely managed company. If you doubt this even for a minute, quickly skim the following questions:

- What if your longtime friend and business partner gets Alzheimer's disease and his caretaker demands to cash out his ownership interest right away?
- What if your business partner gets divorced and his wife ends up with an ownership interest as part of the divorce settlement? What if she tries to interfere with management to get even with her husband?
- What happens if one of your co-owners becomes alcohol or drug dependent, with the result that her conduct is risking the reputation of the company? Can you kick her out?
- What happens if an older co-owner wants to give half of his interest to his notoriously irresponsible son, who has never worked for the company, and elect him to the board?
- What happens if the majority owner of your company wants to sell her share to a stranger, or someone you know well and can't stand?

The answer to all these dilemmas is the same. If you haven't made a sound agreement to anticipate and deal with these issues before they happen, you're taking a risk that friction will arise between owners who will remain at the company and a new owner or a departing owner. Most of the time, this tension occurs because the continuing owners do not want to be forced to work with and share control of the company with a new and unqualified, inactive or unlikeable owner. (After all, most small business owners own their own business because they want to run things their way, or at least share management with co-owners with whom they can comfortably and easily deal.) When such owner-to-owner tension arises, it can lead to serious personal and business discord, which might even be fought out in court or result in the demise of your company.

To avoid these conflicts, you and your co-owners should arrange matters so you'll be able to collectively control who will own and manage the company in the future. In other words, if someone wants to buy into the company, you and the other owners may want to have a say. If an owner wants to give his share to his kids, you and the other owners may want to have a say. If an owner wants to retire but hold on to his interest, you may want to have a say. That's why it's best to set some ground rules ahead of time. Enter the buy-sell agreement, a way that business owners can plan to deal with ownership disruptions in a way that won't wreck their business, by providing pre-established rules for transferring interests.

Attention inactive, unequal or related owners. This book is geared toward companies with two or more owners who are unrelated, who own roughly equal shares of the business and who actively participate in the day-to-day management or operations of the business. If you are an owner of a family business, where your children or the children of relatives will likely some day take over the company; an owner who owns a small minority or a large majority of a business; or a silent investor in a company, you may have some extra concerns that we don't fully address in this book. If this describes you, be sure to have an attorney look over your agreement. We cover finding expert help in Chapter 10.

A. What Is a Buy-Sell Agreement?

Contrary to popular belief, a buy-sell agreement is not really about buying and selling companies. A buy-sell agreement is a binding contract—between you and your co-owners—that controls when an owner can sell his interest, who can buy an owner's interest and what price will be paid for that interest.

Your buy-sell agreement can provide some general guidelines to be used when the ownership and control of your company is on the brink of change. At a time when many people demand that their work be both profitable and personally meaningful, the most common change might be simply that a co-owner wants to sell out because he feels like doing something else. When an owner is contemplating selling or giving away his interest, a good buy-sell agreement steps in to give the continuing owners some control over the transaction, often regulating who can buy the departing owner's interest and at what price, or, sometimes, whether the owner can sell his interest at all. (We discuss these strategies in Chapter 2, *Limiting the Transfer of Ownership Interests*.)

Usually a buy-sell agreement also gives the company and its owners an opportunity to buy out an owner who has stopped working for the company or has died. By so doing it eliminates the possibility that active owners will be forced to share profits with an inactive owner or an unsuitable new owner. A typical buy-sell agreement gives the company and the owners the right to buy out an owner when:

- an owner decides to retire from active participation in the company, or becomes disabled and is no longer able to actively participate in the company.
- an owner dies.
- an owner's ex-spouse stands to receive an ownership interest in the company as part of a divorce settlement.
- an owner's interest is in danger of being confiscated by creditors (because of a personal bankruptcy or foreclosure of a debt).

We discuss these possibilities in Chapter 3, *Providing the Right to Force Buyouts.*

In addition, some buy-sell agreements also give an owner the right to force the company or her co-owners to buy her interest from her under certain circumstances. A buy-sell agreement typically may give owners this right when:

- an owner decides to retire after a certain period of time, or becomes disabled and is no longer able to actively participate in the company.
- an owner dies, and his estate representative or inheritors want to sell his interest back to the company or the continuing owners.

We discuss these options also in Chapter 3, *Providing the Right to Force Buyouts.*

It is your job (along with your co-owners) to decide which of these provisions you want to include in your buy-sell agreement. After reading this book, which shows you the various buy-sell options and how they can be useful, you and your co-owners will select the buy-sell provisions you think are suitable for your company and your situation. These provisions will later instruct and remind you and your co-owners during an ownership transition how you agreed to handle a potential sale or buy-back situation. You'll select provisions for your agreement clauses depending on several factors, including whether you want to keep your company very small and private, how long you expect your business to last and who you expect to succeed you when you die.

After you check the buy-sell options you think best for your business on your buy-sell agreement and sign it, it will then probably sit quietly in a dusty file until an event happens that causes the company or co-owners to want to buy out an owner, or until you or a co-owner wants to part with his ownership interest. When one of these circumstances occurs, the buy-sell agreement will kick in to protect your current way of doing business.

Family Businesses

Buy-sell agreements are just as crucial for family-owned businesses as they are for companies owned by unrelated business associates. Although some family members may not want to consider the chance that there may be disagreements in the future, the truth is that serious disputes can and often do arise in family businesses just as they do in families themselves. In fact, when it comes time to deal with issues of inheritance, succession and estate taxes, family businesses often have an even more pressing need for a buy-sell agreement. We briefly discuss issues that apply to passing the family business from one generation to the next in Chapter 3, Section D.

B. Why Should You Adopt a Buy-Sell Agreement?

We have briefly mentioned several reasons why it is a good idea for most small business owners to agree in advance on buy-sell provisions. Because it is so important, it makes sense to look at the purposes of a buy-sell agreement in more detail. Put bluntly, if you do not have a buy-sell agreement, here is what may happen:

- You may be forced to work with and share control of the company with an inexperienced or untrustworthy stranger who buys the interest of a departing co-owner.
- You may be forced to work with the spouse or other family member of a deceased or divorced owner. While this might be fine, there is always the substantial possibility that the family member would be inexperienced, bitter, immature or air-headed.
- You may be stuck co-owning the company with a bankruptcy trustee or creditor if a co-owner is forced to file for personal bank-

ruptcy or defaults on a personal loan secured by his ownership interest. This can create business delays and prevent you from getting bank loans.

- If you leave the company or die, you or your survivors may be stuck with a small business interest that no outsider wants to buy and for which no insider will give you a decent price.
- You and your co-owners may argue with a departing co-owner or her inheritors over what price should be paid for the interest that is changing hands, resulting in an angry deadlock that spills over into business operations.

Let's look at how a buy-sell agreement can avoid these situations.

1. A Buy-Sell Agreement Can Control Who Can Own an Interest in the Company

An outsider who gains an ownership interest can disrupt business as usual and trigger major problems in any small company's management. For example, a disagreeable new owner, or simply one with different goals, may not see eye to eye with the existing owners on the election of the management team (board of directors, general partners or limited liability managers); the amendment of organizational documents; or the approval of important management decisions. And since unanimous agreement of all owners is required for certain decisions, a new owner could hold up important company actions. Even worse, an unwanted outsider in a corporation, especially one who buys or inherits a large block of shares, can gain control by electing herself to the board of directors (see the sidebar, "How an Outsider Can Take Control of a Small Corporation"). In an unincorporated business, an outsider can sometimes take control automatically by becoming a majority owner in the partnership or limited liability company (LLC).

How an Outsider Can Take Control of a Small Corporation

An outsider who purchases an ownership interest in a small corporation can sometimes gain control by electing himself to the board of directors. Since shareholders cast one vote per share under normal shareholder voting rules, if a shareholder owns a substantial number of shares, the votes she casts for herself as a nominee to the board can be sufficient to ensure her election (since the nominees receiving the greatest number of votes are elected as board members). And once a person becomes a board member, she becomes an equal participant on the board; unlike a shareholder, whose voting power is proportionate to shareholdings, each board member exercises one vote.

Let's look at how an unwelcome outsider can disrupt a company's management.

EXAMPLE: Cousins Xavier and Yolanda incorporate a small business, with Xavier receiving 55% of the corporation's shares, and Yolanda 45%. Each cousin serves as a director of the corporation. Young, healthy and actively involved in the business, the cousins don't give any thought to creating a buy-sell agreement to cope with what happens if one of them wants to move on. A few years later, after the success of their business had far surpassed initial expectations, Xavier and Yolanda have a falling out over whether to significantly expand the business. To escape from the resulting tension, Xavier sells his 55% interest to Richard, a wealthy investor Yolanda doesn't even know, and sets off to spend his days sailing the sunlit Caribbean.

Richard immediately elects himself to the board of directors. (This is possible because he voted 55% of the total number of corporate shares for himself—enough to outweigh Yolanda's vote for a different nominee to the board.) Being a director entitles Richard to participate equally with Yolanda in management decisions. He immediately proposes laying off several loyal employees in order to maximize short-term profits, with an eye towards making a quick and lucrative sale of the company. This horrifies Yolanda, who is interested in the long-term health and growth of the business. Richard and Yolanda quickly reach an impasse in corporate decision-making and Yolanda files a minority-shareholder lawsuit, trying to unseat Richard. This escalates their personal and professional conflicts, with the result that the company's day-to-day operations practically come to a stand-still.

Now we look at how a buy-sell agreement might work to protect the legitimate interests of small business owners.

EXAMPLE: Let's reroll our cameras and give Xavier and Yolanda another chance. Cousins Xavier and Yolanda incorporate a small business, again with Xavier receiving 55% and Yolanda 45% of the corporation's shares. Even though they are young, healthy and actively involved in the business, they realize they don't know what will happen five years down the road. The cousins create a buy-sell agreement to cope with what happens if one of them wants to move on. A few years later, Xavier and Yolanda have a falling out over whether to significantly expand the business. Realizing he can no longer work efficiently with his cousin since they now have different goals, Xavier decides to sell his shares and move on. Xavier lets the word out that his shares are for sale, and Richard, an outside investor, offers him $10.00 a share for his interest. Xavier shows the written offer to Yolanda. Yolanda is wary of Richard, since she doesn't even know him, and decides she doesn't want to share control of the company with him. So she offers to buy the shares from Xavier herself, for $10.00 a share. Xavier, required by the buy-sell agreement to do so, sells her the shares. Yolanda continues business as usual, managing it as the sole shareholder and director, treats her employees well and lives happily ever after.

To prevent these and other unhappy ownership transitions, a well-drafted buy-sell agreement gives owners the power to prevent outsiders from buying in, or to purchase an owner's interest after he dies rather than allow his inheritors to become owners. We look at the ways a buy-sell agreement can grant these rights in Chapters 2 and 3.

Who Does Not Need a Buy-Sell Agreement?

Almost every business with more than one owner should have a buy-sell agreement. In a few situations, however, a buy-sell agreement may not be necessary. If you are a sole proprietor—you own 100% of a company—you probably do not need a buy-sell agreement, unless you plan on selling the business to an employee who is willing and able to take over (see sidebar, "Life Insurance Funding for Sole Proprietorships," in Chapter 5, Section C1). Or, if you and your long-time, highly compatible spouse (with whom divorce is highly unlikely) own 100% of a company, there normally is little reason to bother creating a buy-sell agreement. It's unlikely that either of you will want to get out of the company unless you both do, and if one of you dies while you still own the business, the other person will probably inherit the ownership interest. Likewise, if you own a small business with a child to whom you plan to leave your share of the business at your death, it may be sensible to forego a buy-sell agreement, and just put your wishes in a will or trust. (Unless your estate may owe estate taxes—see Chapter 9, Section B.) But even here there is always the possibility that your child will die, divorce or want to leave the business before you do, so an agreement still makes sense. In short, there may be some situations where it is highly unlikely you'll need the protection of a buy-sell agreement, but you usually take some sort of risk by not having one.

---

2. A Buy-Sell Agreement Can Provide a Guaranteed Buyer for Your Ownership Interest

Besides protecting your company as a whole, a buy-sell agreement can help you individually, if the time comes when you want or need to sell your ownership interest. Having a buy-sell agreement that provides for forced buyouts can end up protecting you and your family from financial hardship and hard feelings.

It shouldn't come as a surprise that it can be quite difficult to sell a less-than-100% share of a small business. Often it is in fact impossible to find an interested buyer, especially if you're trying to sell a minority interest. Why is this so? Remember that a minority share gives an owner little or no control over how the business is run. Think of it this way: If your dream has been to own and run your own business, would you be likely to settle for a tiny piece of someone else's? Probably not—if you are like most people. As a result, if at some point you want to leave the business but your co-owners won't pay a fair price for your interest, you may be stuck with a share of the company that you can't sell, instead of having cash to spend or invest elsewhere. Same goes for your heirs, if they inherit your chunk of the company.

EXAMPLE: Albin, Bertram and Camelia, co-workers in a large cosmetics company, quit their jobs to form a natural cosmetics corporation. Unfortunately, although they spend a lot of time developing a business plan and organizing their business, they adopt no buy-sell agreement or mechanism to fund a buyout should one of them want to sell out.

Three years after the corporation was formed and just when it is beginning to earn substantial profits, Bertram dies, soon after his fiftieth birthday. His wife and two children each inherit an equal number of his shares. But his wife soon becomes strapped for cash, and his kids, still in college, also need money. Neither his wife nor the kids are interested in continuing the business. Albin and Camelia, knowing Bertram's heirs probably can't find an outside buyer, plead poverty and initially refuse to buy the shares. Bertram's wife and kids are stuck, until they eventually sell their shares to Albin and Camelia, who finally agree to buy them for far less than the share of the business was really worth.

This is not an uncommon situation in small businesses. Often, the last thing family members want to worry about is picking up the business where the owner left off. But families who are grieving the loss of a loved one may also suffer financially, from living expenses, funeral costs and death taxes. In that case, it's helpful for an inheritor who does not want to carry on the business to be able to offer her interest to the company and the remaining owners of the company and be guaranteed that they'll buy it for a fair price.

A good buy-sell agreement can be drafted to require that your company or your co-owners buy your ownership share not only after your death, but in other circumstances as well. For instance, if you have to move out of state for family reasons and want to sell your ownership interest, your agreement could require your company or co-owners to buy your share from you. In effect, this type of provision "makes a market" for your interest where one might not naturally exist. If you and your co-owners don't create a buy-sell agreement, there's no guarantee you or any other owner could find an investor willing to pay you a fair price for your share. We look at these situations more thoroughly in Chapter 3.

3. A Buy-Sell Agreement Can Set a Fair Price and a Workable Method for Paying for and Funding a Buyout

An important part of adopting a well-thought-out buy-sell agreement is setting a price at which ownership interests will be transferred. Without establishing a price for the company in advance—or at least a formula for setting this price—lengthy disputes and lawsuits can arise over the value of an ownership interest. Not only are these disagreements almost sure to result in personal ill will, they may even disrupt the ongoing business to the point that the company loses its edge and is in danger of failing.

It can be difficult to value a small or family owned business. Sure, you can add up the value of property, equipment and accounts receivable, but what about the value of your customer lists and your business's reputation? Should these get factored into the equation? And, of course, whatever number you come up with, a departing business partner is likely to have a different idea of the company's worth: perhaps a price based on the high profit she expects the company to bring in next year.

Likewise, a company that doesn't plan *how* it will pay a departing owner (or his family members) can be in for trouble. Having to come up with a large lump-sum payment out of the blue can cause a company to drown in financial hot waters. These issues can be extremely problematic if they are not determined until the time when the ownership interest has to be bought back.

Fortunately, in addition to providing a way to value an ownership interest, a good buy-sell agreement can set forth the mechanics of a buyout—including the specific payment terms and the source of the funding. For instance, if the holder of an ownership interest wants the company to buy back his interest and pay for it on the spot, your company may need to borrow the cash (of course, some can't) or liquidate assets to make the payment. That's why it's often far better to provide in advance that a departing owner (or his family members) can be paid in installments over a period of years. Another alternative is to tie the buy-sell agreement to the purchase of life or disability insurance for each of the business owners —and then use the proceeds to buy an owner out. Without a funding mechanism and a reasonable payment plan, in some cases your company's only other option might be to file for bankruptcy —something you surely want to avoid.

> EXAMPLE: Imagine the same circumstances as the above example, except this time Albin, Bertram and Camelia create a buy-sell agreement at the outset. The agreement protects the owners' inheritors by requiring the corporation to buy back an inheritor's interest at the agreement price—in this case, a price based on the company's book value. It also provides that a company buyout of an inheritor's stock will be funded with company-purchased life insurance. The life insurance proceeds will keep the remaining owners from having to take out loans or sell assets. And thanks to the buy-sell agreement, Bertram's wife and kids receive a reasonable sum for their shares, at no financial strain to the company.

We discuss funding buyouts in Chapter 5, setting a buy-sell agreement price in Chapter 6 and structuring payment terms in Chapter 7.

C. When Should You Create a Buy-Sell Agreement?

Procrastination is a vice most of us share, and that includes many small business owners, no matter how shrewd they may be. Unfortunately, in the area of business planning, it can lead to their financial undoing. Many owners of successful businesses put off creating a buy-sell agreement— because they don't have time, or they think everything's peachy—until it's too late. In short, no matter what stage you're at in the business game, the time to create a buy-sell agreement is now.

When you're forming a new business, by the time you have the notion that you need to talk about "What happens if...," fatigue has probably set in. Often times little energy is left over for hashing out the provisions of a buy-sell agree-

ment. But the key to a buy-sell agreement is that all owners agree to a reasonable plan early on, before anyone knows who will be most affected by it. Think of it this way: At the outset, each owner's concerns are roughly the same, because no owner knows who will be the first to leave. Or put another way, it's only when no one wants to sell out that everyone has the same interest in creating an evenhanded buy-out agreement that's fair to all owners.

Not coincidentally, the best time to discuss these issues is during the formation stage of your company, when you're already discussing other potentially touchy issues—such as the amount each owner will invest, the salaries each owner-employee will take home and the policies that will guide your company.

New owners sometimes worry that focusing on problems surrounding an owner's leaving casts a shadow over their new business. Just the opposite is true. Fortunately, facing the fact that problems can arise and that negative things do happen can be healthy for your business relationship. Airing concerns, and perhaps a little dirty laundry, often helps you to head potential problems off, or if that's impossible, to be sure they will be handled smoothly without putting your business's survival at risk. In short, knowing that possible changes are covered and planned for can act as a reality check and a stabilizing force.

1. Start Small

Hopefully you've decided not to put off until tomorrow what you can do today, and will dive into creating a buy-sell agreement with us. If your business is brand new and will start small, you and your co-owners probably want to create a very simple buy-sell agreement at the outset. Your agreement should concentrate on giving your company and/or continuing owners the right to buy a selling or departing owner's share at a fixed price, or a price to be set according to a simple formula, such as book or appraised value.

There's no need to spend a lot of time on complex valuation formulas (for example, the capitalization-of-earnings method) at this point. In fact, you couldn't use one of the more complicated formulas early on even if you wanted to—they require that you be in business for a few years. Later, as the worth of your company grows, and as you develop an earnings history, you can refine your valuation formula to reflect changes in the company's assets and earnings.

 Older owners may want to mesh their buy-sell agreement with estate planning needs. If you and your co-owners are forming a new company, are contributing a lot of cash or property and are in your fifties or sixties, you may want to consult an estate planner before you adopt your agreement. In particular, choosing the right valuation formula early on can have a minimizing effect on estate taxes when you or a co-owner dies. We discuss estate taxes as they relate to buy-sell agreements in Chapter 9, Section B.

2. A More Sophisticated Agreement

If you've been in business at least two or three years, you might want to make a more complex agreement now. Same goes anytime one of the following is or becomes true:

- your company's assets are quite valuable, or
- limiting the impact of estate taxes is an issue for older owners (see Chapter 9, Section B).

If one of these statements reflects your situation, plan on making a more developed buy-sell agreement, complete with a detailed valuation method (that includes the worth of your company's goodwill) and a sophisticated way to fund a buyout that takes tax strategies into account. We cover these issues in the chapters to come.

 If you think your circumstances warrant a sophisticated and complex agreement, you'll need a small business lawyer's help. See the tip entitled "Check Your Agreement With an Expert," near the end of this chapter.

D. Where Should You Put Your Buy-Sell Provisions?

No, we don't mean whether you should put your buy-sell agreement in an attic drawer or in a safety deposit box (but a file cabinet will probably do). Here we're talking about what kind of document should hold your buy-sell provisions— a separate buy-sell agreement or an existing document such as your corporate Bylaws, your LLC operating agreement or your general or limited partnership agreement. Because corporations, LLCs and partnerships are such different animals, sometimes we have different advice for owners of these different types of businesses. This is one of those times.

1. Corporations

If you do business as a corporation, you can add your buy-sell agreement to your organizational documents—either your Articles of Incorporation or, more likely, your Bylaws (since changes to your Articles must be filed with the state). Or as an alternative, you can adopt your buy-sell provisions as a separate agreement—often called a shareholders' agreement in the corporate context. This type of agreement is signed by all shareholders and is just as valid and binding on the owners of a corporation as the provisions of corporate Articles and Bylaws.

We believe the latter approach—adopting a distinct agreement—is best. By keeping your agreement separate from your organizational documents and having each owner sign it, you emphasize the importance of its buy-sell provisions. With full disclosure thus assured, an owner can't later claim surprise when she wants to sell to an outsider and her co-owners invoke the terms of the buy-sell agreement.

To adopt the buy-sell provisions as a separate buy-sell agreement, when you're ready, have all shareholders date and sign the agreement at the bottom, using the signature page included at the end of the buy-sell agreement that comes with this book (as a tear-out form in Appendix C and as a word processing document on the accompanying disk).

Refer to your buy-sell agreement in your corporate Bylaws. If you adopt your buy-sell provisions in a separate buy-sell agreement as we suggest, we strongly recommend that you add a provision to your current Bylaws that refers to the existence of your buy-sell agreement (legally this tactic is called "incorporating your buy-sell agreement by reference" into your Bylaws). Doing this helps to cover all the legal bases, and can help avoid a challenge to your buy-sell agreement by someone looking for a legal way out of its enforceability. To do this, amend your Bylaws by adding a sentence that recognizes that a separate agreement exists to control and regulate the ownership of interests in the corporation. One simple way to phrase this new bylaw provision is:

> "The provisions of the agreement among the shareholders dated _[insert date of signing of your buy-sell agreement]_, which regulates the transfer of ownership interests in the corporation and other related matters, is hereby incorporated by reference into these Bylaws and shall be binding on the corporation, its creditors, its shareholders and their assigns and successors and other parties as provided in the agreement."

If, instead, you decide to add your buy-sell provisions to an existing organizational document of the business (such as your Bylaws), simply cut and paste the buy-sell provisions into the existing document, without the signature page. We recommend that you add them to the end of the existing document, but you can insert them anywhere you wish. Of course, when adding these provisions to the document, you will want to change the paragraph numbering or lettering of the buy-sell provisions to conform to the numbering or lettering scheme of your existing organizational document. Remember to have all owners (and their spouses) sign the new agreement.

Whichever approach you take, you'll need to make sure that your buy-sell provisions do not conflict with the existing provisions of your Articles and Bylaws (see the sidebar, "Perform a Consistency Check on Your Buy-Sell Provisions," below). Performing this type of consistency check is a bit of a legalistic chore, and you may want to turn this task over to a lawyer once you've drafted the final version of your buy-sell provisions.

Lastly, if you've amended your Articles or Bylaws—whether you've added the buy-sell provisions directly to one of the documents or you've just "incorporated them by reference"—the shareholders need to approve that amendment. You should meet any special voting requirements under state law and in your Articles or Bylaws for shareholder approval of such an amendment. Shareholder approval to amend your Articles or Bylaws can be obtained in two ways: 1) at a formal shareholders' meeting, documented by written minutes, or 2) by having each shareholder sign a written consent form that says they approve the buy-sell provisions attached to the consent. While not always required under state law or corporate Articles or Bylaws, we also recommend that all directors of the corporation separately approve the amendment also. Just hold a directors' meeting or prepare a written consent for directors to sign as you did with your shareholders.

If these corporate formalities are over your head, or you want a ready-made minutes or consent form to use to approve your Articles or Bylaws amendment, see Nolo's *Corporate Minutes Book*, by Anthony Mancuso.

Another task you'll need to perform after adopting your buy-sell provisions is to update your stock certificates (both the blank ones sitting in your corporate records binder and the certificates that have already been issued to existing shareholders). Specifically, to give notice of the buy-sell restrictions on the shares and the limit on their worth to potential creditors and buyers, you need to add language to each certificate stating that the shares are subject to the terms of a shareholders' agreement. This statement is called a stock certificate "legend," and we show you how to add one to your stock certificates in Chapter 8, Section B.

2. LLCs and Partnerships

For general and limited partnerships, the partnership agreement, and for LLCs, the operating agreement, is the primary (and, usually, only) agreement among the owners of the business. It sets outs the capital contributions of the owners and their rights and responsibilities with respect to each other. For these types of businesses, we recommend you place your buy-sell provisions directly into the partnership or LLC operating agreement.

To accomplish this, simply cut and paste the provisions into the existing organizational document (leaving out the signature page). We

recommend that you add them to the end of the existing document, but you can insert them anywhere you wish. Of course, when adding these provisions to the document, you will want to change the paragraph numbering or lettering of the buy-sell provisions to conform to the numbering or lettering scheme of your existing organizational document.

Before finalizing your agreement, you'll need to make sure that your buy-sell provisions mesh well with the existing provisions of your partnership or LLC operating agreement (see the sidebar, "Perform a Consistency Check on Your Buy-Sell Provisions"). Performing this type of consistency check is a bit of a legalistic chore, and you may want to turn this task over to a lawyer once you've drafted the final version of your buy-sell provisions.

You and your co-owners will then need to approve the additions to your partnership or LLC operating agreement. All current owners (for a limited partnership, this includes general and limited partners) should date and sign the amended agreement. This new agreement, which contains your buy-sell provisions, is your new partnership or LLC operating agreement. If spouses of the owners or any additional nonowners (such as LLC managers) signed the original agreement, make sure they sign the new agreement as well.

If you decide instead to adopt the buy-sell provisions as a separate document, when you're ready, have the owners of the business date and sign the agreement at the bottom, using the signature page included at the end of the buy-sell agreement that comes with this book (as a tear-out form in Appendix C and as a word processing document on the accompanying disk).

For further information on partnership and LLC operating agreements, be sure to check out Nolo's books: *The Partnership Book,* by Ralph Warner and Denis Clifford; *Form Your Own Limited Liability Company,* by Anthony Mancuso; and *Your Limited Liability Company: An Operating Manual,* by Anthony Mancuso.

Perform a Consistency Check on Your Buy-Sell Provisions

Whether you adopt your buy-sell provisions as part of a separate agreement or add them to an existing organizational document, make sure they do not conflict with the current provisions of your organizational documents—your corporate Articles and Bylaws (for corporations) or your current partnership or LLC operating agreement. Mostly, you want to check to make sure an existing provision does not prohibit, or impose additional rules on, any of the buyout procedures covered in your buy-sell provisions. For example, if your corporate Bylaws prohibit the transfer of shares in your corporation, but you check the option in the buy-sell provisions to allow an owner to sell to an outside buyer under certain circumstances (covered in Chapter 2), you will want to amend your Bylaws to delete the restriction on transfers. Similarly, if your LLC operating agreement prohibits an LLC member (owner) from selling an LLC membership (ownership) interest without the approval of all nonselling members, but you check the option in the buy-sell provisions to allow the estate of a deceased owner to force the company to purchase the deceased owner's interest (see Chapter 3), you will want to remove the conflicting restriction on transfers from your LLC operating agreement.

For partnerships and LLCs, working out whether your buy-sell provisions are consistent with the other provisions in your agreement can get particularly complicated and legalistic. The reason is that state partnership and LLC laws contain "default" provisions—rules that apply in the absence of a contrary provision in the partnership or LLC operating agreement—that affect ownership transfer rights in a partnership or LLC. Consequently, many partnership and LLC agreements adopt specific clauses that override, repeat or customize the default state law, and these may conflict with your buy-sell provisions. Here are some of these special state-law based provisions to look out for in a partnership or LLC operating agreement:

Restrictions on Transfer of Full Ownership Rights: One common state default rule is that, in the absence of a contrary provision in a partnership or LLC agreement, a person who is transferred an ownership interest (the legal term is a "transferee" or "assignee") only receives economic rights in the business—that is, a right to receive profits and any distribution of cash or property made by the partnership or LLC. The transferee or assignee does not get any voting or other management rights attached to the interest unless the nontransferring owners approve this at the time of transfer. Obviously, you want future transferees to get the full ownership rights accorded under your buy-sell provisions (our buy-sell provisions provide both economic and management rights to buyers of an ownership interest), without having to obtain the consent of all owners at the time of transfer. If you find a clause in your partnership or operating agreement that requires the approval of all owners for transfers of management rights, you'll probably want to delete it (or have a lawyer make our buy-sell provisions mesh with that requirement).

Termination of Business on Dissociation of Owner: This one is particularly legalistic. The law in some states is that, absent a contrary provision in the partnership or the LLC operating agreement, the business legally dissolves when an owner is "dissociated"—this means when an owner transfers an interest, dies, withdraws, is expelled, files for bankruptcy or otherwise ceases to hold an ownership interest—unless the remaining owners vote to continue the business. Admittedly, this is a bizarre rule. But you will want to check your agreement to see if it repeats this voting requirement. If you find it, you probably will wish to delete it (after checking with your tax advisor to make sure it isn't needed for state income tax classification purposes). If you keep it in your agreement, it will conflict with our buy-sell provision that says the company does not terminate when an owner is "dissociated" (and your partnership or LLC may be subject to automatic legal dissolution whenever an ownership interest is transferred under your buy-sell provisions). (See Chapter 9, Section A4, for a bit more on legal terminations.)

If your partnership or LLC operating agreement is silent on these issues, then you should be fine including your buy-sell provisions in your agreement, at least with respect to these state default rules. Why? Because by including your buy-sell provisions, you are implicitly saying you do not want any state default rules that would interfere with the operation of your buy-sell provisions to apply.

Pay a lawyer to help you check for legal consistency. Finding contradictions and inconsistencies between your buy-sell provisions and your organizational documents is not always an easy task, and as discussed above, can be particularly troublesome when analyzing partnership and LLC agreements. This is one of the times when it makes sense to pay a lawyer to do the dirty work for you. Give the lawyer your proposed buy-sell provisions and copies of your organizational documents, and let her root out any inconsistent language. You have to pay extra for this type of legal scrutiny, but we think it's worth it.

E. How to Use This Book

Throughout the text, we present and explain various provisions you can use to handle ownership transition issues, from deciding which potential problems may affect you and your company to choosing how you'd prefer to handle these dilemmas.

We provide a lot of the legal and tax information you need to make informed choices about the future of your company, including the following major issues that will help you decide on the terms of your buy-sell agreement:

- how to put limits on whom an owner can transfer his interest to (Chapter 2)
- how to provide for forced buyouts in certain circumstances (Chapter 3)
- how to set the procedure for future buyouts (Chapter 4)
- how to fund future buyouts (Chapter 5)
- how to set the price that will be paid for ownership interests (Chapter 6)
- how to set the terms of payment (such as installment plans) (Chapter 7)
- how buy-sell agreements can affect ordinary income and capital gains taxes and estate taxes (Chapter 9).

Throughout the book, after introducing you to these concepts, we advise you in choosing the provisions that are right for your company. To help you keep track of the options that interest you, and any related thoughts you may have, we provide you with a worksheet that follows the order of the chapters and the issues we discuss. Before you start reading Chapter 2, tear out the worksheet from Appendix B, and keep it by your side while you're reading. The text will prompt you to check various options and jot down any relevant notes on your worksheet. Later, when you're filling out the buy-sell agreement we provide (as a tear-out form in the back of the book and as a word processing document on disk), you can refer to the worksheet to refresh your memory.

Icons Used in This Book

Throughout this book, these icons alert you to certain information.

 Fast Track. We use this icon to let you know when you may skip information that may not be relevant to your situation.

 Warning. This icon alerts you to potential problems.

 Recommended Reading. When you see this icon, a list of additional resources that can assist you follows.

 Tip. A legal or common sense tip to help you understand or comply with legal requirements.

 See an Expert. Lets you know when you need the advice of an attorney, accountant or other expert.

 Cross-Reference. This icon refers you to a further discussion of the topic elsewhere in the book.

 Worksheet. When you see this icon, the text will tell you to make a notation or check an option on your worksheet, as explained above.

One practical suggestion: Take it easy. As you read through the book for the first time, you may feel a bit discombobulated by the numerous possibilities that can be covered in a buy-sell agreement. Expect to feel a bit overwhelmed. Not every company needs to cover every contingency. And there's no need to grasp every detail the first time through. Start by reading the entire book to get a rough understanding of what's involved and making a few observations on your worksheet

about what situations or provisions might be particularly applicable to you.

Then spend time considering what you want to happen to your business when you are no longer in charge; creating a buy-sell agreement has important, long-term consequences for you and your family, and your finances. Allow plenty of time for discussions with your co-owners—talk, argue and speculate. When you're ready, go back, focus on the areas of most concern and begin to pin down exactly what you want in your agreement.

When you've made your decisions, you'll be able to transfer your choices from your worksheet to the blank buy-sell agreement we provide. You'll end up with an agreement that can handle all the predicaments that we discussed above, as well as a few more.

 Check your agreement with an expert. While we provide a lot of information, we cannot provide the depth of advice, especially in the tax and estate-planning realm, that a buy-sell or financial planner or a tax expert can provide. And of course, since we don't know you and your particular business, we can't customize an agreement for you that exactly suits your company's and each owner's individual needs, though we do make every attempt to provide different alternatives and tips on customizing your own agreement.

So, in general, we recommend you bring your draft buy-sell agreement to a small business tax or legal advisor before putting your finalized agreement into action. Consultations of this sort are invaluable to make sure that you have considered all the relevant tax angles and the contingencies that apply to your particular business. And, if the needs or circumstances of the owners are substantially different, each owner may wish to check out the tax and estate-planning repercussions with his or her individual tax advisor or financial planner. Although you must pay professional fees for document review and any additional individual consultations with your tax specialist, you'll still save thousands by not asking a small business lawyer or tax advisor to create your buy-sell agreement from scratch. In Chapter 10, we discuss how to find a legal "coach"—a helpful professional who will review your papers and double-check your self-help legal efforts.

Or, if you decide to have an expert prepare your buy-sell agreement, you'll benefit greatly by knowing the critical issues and what your options are. You may want to create a draft of a buy-sell agreement anyway and bring it with you to your first meeting, along with any questions you have—it will help your planner immensely in knowing where you're at and what you want out of an agreement, saving you time and money.

Of course, planning in advance to contend with likely disputes is not the same thing as saying you can prevent change. For good or bad, your ownership situation is almost sure to be different five years hence. The point is that crafting a good buy-sell agreement can make this process as positive as possible, and will help you avoid change's most unfavorable aspects. So, as you read about all the horrible things that can happen to a company and its owners, don't let the specter of changes of ownership and resulting conflicts get you down.

Remember why you started your own business. Doing your own thing allows you to work with people you enjoy and to control your own destiny. A buy-sell agreement will make sure it stays that way. Getting along with your co-owners and making decisions together from the start can make a world of difference in the future of your company. Begin by being frank with your co-owners and family members now—we are confident that reading this book closely with your co-owners will leave you with a comprehensive buy-sell agreement that will protect you and your co-owners for years to come.

Companion Disk

Included at the back of this book is a 3½" PC-formatted computer disk containing files with word processing (rich text format) and text-only versions of the tear-out forms included in Appendixes B and C. For specific instructions on using the forms disk, see Appendix A.

Macintosh Users: Most newer Macintosh computers (with a 3½" SuperDrive) can also read the enclosed disk.

Limiting the Transfer of Ownership Interests

In an age when many people change jobs or even careers a number of times during their adult life and when businesses are opened and closed with head-spinning speed, it's a bit of a risky bet that you and your co-owners will all be doing the same thing even five years from now. Or put bluntly, at some point during the life of your business, you or one of your business's co-owners will probably want to sell your interest in the business, and move on to do something else. For that reason, the most common event that can disrupt a small business involves an owner's wanting to sell or transfer her interest in your company.

A. Transferring Ownership Interests

One way an owner might try to transfer her interest is to sell it to an outside buyer (anyone not a current owner)—assuming she's lucky enough to find one. Another, probably more likely, sales scenario is for one or more of her co-owners to purchase her share (or for the company itself to buy the interest back). Or, an older owner may want to transfer all or part of her ownership interest to a trust, or give it to her children or long-time employees as part of her estate planning. The buy-sell provision we discuss below covers all these scenarios; essentially, it covers any attempt by an owner to transfer an ownership interest in the company—by sale, gift or otherwise.

Whenever an owner contemplates selling or giving away her ownership interest, the management rights that go with it are usually also up for grabs. As we mentioned in Chapter 1, it's important for all owners to plan in advance so these management rights don't fall into the wrong hands, mainly because continuing owners do not want to risk being forced to share control of the company—and possibly even work—with an unknown person or an incompatible person who may be poorly qualified (revisit Chapter 1, Section B for other reasons).

To help you and your co-owners maintain control of your company, it's essential to create in advance an impartial method for reviewing potential ownership transfers and blocking any undesirable ones. The best way to do this is to adopt a buy-sell provision to do one of the following:

- Give the company or co-owners the right to buy an owner's interest before it's sold, given away or otherwise transferred (called a "Right of First Refusal"), or
- Give the company or co-owners the right to approve or veto an owner's transfer of her interest, or
- Place sensible restrictions on who can buy or take over an ownership interest in your business.

Let's look at each type of restriction in more detail, with an eye towards your being able to pick the one that best fits your business.

B. Right of First Refusal

To avoid the scary possibility that an unwanted person might buy (or otherwise be transferred) an interest in your business, most buy-sell agreements very sensibly contain a "Right of First Refusal" provision requiring an owner to first offer his interest for sale to his company and co-owners before selling it or transferring it to anyone else. Depending on the needs of your company, you may want this type of restriction to apply only when an owner considers transferring his interest to an outsider. But there can also be reasons why you might want this type of restriction to apply when an owner is considering transferring his interest to an insider—a current owner.

Voluntary transfers only. Realize that our Right-of-First-Refusal provision only applies to a voluntary, lifetime transfer of an interest by an owner by sale, gift or otherwise, not to a court-ordered transfer to an ex-spouse as part of a divorce, to a transfer to an owner's estate or beneficiaries upon death or to other *involuntary* transfers. Other buy-sell provisions in our agreement, discussed in Chapter 3, cover these additional types of transfers.

1. What If an Owner Wants to Sell Her Interest to an Outside Buyer?

Should a co-owner have the unconditional right to transfer his interest in the business to someone who is not already an owner of the company? Although at first thought you might be tempted to say, "Why shouldn't an owner be able to do whatever he wants with his interest?"—think again. Consider that if you happen to be one of the continuing owners in the company, you'd almost surely be horrified if a co-owner were to sell out to an unqualified, uninformed or just plain ornery new owner, who—even if she purchased a minority share—would have much power to make your life miserable. And, of course, things would be far worse if an outsider stood to gain a majority interest in your company, since this would give her an opportunity to all but take your company away from you.

> EXAMPLE: Brothers Frank and Eldon, along with Eldon's wife, Ethel, open a boutique computer store and service business. They create a corporation with each relative owning a one-third stock interest and each serving as a board member. No buy-sell agreement is prepared. A few years later, after the service part of the business has become very successful, they receive a favorable buyout offer from a competitor—an owner of a chain of inexpensive computer stores. Frank has no interest in selling his shares—he wants to keep the business in the family and eventually have his daughter Emily succeed him. Eldon and Ethel, on the other hand, have been looking forward to early retirement and jump at what they see as a golden opportunity to cash out. Since neither the corporate law in their state nor the corporation's Bylaws require the approval of all owners to a transfer of an owner's shares in the corporation, Eldon and Ethel quickly sign a contract to sell their two-thirds ownership in the company to the chain operator. The new owner quickly votes her newly acquired, two-thirds controlling interest to elect herself and her husband to fill the two recently vacated board seats. Frank is left with a one-third interest in a business that he can no longer run independently.

While putting an absolute ban on transfers of ownership interests would prevent an outsider from being able to buy into the company, we think it's a poor idea. Banning an owner from selling her interest can lock an owner into owning a chunk of the business when she is no longer interested in helping it to succeed, or when she no longer gets along with her co-owners—both situations that can't be healthy for the company. (We discuss banning sales briefly in Section C, below.)

Rather than banning or restricting transfers to outsiders outright, a more reasonable way to regulate these sales is to adopt a "Right-of-First-Refusal" provision. As mentioned above, this type of provision gives the company, and usually the continuing (nontransferring) owners individually, the choice to buy—or not buy—a co-owner's interest before an outsider is allowed to make a purchase or otherwise receive an interest in the company. If the continuing owners decide they do not want to work with a prospective new owner, the company or the owners individually can exercise their right to buy the transferring owner's interest. On the other hand, if the owners approve of the transferee (the person to whom the interest will be transferred), they can elect not to buy the co-owner's interest—essentially, approving the transfer.

Our Right-of-First-Refusal clause provides that either the company or the continuing owners can buy an owner's interest to stop the transfer of an owner's interest. In the case of a corporation, if the corporate entity, rather than the continuing owners, buys an owner's shares, it "cancels" them, which means the remaining owners' percentage of ownership in the company increases accordingly. Similarly, in the case of partnerships and LLCs, if the company buys the departing owner's interest, that interest is "liquidated." Compare this to the situation where the remaining shareholders, partners or LLC members decide to individually buy the transferring owner's interest. When this happens, the transferring owner's shares or interest is not canceled or liquidated, but is reallocated among the remaining owners.

> EXAMPLE: Kate, Nancy and Lisa own and operate a small, member-managed LLC as equal one-third owners. Kate decides she wants to leave the LLC, and finds a willing buyer who signs a written offer to buy her LLC interest for cash. If the LLC, under the Right of First Refusal in its buy-sell provisions, buys back Kate's interest, Nancy and Lisa become equal one-half owners of the business after the purchase. The same percentage result occurs if Nancy and Lisa both decide to individually buy back one-half of Kate's interest.

In Chapters 4 and 9 we discuss the procedure and issues (mainly tax advantages and disadvantages) relating to who the buyer will be—the company or the continuing owners. For now, just understand that it's best to use a procedure that allows for both approaches (ours does), leaving the determination as to who should be the buyer to be made at the time of a buyout.

Here are the details of how our Right-of-First-Refusal provision works with respect to potential sales of an interest by an owner to an outsider. (We discuss how our clause covers sales to insiders and gifts of interests—the two other most common types of transfers—later in this chapter). When an owner receives an offer from an outsider to buy his ownership interest, a Right-of-First-Refusal provision requires that owner (let's call her the "transferring owner") to submit written notice to the company of her intent to sell her interest, along with the terms of the proposed sale. (A signed copy of the outsider's offer must be attached to the notice—more on this requirement below). The company and the continuing owners then have an option to buy the interest (at the same or a different price than that offered by the outsider, depending on which price option is checked in the buy-sell agreement—also discussed below).

If the company and the continuing owners decline to purchase all of the transferring owner's interest, the transferring owner is free to sell her interest to the outsider. The transferring owner must, however, transfer her interest to the outsider within 60 days, at the same price and terms stated in her Notice of Intent to Transfer, or she must start the whole process over again before transferring her interest. For example, if the transferring owner wishes to lower the price to be paid by the outsider for her interest, or wishes to change other terms of the sale to the outsider to more favorable terms (for example, a lower interest rate on installment payments, or a longer payment term), she must submit to the company a new notice and copy of the new offer—essentially starting the process over again for the transfer of the interest under the new terms.

On the other hand, if the company and/or the continuing owners decide they do want to purchase the entire ownership interest, the outsider is out of luck. The company and/or the continuing owners then buy the interest from the transferring owner within a certain period of time.

> EXAMPLE: Jason, Tim, Chris and Bart are four equal shareholders and directors of a small travel-adventure corporation called Run-a-Muck. Jason wants to sell his shares to an outsider, Kacey. According to the Right-of-First-Refusal provision in their corporate buy-sell agreement, Jason must first get a signed written offer from Kacey, then notify the corporation of his intent to sell his shares to Kacey. The terms of the proposed sale must be included in the notice, with a copy of Kacey's

offer attached. Jason's notice of proposed sale presented to the corporation is simple, and it reads as follows:

> I, Jason Abercrombie, propose to sell 250 shares in Run-a-Muck to Kacey Gardner within 60 days of the date of this notice for $2,500.00 cash ($10.00 per share). Payment of the purchase price by Kacey Gardner is to be made in cash on the date of the transfer. A copy of the offer to purchase these shares on these terms, signed by Kacey Gardner, is attached to this notice.

Run-a-Muck's Right-of-First-Refusal provision states that the corporation and the continuing shareholders have 60 days from receipt of the notice to purchase all of Jason's shares. If they don't elect to purchase the shares, Jason is free to sell them to Kacey according to the terms of Kacey's offer. Faced with Jason's notice of a proposed sale, Tim, Chris and Bart promptly meet as board members and decide that Run-a-Muck, Inc. itself will purchase Jason's shares, shutting Kacey out of the company. Run-a-Muck then buys and cancels Jason's shares.

 Not every buyer is a bum. We focus here on what happens if the continuing owners don't want to allow a sale to an outsider, in which case they or the company itself will try to buy out the transferring owner. But in the real world, the continuing owners may think highly of a person who wants to buy the transferring owner's share. And, of course, there can be a real incentive for the continuing owners to allow a new owner to buy in, since it means they won't have to reach

---

Section II: Limiting the Transfer of Ownership Interests

☐ **Option 1: Right of First Refusal**

(a) No owner ("transferring owner") shall have the right to sell, transfer or dispose of in any way any or all of his or her ownership interest, for consideration or otherwise, unless he or she delivers to the company written Notice of Intent to Transfer the interest stating the name and the address of the proposed transferee and the terms and conditions of the proposed transfer. Delivery of this notice shall be deemed an offer by the transferring owner to sell to the company and the continuing owners the interest proposed to be transferred.

   If the proposed transfer is a sale of the owner's interest, these terms shall include the price to be paid for the interest by the proposed transferee, and a copy of the offer to purchase the interest on these terms, dated and signed by the proposed transferee, shall be attached to the notice.

(b) The company and the nontransferring owners then have an option, but not an obligation (unless otherwise stated in this agreement), to purchase the interest proposed for transfer, and may do so within the time and according to the procedure in Section IV, Provision 1 of this agreement.

   If the company and the nontransferring owners do not elect to purchase all of the interest stated in the notice, the transferring owner may then transfer his or her interest to the proposed transferee stated in the notice within 60 days after the end of the nontransferring owners' purchase option, according to the procedure in Section IV, Provision 1 of this agreement.

Excerpt 1

into their own pockets to pay the transferring owner or ask their company to pony up the cash.

The Right-of-First-Refusal clause included in our buy-sell agreement is shown in Excerpt 1, above.

If you are interested in requiring this Right of First Refusal option before an owner can transfer his interest, check Option 1 on your worksheet now. (Section II, Option 1.)

a. Price of the Ownership Interest

What about price? How much should a transferring owner be paid for her share? Often a Right-of-First-Refusal provision gives the company and the nontransferring owners the right to purchase the transferring owner's interest at the price the proposed buyer is willing to pay (assuming the interest is being sold, not gifted). In other words, they've got to match this price or allow the sale to take place.

One potential problem with this approach is that a disaffected owner may be tempted to solicit a phony outside bid, perhaps from a good friend or relative, to prod her co-owners into buying her ownership interest at an inflated price. To help cope with this possibility, our Right-of-First-Refusal provision requires that a written offer for the purchase of an ownership interest, signed by the proposed buyer, be attached to the transferring owner's Notice of Intent to Transfer. Of course, this is no real guarantee that the offer is genuine, but at least it makes the purported buyer sign a commitment to buy the interest—most people will not want to sign such a statement unless they truly intend to buy the interest.

You can also require a down payment. Some owners may want to go even further and require that the proposed buyer tender a significant down payment to the transferring owner as evidence of good faith, and that the transferring owner present evidence of this payment (check,

money order) with the copy of the signed, written offer presented to the company. This may seem like an excess of caution to many, but it can help avoid the problem of an owner's soliciting a written "offer" from a relative or close friend of the seller who is not serious about purchasing.

You can avoid this problem altogether by having your agreement provide that the company or continuing owners can buy an owner's interest under a Right of First Refusal at the "Agreement Price"—a price predetermined in the buy-sell agreement itself (we cover the Agreement Price in Chapter 6). In short, even if the transferring owner receives a higher offer from the outsider, she must sell to the company or the continuing owners at the agreement price, if they so desire. This variation has the virtue of protecting the continuing owners from being forced into business with an outsider who is willing to pay an inflated price— one that the continuing owners can't afford or aren't willing to match. Of course, this provision is weighted heavily toward the interests of the continuing owners and is less favorable to a transferring owner, who could end up selling her interest for less than it's really worth.

Using the agreement price can help avoid estate taxes. In limited circumstances, there is an additional reason to require the transferring owner to sell at the agreement's predetermined buyout price, rather than requiring the company or continuing owners to match an outsider's price. By requiring any and all departing owners to sell out at the Agreement Price, you take a big step towards establishing a reasonable value for the company for estate tax purposes. (Estate taxes are the taxes that may be owed to the government upon a person's death.) See Chapter 9, Section B3, Rule 3, for more on this.

The options in our agreement that cover the price to be paid by the company and the continuing owners when exercising their Right of First Refusal are shown in Excerpt 2.

(c) Price and terms

☐ **Option 1a: Price and terms in offer**

If the proposed transfer is a sale of the owner's interest, the company and the nontransferring owners shall have the right to purchase the interest of the transferring owner only at the purchase price and payment terms stated in the Notice of Intent to Transfer submitted to the company by the transferring owner. The price and terms in this notice override the general Agreement Price selected in Section VI of this agreement and the agreement terms selected in Section VII.

If the proposed transfer is a gift of the owner's interest, the company and the nontransferring owners shall have the right to purchase the interest of the transferring owner at the Agreement Price selected in Section VI and according to the manner of payments and other terms of the purchase as established in Section VII of this agreement.

☐ **Option 1b: Price and terms in agreement**

The company and the nontransferring owners shall have the right to purchase the interest of the transferring owner at the Agreement Price selected in Section VI and according to the manner of payments and other terms of the purchase as established in Section VII of this agreement.

Excerpt 2

 If you checked Option 1, "Right of First Refusal" in Section II, also:

- check Option 1a if you want your Right-of-First-Refusal clause to require the company and the nontransferring owners to match any amount offered by a buyer, or
- check Option 1b if you want your Right-of-First-Refusal clause to require the company and the nontransferring owners to pay only the buyout price set forth in the agreement and not be bound to match any amount offered by a buyer.

b. Effect on Minority Owners

If you are a minority owner, it's especially important to understand that a Right-of-First-Refusal provision alone does not guarantee you'll ever be able to sell your interest—either to an outsider or to your co-owners. In fact, this type of provision can have the effect of preventing a minority owner from selling her interest (except to the company or the majority owners at a dirt-low price).

Here's why. A Right-of-First-Refusal provision is only triggered when you get an offer from someone who wants to buy your interest. But for most types of small businesses, there is a very thin—or often no—market for minority interests. In short, a minority owner may find it virtually impossible to find a buyer who will make a legitimate offer for her interest at anything but a flea-market price. And if a minority owner can't get an offer, he can't trigger the contractual provision that allows the company or the nontransferring owners to buy his interest. To guarantee that you'll be able to cash out your interest, it's important to also include a "Right-to-Force-Sale" clause in your buy-sell agreement (discussed in Chapter 3).

The flip side of the coin is that, for minority owners, a Right-of-First-Refusal provision may not even fulfill its main purpose—to give the owners the ability to control the ownership of their company. That's because all Right-of-First-Refusal provisions rely on purchasing power to regulate transfers of interest. Because of lack of company or personal funds, minority owners armed only with a Right-of-First-Refusal provision may not be able to prevent a majority owner from selling to a proposed buyer. Put bluntly, if the company itself or the minority owners don't stand a chance of being able to pony up a healthy sum to buy out the majority owner, their Right of First Refusal doesn't mean much. They could be stuck with a new controlling owner who is a tyrant, a competitor or simply an inactive owner who will reap the benefits of their work. This is a good example of why minority owners should check with a small business attorney to investigate the pros and cons of any Right-of-First-Refusal provision before signing a buy-sell agreement.

Check with your attorney. Again, most of our advice is tailored to small businesses where the owners own largely equal shares of the company, and where all actively participate in the company's day-to-day operations. If you are a minority owner, be sure to have an attorney look over your agreement. We cover finding expert help in Chapter 10.

2. What If an Owner Wants to Sell Her Interest to a Current Owner?

As mentioned above, when an owner tries to sell his small business interest, he may not have much luck finding an outsider who's willing to make an offer. A situation where a co-owner buys an owner's interest—let's call that an interowner transfer—is more likely.

Many companies allow co-owners to transfer their interests between themselves freely—without being subject to a Right-of-First-Refusal or other buy-sell provision. After all, a transfer to a current owner would not bring a stranger into the ownership ranks—the current owners already share management duties with each other. But in

situations where there are more than two owners, there's another reason to establish rules governing interowner transfers. Without rules, there is no mechanism to prevent one or two co-owners from snapping up a transferring owner's share, grabbing control of the business. Here's how this can happen:

EXAMPLE: Serena, Petra and Alex start a small corporation that sells mailing lists, with each owning 333 shares of the 999 shares that were initially released. They do not create a buy-sell agreement. After suffering through several management quarrels with Petra, and deciding that the work is not personally meaningful to him, Alex decides he wants to cash out his interest and go to cooking school. Needing a large chunk of change for tuition, he secretly negotiates a deal with Serena, who agrees to buy his shares without telling Petra, for whom Alex and Serena have developed a general distaste. The result is that Serena is able to purchase all of Alex's interest without Petra knowing, and ends up with a total of 666 shares and control of the company. Poor Petra no longer has a say in managing the company.

To avoid situations where an equal owner suddenly and surprisingly becomes a majority owner, you can have your Right-of-First-Refusal clause apply to sales to current owners as well as outsiders. In other words, you can give *all* co-owners the right to buy an owner's interest whenever it is offered for sale to a current owner. The language that covers this choice in the agreement is shown in Excerpt 3.

 If you checked Option 1, "Right of First Refusal," in Section II, also:

- check Option 1c if you want your Right of First refusal to apply to sales to outsiders and current owners alike, or
- check Option 1d if you want your Right-of-First-Refusal clause to apply only to sales to outsiders.

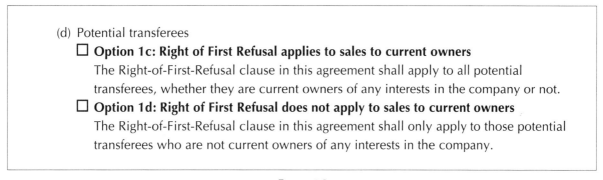

(d) Potential transferees
- ☐ **Option 1c: Right of First Refusal applies to sales to current owners**
  The Right-of-First-Refusal clause in this agreement shall apply to all potential transferees, whether they are current owners of any interests in the company or not.
- ☐ **Option 1d: Right of First Refusal does not apply to sales to current owners**
  The Right-of-First-Refusal clause in this agreement shall only apply to those potential transferees who are not current owners of any interests in the company.

Excerpt 3

3. What If an Owner Wants to Give Away Her Interest (or Put It in a Trust)?

There are two common approaches a buy-sell agreement can take with regard to gifts of ownership interests and transfers to trusts. One, your agreement can make gifts of ownership interests and/or transfers to trusts subject to the same Right-of-First-Refusal provision that sales are subject to. Two, your agreement can exempt gifts and/or transfers to trusts from the Right-of-First-Refusal procedure, essentially giving owners free rein to give away their ownership interests.

a. Estate Planning and Living Trusts

Let's first take a brief look at estate planning in the context of why allowing owners the flexibility to give away their ownership interests freely, or to put them into trusts, may be important to you and your co-owners.

One aspect of estate planning is avoiding probate. Probate is a costly and time-consuming court process during which a deceased person's will is proved authentic, all property subject to the will is inventoried and appraised and relatives and creditors are notified. Finally, the property is distributed to the people entitled to inherit it. Probate can take months or even years and can

cost as much as 5% of the value of the probated property. If the family members or business partners of a deceased owner have to wait one or more years to gain title to their ownership interests from a probate court, business can grind to a halt. For this reason, keeping ownership interests—and the controlling voting power and management of the company—out of probate is essential to ensure the smooth transition of the business. Estate planning, or, specifically, giving away part or all of your ownership interest or putting it into a probate-avoidance living trust before you die (see below), can avoid the hassles of probate.

Another equally important aspect of estate planning is reducing or eliminating federal estate taxes. Federal estate taxes are a form of inheritance or death tax, which are taken from your estate after you die. Whatever property you leave behind, including an ownership interest in a small business, is subject to federal estate taxes—although the federal government generally exempts the first $650,000 (increasing to $1 million by 2006) from the tax (and, if you're very lucky, your business may qualify for the federal family business estate tax deduction—discussed in Chapter 9, Section B2). To oversimplify greatly, giving away part of your ownership interest to family members in $10,000 chunks each year is one excellent method of avoiding estate taxes. (We discuss estate taxes more fully, including whose estate may incur them and several common methods of eliminating or lowering them, in Chapter 9, Section B.)

Putting an ownership interest into a living trust can be an integral part of avoiding probate and, sometimes, estate taxes. Here's how probate-avoidance living trusts work: When a business owner is at an age where estate planning becomes practical, he signs his ownership interest over to a legal entity called a trust. The business owner is the trustee of the trust and has control over the ownership interest, just as if he owned it in his own name. Upon his death, the ownership interest is transferred to the beneficiaries of the trust—usually the owner's spouse and/or children—without having to go through probate. Also, certain tax-avoidance trusts, such as "marital" or "AB" trusts, are a routine way for couples to plan to reduce estate taxes. (Tax-avoidance living trusts are discussed further in Chapter 9, Section B2.)

Because putting ownership interests in living trusts usually doesn't threaten the company or the continuing owners with an actual change of ownership—it's really just a paper transfer—many companies exempt from the Right-of-First Refusal an owner's transfer of his interest to a trust, as long as the following conditions are met:

- the power to revoke the trust remains with the grantor (the owner of the interest), and
- the grantor (the owner of the interest) is a trustee of the trust.

If, however, the owner ceases to be a trustee of the trust (for example, a new trustee takes over

because the owner becomes mentally incompetent), the new trustee would control the owner's interest, and be able to vote on the management of the company. Therefore, this change should be considered an ownership transfer that causes the Right-of-First-Refusal clause to kick in, giving the company and the other owners the right to buy the interest back.

Our Right-of-First-Refusal covers transfers to trusts in subsection (e) of Option 1. It is shown in Excerpt 4.

If you want transfers to trusts to be *exempt* from the Right-of-First-Refusal, you do not have to do anything. If you want transfers to trusts to be *subject* to the Right-of-First Refusal, you can simply cross out subsection (e), or remove it from your word processing file. (Section II, Option 1.) If so, make a note to do this on your worksheet.

(e) This Right-of-First-Refusal provision shall not apply to an owner's transfer of an ownership interest to a trust as long as the following conditions are met:
  i) the power to revoke the trust remains with the grantor (the owner of the interest), and
  ii) the grantor (the owner of the interest) is a trustee of the trust.
       If either of the above conditions ceases to be true, this change will subject the ownership interest to this Right-of-First-Refusal.

Excerpt 4

b. Restricting Gifts of Ownership Interests

The provision allowing transfers to living trusts above does not address the matter of gifts—giving ownership interests to relatives or long-term employees, usually for estate planning purposes. Our Right-of-First-Refusal clause does not exempt gifts (which, unlike living trusts, do actually transfer ownership) from the Right-of-First-Refusal procedure. In other words, any owner who wants to give away part or all of his interest must first submit a Notice of Intent to Transfer the interest to the company, giving the company and the nontransferring owners a chance to buy the interest. We recommend this approach because most owners do not want their co-owners to be able to transfer their interest to outsiders without any kind of oversight or approval process—even if the outsiders in this case are children or other relatives. The reasons for this are the same as for restricting any transfer—mainly so that you don't have to work with and share control of the company with a new, untested owner (see Chapter 1, Section B for other reasons). Supplying the company and the continuing owners with the discretion to allow or disallow such gifts allows those whose livelihood could be affected by ownership changes to make that decision.

Our Right-of-First-Refusal clause works with respect to proposed gifts in almost the same way as it does for proposed sales. Before giving part or all of her interest away, the owner who is considering giving a gift of her interest (the "transferring owner") must give notice to the company of the proposed transfer, including the proposed recipient's name and address. However, the provision says that in this case the price and terms at which the company or the nontransferring owners can purchase the interest are the standard agreement price and terms established in other sections of the buy-sell agreement (we cover the Agreement Price in Chapter 6). If the company and the other owners decline to purchase the ownership interest, the transferring owner is free to give away her interest. But if the company or other owners decide they don't want the transfer to go through, they must pay the owner for the interest according to the price and terms in the agreement. Keep in mind that, if the company or the nontransferring owners buy the interest, the transferring owner will probably have cash available from her sale proceeds that she is free to give away to relatives for estate planning purposes.

Many older business owners want the ability to plan their estates to best avoid probate and estate taxes, and so should beware of how a buy-sell agreement can hinder an estate plan unless it is properly drafted. If you are of an age where estate planning is high up on your to-do list, you should have your estate planner look over your buy-sell agreement before you sign it, to make sure it won't conflict with your estate-planning goals.

If you want gifts of ownership interests to be subject to the Right of First Refusal discussed above, you don't need to check anything on your worksheet or change anything in the buy-sell agreement.

c. Allowing Unrestricted Gifts of Ownership Interests

Knowing that the ability to give gifts is key to estate planning, you and your co-owners may not be comfortable parting with the right to give away your interests to whomever you please. (Of course, in allowing the unchecked gifting of ownership interests, owners give up some of their collective control over the ownership of the company.) If you and your company choose not to place restrictions on the transfer of owners' interests to their family members, you can simply check a box in your agreement so that the Right-of-First-Refusal provision does not apply to gift-giving. The option from our agreement is shown in Excerpt 5.

☐ **Option 2: Transfers to relatives can be made without restriction or approval notwithstand-ing any other provision in this agreement.**

Excerpt 5

If you are interested in allowing owners to give away their ownership interests to their relatives freely, not subject to a Right of First Refusal, check this option on your worksheet now. (Section II, Option 2.)

C. Absolute Transfer Restrictions

Just saying "no" to the possibility of all ownership transfers, including gifts and sales to outsiders and current owners, is obviously another way that owners can keep control of company ownership. But we don't normally recommend this all-or-nothing approach. Not only is it inflexible, but also, barring all transfers under all circumstances doesn't reasonably balance the desires of an individual owner with those of the continuing owners. Just the same, because this approach may work well in a few situations, we discuss it briefly.

A complete ban on the transfer of ownership interests prevents any owner from selling, gifting or otherwise transferring her interest (unless, of course, her co-owners agree to change or ignore the buy-sell agreement later). A similar clause that has the same effect—called "No Transfers Without Consent"—requires an owner to get the approval of her co-owners before selling to an outsider or making other transfers. No question, either of these provisions gives a huge amount of power to the other owners; they really can "just say no" to the owner who wants to sell, without even having to buy his interest. (At least with the Right-of-First-Refusal clause, discussed above, the continuing owners have to fork out some cash to stop a transfer, meaning it's less likely they'll disallow a sale on a whim.) One nasty result of a No-

Transfers-Without-Consent clause may be that the majority owners withhold their consent to a sale and then pressure a minority owner to sell his ownership interest to the company or to them at an unfairly low price.

It's unwise to overly restrict sales of ownership interests. If, despite your care-fully crafted buy-sell agreement, a court dispute ever arises about whether an owner can sell an interest in her company to an outsider, the court is likely to scrutinize a restrictive buy-sell clause carefully. A court may hold the clause to be unenforceable if it concludes it puts too great a limit on an owner's right to sell. Specifically, the courts dislike buy-sell provisions that make it difficult for an owner to sell her interest in the company to anyone for a reasonable price. (Believe it or not, lawyers call this an "unreason-able restraint on alienability.") In at least some states, courts have refused to enforce strict prohibitions on the sale of ownership interests. (But the Right-of-First-Refusal clause that we discussed in Section B, above, has been held to be reasonable by most courts.)

A restriction that provides a little more flexibility is a clause that provides for "Transfers to Qualified Buyers Only." Here, you and your co-owners have the opportunity to define the term "qualified buyer" in advance in your buy-sell agreement. For example, your agreement could require a potential buyer to hold a license for a particular profession or have a certain number of years of experience in your particular field. But keep in mind that while this restriction protects the nontransferring owners from having to share management with an obviously unqualified person, most business owners feel that it doesn't offer them adequate protection. The other owners have no right to veto a sale to a new owner who, despite having a dozen degrees and loads of experience, may still be a flake or a jerk.

The opposite of this restriction is a "No-Transfers-to-Certain-Persons" clause. Typical uses of this type of provision would be to prohibit a sale to a "competitor," to any "existing owner" who would then own a share greater than 50% or to any buyer whose purchase would jeopardize a key tax election or violate state law. For example, if your company is an S corporation—a corporation that made a tax election with the IRS to be taxed more or less as a partnership—you may prohibit a sale to a non-US citizen, a corporation or a partnership, all of whose ownership would terminate S corporation tax treatment. This type of restriction is normally legal as long as you do not prohibit transfers to outsiders based on discriminatory or unreasonable criteria such as a buyer's race or sex.

Here are a few samples of such transfer restrictions:

☐ **No Transfers Without Consent**
No owner shall sell, transfer or in any way dispose of any of his or her ownership interest or any right or interest in the company without obtaining prior written consent of the company and of all other owners.

☐ **Transfers to Qualified Buyers Only**
No owner shall sell, transfer or in any way dispose of any of his or her ownership interest or any right or interest in the company except to a buyer or other proposed transferee who has _____ *[insert qualifications, such as "five years, full-time experience in selling real estate"]* .

☐ **No Transfers to Certain Persons**
No owner shall sell, transfer or in any way dispose of any of his or her ownership interest or any right or interest in the company to a buyer or other proposed transferee who is *[insert restricted class, such as "an existing owner who would, after such transfer, own 50% or more of the company"]* .

⚠ **These transfer restrictions are not included in our buy-sell agreement.** Since we remain unconvinced that these clauses provide flexible and intelligent solutions for controlling the ownership of small companies, we do not include them in our agreement. (A Right-of-First-Refusal clause does a good job of restricting ownership in most cases.) If you are interested in using one of the clauses, get the advice of a small business lawyer or other expert before you do so. We cover finding expert help in Chapter 10. ■

CHAPTER

3

Providing the Right to Force Buyouts

Over the course of its business life, your company will probably experience a few bumps in the road, and maybe even a pothole or two. Many of the resulting, unwelcome jounces will involve the business itself, such as problems with sales, employees or product quality. But often the most troublesome shocks will occur when an owner's personal situation changes from when he started or joined the company. In this chapter we look at some of the common life changes that can upset any business, and we discuss ways your buy-sell agreement can be structured to avoid, or at least cope with, such predictable upheaval.

A. Why Provide the Right to Force the Sale of an Ownership Interest?

In Chapter 2 we discussed how a buy-sell provision can control or prevent an owner from selling, gifting or otherwise transferring his interest when he wants to. In this chapter, we discuss events—usually changes in an owner's life—that can upset the functioning of a small, closely managed company. For example, if an owner becomes disabled or loses his needed vocational license, or simply retires, the fortunes of all owners will be affected. Other events, like an owner's divorce, death or personal bankruptcy, which can cause the owner's business interest to be transferred to an outsider, can also be traumatic, for both the affected owner and the company as a whole. For instance, if an owner gets divorced, she might be forced to give her ex-husband half of her owner-ship interest as part of their divorce settlement, or, if an owner files for bankruptcy, the bank-ruptcy trustee may take over all of her ownership interest. (Again, note that these situations, which involve involuntary transfers, are distinct from those where an owner simply wants to sell or give away her share, which we covered in Chapter 2.)

1. Restoring Control Over the Company's Ownership

One common reaction to a disruptive ownership change is for the company or the continuing co-owners to want to readjust the ownership of the company to restore it to something closer to what it was before the change in circumstances upset the status quo. For instance, in the case where an ownership interest is transferred to an ex-spouse or a bankruptcy trustee, the company or co-owners understandably might want the right to buy back that interest, to able to restore control to the original owners of the company. Similarly, should an owner no longer be able to work, perhaps because he has become disabled, lost his license or retired, the company or continuing co-owners might want the right to purchase ("buy out") his interest, to keep control of the company in the hands of active owners.

Not every ownership change is bad. In planning to limit the possibly damaging effects of a change in ownership, don't be too paranoid. Sometimes a change in ownership is just what's needed to pep up a sleepy or flagging business. It may work out that everyone is happy with whatever new ownership situation comes about. If so, no reshuffling is necessary.

Many times these disruptions are handled in a collegial fashion, with the company or continuing co-owners simply agreeing to buy out the share of the departing owner (or his estate), and the departing owner (or his estate) agreeing to sell out at a fair price. But it's also common that owners don't see eye to eye. For example, perhaps a retiring owner, an ex-spouse or an inheriting son demands an outrageous price for his interest, threatening to sell to an outsider if the lump-sum amount isn't promptly forthcoming. No question, bickering over the terms of a buyout, or even whether one should occur, can use up a lot of the company's important time and, should lawyers become involved, money. Such disputes can also weaken bonds between ongoing owners and even lead to the failure of a company. In these cases and others like them, a lot of grief can be avoided if one owner or group of owners can simply turn to their buy-sell agreement to force a buyout at a pre-established price. The continuing owners as a group then might be able to force an unwilling owner to sell his interest to them (only under certain circumstances), or a departing owner could force the company or continuing co-owners to buy his interest.

To plan to avoid bitter fights over ownership in the future, it's best for all owners to adopt these rules for forced buyouts well in advance of the need to use them. Usually when the business is being formed or in its early days, no owner knows whose circumstances will change first—or how they'll change—so it's usually not difficult to do this. Since each owner could be the first or last to leave, all are motivated at that time to adopt an even-handed agreement.

2. When a Situation Calls for a Forced Buyout

While all sorts of specific events can trigger or call for a change in the ownership of a company, a few broad scenarios are likely to affect most small businesses. In the rest of this chapter we consider the common types of business-disrupting events and discuss the various ownership transition issues that arise with each one. To prepare you to choose the most appropriate buy-sell provision to deal with each type of scenario, we also explain and present ways to provide for forced buyouts, including those that offer:

- the option for your company and its owners to purchase an ownership interest from an owner or her estate or her family members under certain circumstances (called an "Option to Purchase an Owner's Interest"). Here, the company and the continuing owners have the right, but not the obligation, to purchase all or part of a departing owner's

interest within a certain time period, at the price and terms that are pre-established elsewhere in the buy-sell agreement. (In other words, the company and continuing owners can force a departing owner to sell out.)

- the *obligation* of the company or its owners to buy out an ownership interest from an owner or her family members under certain circumstances, if the departing owner or his family members so request. Here, the departing owner may demand that the company or the continuing owners buy his ownership interest. The company or the continuing owners then must purchase all or part of the retiring owner's interest within a certain time period, at the price and terms that are pre-established elsewhere in the buy-sell agreement. (In other words, a departing owner can force a buyout by the company or the continuing owners—that's why we call this optional clause a "Right to Force a Sale.")

Of course, as you read this material you'll want to think about the ownership transition problems that are most likely to occur in your company. Then, as you prepare your buy-sell agreement, you'll want to be sure you address not only the several types of ownership transition problems likely to be faced by lots of small businesses, but also the specific issues that concern you. Remember, you can include any or all of our clauses and options, or custom-tailor them to fit your situations.

All buyout provisions must contain important details, such as the price to be paid for ownership interests (or a formula to calculate that price), terms for payment (an installment plan, for example) and often a source of funding (for example, life and disability insurance). We discuss the details of these issues in Chapters 5, 6 and 7.

Our forced buyout provisions provide that, in any potential buyout situation, either the company or the continuing owners may buy a departing owner's interest. What happens if the company itself buys an owner's interest? In the case of a corporation, the shares would be cancelled, and the remaining shareholders' percentage of ownership in the company would increase accordingly. Similarly, in partnerships and LLCs, if the company itself buys an owner's interest, the interest would be liquidated.

In Chapter 4 we discuss the procedure for deciding who the buyer will be—the company or the continuing owners. We also discuss the issues —mainly tax advantages and disadvantages—that will affect that decision. For now, just understand that it's a determination that will be made jointly by the company and the continuing owners at the time of a buyout.

Now let's jump into the scenarios that can cause business disruptions, and discuss possible solutions for each.

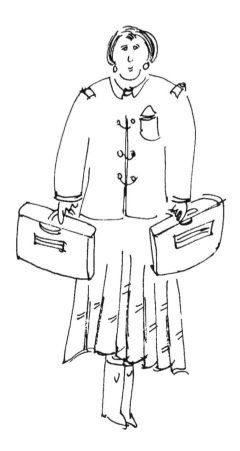

Majority Owners Beware

Most of our advice is aimed at companies that were started by several owners with roughly equal power. But when a controlling owner runs the business along with one or more small minority owners, things change a bit. A majority owner may not want to be subject to the same restrictions that the minority owners are subject to. And indeed, there is no rule that says all owners must be treated alike in the buy-sell agreement (except perhaps as they pertain to estate taxes—we discuss special requirements of buy-sell agreements regarding estate taxes in Chapter 9, Section B3).

For instance, a majority owner may want her children, but not the minority owners' children, to be able to take over the business after her death. In that case, she wouldn't want the company or the remaining owners to be able to force *her* children to sell their interest subject to an Option-to-Purchase provision. (We discuss this scenario in Section D, below.)

If you are a majority owner and want to avoid being restricted under a certain provision, you'll want to suggest to your co-owners that you will add a sentence at the end of the provision saying: "This section applies only to owners of less than 50% of the interests in the company." (Note that if you do this, the agreement price will not set the value of the ownership interests for estate tax purposes. We discuss setting the value for estate tax purposes in Chapter 9, Section B3.)

And of course, as a majority owner, you should consult a small business legal expert before signing a buy-sell agreement. Otherwise you may give up important elements of control unintentionally and unnecessarily.

B. What If an Owner Wants to Retire or Stop Working?

At a time when some people hope to retire in their 50s, and when many of us will change fields several times, it's common for an owner to simply stop working for your company.

1. Option of Company and Continuing Owners to Purchase a Retiring Owner's Interest

Most, but not all, of the time, an owner who wants to leave will also want to take his marbles (cash) with him—usually by having the company or the continuing owners buy out his interest. But sometimes an active owner (as opposed to a passive investor) who wants to retire or stop working for the company also wishes to retain all or part of his ownership stake. In some situations this may be just what the continuing owners want, since this allows them to keep the retiring owner's capital in the business and means they don't have to come up with money for a buyout. But in other situations the remaining owners may hate this arrangement, reasoning that they don't want a passive investor to reap the benefits of their continuing hard work.

One thing is sure, it's hard to know how one owner's deciding to retire or quit will be viewed in the future. A lot will probably depend on whether the departing owner and the remaining owners are on good personal terms. But just because you can't predict the future doesn't mean you shouldn't prepare for it. The best approach is to establish an orderly legal framework to answer the following questions:

- If an owner wants to leave the company, can he just walk away, taking his ownership interest with him?
- Or does an owner who puts your business in her rearview mirror have to sell her ownership interest to the company or the remaining owners if they wish to her out? If so, what price is she entitled to?

While there is no one right answer to these questions, on balance it's usually best to provide that, when an owner quits her active duties, whether as an officer or employee, the company and the continuing owners have the option to purchase her interest. If you doubt this, consider what might happen if a departing owner stops working for your business under less than amicable circumstances and is poised to make trouble for management. Even if circumstances are initially friendly, tensions may eventually arise between the active owners, who may be working long hours to build up the company, and an inactive owner, who may still want to have a say in things and retain her right to a share of the profits.

EXAMPLE: Andromache and Eddie leave their management positions at a large software company to form a small custom-programming shop (Scripts Are Us). They convince a programmer, Mark, to work with them by offering him a minority interest in the new company. After two years, during which Scripts Are Us is modestly successful, Mark and the majority owners no longer see eye to eye on product development issues. As a result, Mark quits to follow his own dreams.

In the absence of a buy-sell agreement, Mark can—and does—refuse to sell his minority interest to Andromache and Eddie, apparently believing that even though they are not as farsighted as he is, Scripts Are Us is likely to enjoy a profitable future. Unfortunately, Mark doesn't go quietly into the night. Instead, Mark's continual kibitzing becomes a constant annoyance to Andromache and Eddie, who particularly resent his periodic demands to inspect the company's books. Finally, after several nasty spats at shareholders' meetings over the reinvestment of profits, Mark brings a lawsuit against Andromache and Eddie claiming they breached their "fiduciary duty to him as a minority shareholder."

No question that Andromache, Eddie and Mark would have been far better off if, at the time their business was formed, they'd adopted a buy-sell agreement covering the eventuality that one of them might cease to be active in the business—specifically, one that provided the company and the continuing owners with an option to buy a retiring owner's interest. Such a provision doesn't *obligate* the company or the continuing owners to purchase the departing owner's interest, but it gives them that option. We include a clause that provides for this in our buy-sell agreement. It's called an "Option to Purchase" clause, and it is shown in Excerpt 1, below.

Not for silent investors. If your company is owned by both inactive, "silent" investors and actively participating owners, this buyout option may not suit your needs. (If an investor was not working in the first place, retirement should not change his situation with regard to the company.) Since most of our advice is tailored to small businesses where the owners are active in the business, we don't deal in detail with the special needs (or problems) of investors. If you face this situation, be sure to have an attorney look over your agreement. We cover finding expert help in Chapter 10.

If you are interested in giving the company and the continuing owners the option to buy a retiring owner's interest, check Option 1 on your worksheet now. (Section III, Scenario 1.)

How much of an owner's interst can be bought? You can require that the company or continuing owners buy either all of the retiring owner's interest or none of it with an Option to Purchase. But this can lead to undesired results. For example, if the company and continuing owners can only afford to buy half of the retiring owner's interest, they would end up with none of it. For this reason, our agreement allows the company and continuing owners to buy any or all of the retiring owner's interest.

Section III: Providing the Right to Force Buyouts

Scenario 1. When an Active Owner Retires or Quits the Company's Employ

☐ **Option 1: Option of Company and Continuing Owners to Purchase a Retiring Owner's Interest**

(a) When an owner voluntarily retires or quits the company's employ, he or she is deemed to have offered his or her ownership interest to the company and the continuing owners for sale. The company and the continuing owners shall then have an option, but not an obligation (unless otherwise stated in this agreement), to purchase all or part of the ownership interest within the time and according to the procedure in Section IV, Provision 1 of this agreement. The price to be paid, the manner of payments, and other terms of the purchase shall be according to Sections VI and VII of this agreement. An owner who stops working for the company is referred to as a "retiring owner" below.

Excerpt 1

2. Right of Departing Owner to Force a Sale

Rather than having trouble buying out a departing owner, it's far more likely that, when a co-owner decides to leave a business, she'll be anxious to sell her interest, either to an outsider or back to the company or the continuing owners. If she has no luck finding an outsider to buy her interest, she'll probably approach the company and the continuing owners. Sometimes the company or the continuing owners may be happy to buy the departing owner out—perhaps the company is now quite profitable and the remaining owners are pleased to increase their shares. Or, perhaps the departing owner is leaving precisely because she wasn't getting along with the other owners and they're glad to see her go, even if it means they have to pay her for her share of the company. In these and other workable circumstances, an ownership buyout is normally a fairly straightforward situation. Once the deal is done, it's business as usual with one less owner.

But it's not always so simple. What if the remaining owners don't want to, or can't afford to, buy a departing partner out? In this situation the question often becomes: Can the departing owner force the continuing owners to purchase his share? As you've probably guessed, the answer is: not unless there is an agreement requiring it. To adopt a buy-sell provision that will deal with this situation, you and your co-owners should ask yourselves a simple question: Do you want an owner (who, after all, could be any of you) to be able to force the company and the continuing owners to buy her interest if she decides to leave?

Especially if you're a minority owner, your answer is likely to be yes. It can be hard enough to sell a majority interest in a small business, but it can be next to impossible to sell a minority stake—or even a 50% share.

EXAMPLE: Luis and Marta are equal partners in a successful burrito shop that caters to the business lunch crowd. After a few years of long hours and hard work, Marta decides she wants to sell her interest to Luis and get a job where she can work shorter hours and spend more time with her kids. Luis, who feels personally abandoned, is reluctant to further stretch his already tight finances and is worried about competition from a new deli that is about to open in the area. He shrugs and says he's not interested in buying Marta's interest. Since she and Luis didn't sign a buy-sell agreement, Marta has to search for an outside buyer. She hires a business broker and spends money advertising, but finds out that no one wants to buy only half of a burrito shop. Potential buyers want the whole enchilada or nothing. After looking for a buyer for months, Marta finally ends up selling her share to Luis's cousin for far less than it was worth.

One way to deal with a problem like Marta's would be to include a buy-sell provision that requires either the company or its remaining owners to buy out an owner who wants to leave—no ifs, ands or buts. This type of clause—we call it a "Right-to-Force-a-Sale" clause—can protect a departing co-owner (who, after all, may be leaving as the result of personal or financial distress) by guaranteeing a buyer for his ownership interest. The clause included in our buy-sell agreement that covers this option is shown in Excerpt 2.

If you are interested in giving a retiring owner the power to force a sale of her interest to the company and continuing owners, check Option 2 on your worksheet now. (Section III, Scenario 1.)

All or none of the interest can be offered. Note that our Right-to-Force-a-Sale provision does not allow a retiring owner to require the company and the continuing owners to buy a portion of her interest. A retiring owner can request the company and continuing owners to buy all of her interest or none of it.

☐ **Option 2: Right of Retiring Owner to Force a Sale**

(a) When an owner voluntarily retires or quits the company's employ, he or she can require the company and the continuing owners to buy all, but not less than all, of his or her ownership interest by delivering to the company at least 60 days before his or her departure a notice of intention to force a sale ("Notice of Intent to Force a Sale"). The notice shall include the date of departure, the name and address of the owner, a description and amount of the owner's interest in the company and a statement that the owner wishes to force a sale due to the owner's retirement as provided in this provision. The procedure for purchase of the ownership interest shall be according to Section IV, Provision 2 of this agreement. The price to be paid, the manner of payments and other terms of the purchase shall be according to this section and Sections VI and VII of this agreement. An owner who requests that his interest be purchased is referred to as a "retiring owner" below.

Excerpt 2

⚠ **Not for silent investors.** Again, most of our advice is tailored to small businesses where the owners all actively participate in the company's day-to-day operations. If you are an inactive investor, be sure to have an attorney look over your agreement. (We cover finding expert help in Chapter 10.) Generally, if your company is owned by both inactive, "silent" investors and actively participating owners, this clause may not suit your needs. (After all, if an investor was not working in the first place, retirement alone should not allow him to force a buyout.)

No question, this type of provision allows all co-owners lots of leeway in deciding if and when to leave the business. But also consider that personal flexibility is not necessarily a good thing for your company or for the owners who are left behind when one owner quits. Leaving aside the fact that it may weaken all owners' commitment to their company, it creates the real possibility that one or more owners will demand to be cashed out precisely at a time when the company is doing poorly or needs every bit of its cash for another purpose, such as expansion.

Recognizing that a required buyout may be highly problematic, you may decide to head in the opposite direction and say that a departing owner can never force the company or other owners to buy him out. But, of course, that brings you right back to the worry you started with: the possibility of getting stuck forever owning a share of a business you no longer want, or selling your share at a huge discount because you're so desperate to get out. This prospect is so unattractive—and potentially unfair—that it can even lead to horrendous results.

EXAMPLE: Dakon and Jed each contribute $20,000 of their savings to open a climbing-gear store in Colorado. To purchase inventory and cover other start-up costs, they also take out a bank loan. From the start they are successful enough to pay the bills and eke out small salaries, but not much else. Near the end of the first year, Dakon tells Jed he wants out of the business and would like his $20,000 back—running a business, it turns out, doesn't give him enough time to hit the peaks. Jed can't figure out a way to give Dakon his investment back without selling off badly needed inventory at fire-sale prices (and perhaps having to close the shop). Refusing to do this, he tells Dakon that he can't take his money out of the business so soon and on such short notice. This angers Dakon—after all, he has worked hard at low pay for almost a year! So one night Dakon grabs what he guesses is $20,000 worth of climbing gear from the store, loads it into his Jeep and takes off. On the counter he leaves a note saying that the store now belongs 100% to Jed. Left with inadequate inventory, Jed can't pay the store's debts and has to file for bankruptcy. Of course, Jed has a claim against Dakon, but with Dakon off climbing mountains in Chile, Jed is unlikely to collect anything.

You can include both Option 1 and Option 2 for retiring owners in your agreement. It's possible, and perfectly valid, to include both Option 1—option for the company and continuing owners to buy out a retiring owner—and Option 2—a retiring owner's right to force a sale—in your agreement. For practical purposes, however, you and your co-owners will probably adopt a buy-sell agreement that either leans toward protecting the long-term interests of the company as a whole to control ownership of the company (and uses Option 1) or that protects the interests of individual owners to be able to cash out their interests (and uses Option 2).

a. Providing Disincentives to Leaving Early

Although it's impossible to prevent a business associate from acting as badly as Dakon did, you can reduce the likelihood that this will occur, while at the same time not going to the other extreme of allowing an owner to demand her money back at any time. To accomplish this, it's usually best to tailor your Right-to-Force-a-Sale clause to let an owner cash in her interest only after a reasonable period of time. For instance,

your clause can require the company to buy out an owner only if he has been an active owner in the company three years or more. Or, you could provide that if an owner leaves before the expiration of a required time period, the company will be required to buy him out, but only at a lowish price (say, 50% of the business's appraised value). This makes it clear to the owners that, by going into business, they are making a financial commitment to stick it out until the business becomes profitable—if they don't, they may lose all or part of their investment.

EXAMPLE: Let's reroll our cameras and give Jed and Dakon a legal framework designed to cope with change. Knowing that Dakon is highly susceptible to the call of the wild, early on Jed raises the subject of what would happen if one of them becomes unhappy with the business and wants out. They jointly decide that to get the business past its start-up pains, each must make a minimum two-year commitment. To enforce this point, they adopt a buy-sell clause stating that if one of them decides to leave during the first year, the other will buy him out at a price that is 40% of the standard buyout price set in the agreement. If one of them leaves during year two, he gets 60% of the agreement price. Only if a co-owner stays with the business into the third year is he eligible to force a purchase for 100% of the full agreement price.

The good news is that Dakon, realizing he is committed, hangs in for almost three years, at which point Jed has no trouble borrowing the money to buy Dakon's share for 100% of the Agreement Price.

Choosing the required time period. The length of time you choose for a departing owner to receive 100% of the agreement price can vary with your type of business. For example, if yours is the type of business likely to take five or more years to fully establish, you may want to pay a departing owner 100% of her interest's value under your buy-sell agreement only after this period is over.

There are, of course, times when an owner really needs to leave and be cashed out, as opposed to simply wanting to bail out to do something else. For example, an owner with a sick child may need to move closer to a particular medical center, or an owner whose own health is declining may be advised to quit working. In situations like these, should the departing owner be subject to the same discounts or punishments that would apply to an owner who leaves his spouse and runs off to the Cayman Islands? If your answer is no, you'll probably want to draft an agreement providing that an owner who leaves for a short list of personal or family reasons is entitled to a better deal than an owner who leaves on a whim.

EXAMPLE: Let's rewind one more time. Dakon and Jed are running their climbing-gear business with a solid buy-sell agreement in place that outlines what will happen if one of them leaves the business. Dakon learns that his elderly mother has severe multiple sclerosis. He decides he has to move back east to help out his parents. Even though he and Jed have only been in business less than a year, Dakon points out that in case of a serious illness of a co-owner's spouse, child or parent, their agreement provides that a departing owner is entitled to 100% of the agreement price for his interest.

The language included in our buy-sell agreement that gives you a choice of disincentive options, one with a release clause in case of injury or illness and one without, is shown in Excerpt 3.

If you want a retiring owner to receive a discounted price if he leaves within a certain time period for any reason, check Option 2a on your worksheet. (Section III, Scenario 1, Option 2.) If you want a retiring owner to receive a discounted price if he leaves within a certain time period, *unless he is leaving because of a*

(b) Disincentive option

☐ Option 2a: Disincentive period, with illness/injury exception

If a retiring owner gives notice that he or she wishes his or her ownership interest to be bought before the end of _[insert number of months, such as "24"]_ , months of ownership of the company, he or she is entitled to receive only _[insert percentage, such as "50"]_ % of the Agreement Price for the sale of ownership interests in this company under this agreement, unless he or she is required to leave because of serious personal illness or injury or the serious illness or injury of a spouse, parent or child, in which case he or she is entitled to 100% of the Agreement Price.

☐ Option 2b: Disincentive period, without illness/injury exception

If a retiring owner gives notice that he or she wishes his or her ownership interest to be bought before the end of _[insert number of months, such as "24"]_ months of ownership of the company, he or she is entitled to receive only _[insert percentage, such as "50"]_ % of the Agreement Price for the sale of ownership interests in this company under this agreement.

Excerpt 3

personal or family illness or injury, check Option 2b on your worksheet. If you check one of these options, also:

- insert the amount of time an owner must be with the company before being able to sell out for the full Agreement Price, usually at least one or two years, maybe more.
- insert the amount of the discount to be taken off the Agreement Price if an owner leaves before the end of the required time period.

Having a flexible payment plan for buyouts often allows continuing owners to pay a selling owner a higher price. You may be wondering how Jed could afford to pay Dakon 100% of the agreement price after being in business less than a year. As you'll see in Chapter 7, the best way to accomplish this and most other types of sudden buyouts without bankrupting the business is to pay a departing owner in installments over several years. When a death or disability is involved, planning in advance to fund a buyout with insurance is also an option. We cover funding in Chapter 5 and payment plans in Chapter 7.

b. Requiring Advance Notice of Intent to Leave

Another smart way to ease the burden of a forced buyout is to require an owner who wants to quit or retire to give the company advance notice of her intention to leave (except in the case of death or sudden illness or disability, of course). In some companies, requiring a six- to twelve-month advance notice is often considered reasonable. Our agreement requires a 60-day notice. This should be adequate time for the remaining owners to take a collective deep breath and devise a plan to buy out the owner and continue the business. Of course, if you and your business partners think you'll need more notice, you can change the agreement to reflect this.

If you are interested in providing for a longer notice period, make a notation on your worksheet to change this time period. (Section III, Scenario 1, Option 2, Paragraph (a).)

Be Ready to Customize Standard Clauses to Fit Your Situation

Throughout this book we provide technical language and options to solve common buy-sell situations. But since every situation contains its own nuances, you may want to tinker with our clauses and clause options to be sure your agreement fits like a custom-made glove, not a one-size-fits-all handcuff. For instance, as noted in the text, a well-drawn buy-sell agreement will balance the desire to protect each owner in case of personal problems with the need to protect the financial integrity of the business. We've talked about several ways to approach this balance. But only you and your co-owners know what's best for your company.

If you want to provide a market for a departing owner without overburdening the company, and aren't satisfied with the options we suggest, such as requiring advance notice, a lower price for leaving early and an installment payment plan, you can create your own contractual language. For example, a customized Right-to-Force-a-Sale provision might state that the departing owner must first try to find an outside buyer for her interest who is acceptable to the other owners. Assuming no buyer comes forward after six months, your agreement could then provide that the company or the continuing owners must purchase the departing owner's interest, at a price discounted by 20% of the full Agreement Price. This discount gives the departing owner some incentive to find an outside buyer first, and lessens the immediate financial burden on the company and remaining owners.

C. What If an Owner Becomes Mentally or Physically Disabled?

The next business-disrupting event we consider and help you plan for is the possibility that an owner becomes disabled. Disability, of course, includes physical injuries and illnesses, but also can be caused by mental illness, such as clinical depression, Alzheimer's disease and other forms of dementia or incapacity. Below, we discuss how your agreement can deal with the tricky question of whether an owner is truly "disabled."

 Disability and retirement buyout clauses should be looked at together. If an owner feels he cannot work and wants to be bought out, but does not fit under a doctor's or the disability insurance company's definition of disability, arguments can arise. These conflicts can often be defused in advance if you have also adopted a clause allowing an owner to force a sale due to retirement (discussed in Section B2, above).

1. Option of Company and Continuing Owners to Purchase a Disabled Owner's Interest

What happens if an owner becomes injured, develops a chronic illness or is otherwise unable to participate in company affairs for an extended period of time? If the owner is an investor and was never involved in the day-to-day operations of the business, the answer may appropriately be: "nothing"—after all, it probably makes little difference to the company whether an inactive investor is or isn't disabled.

But assume the owner has been active in the business and draws a salary from it. For an owner who can no longer work but draws a regular paycheck, there are obvious reasons why the other co-owners might sooner or later want to replace her. Of course, after a decent interval the co-owners could stop the salary of the disabled owner (who, after all, is no longer earning it), but

allow him to continue to own his share of the business. But the co-owners of a small company may not want to share future successes and management decisions with an owner who is no longer adding anything to the company. In this situation, the co-owners might want the right to buy out the disabled owner.

Absent this right, there can be highly emotional disagreements when a disabled owner does not want to be bought out (he may even disagree as to whether he is unable to perform his duties). It is because of the debilitating nature of these disputes that you absolutely need to have a disability-triggered buy-sell provision in place. Normally you'll simply want to adopt a clause that allows the company and the other owners to be able to require a disabled owner (or the owner's conservator, guardian or other legal representative) to sell her ownership interest back to the company or to the other owners on demand. This protects the nondisabled owners of the company from having to share management with someone who can't handle the requirements of the job, or simply from having to support that person.

EXAMPLE: George has been a partner of a printing company for ten years, along with his longtime friends Martha and Stew. Now in his 70s, he frequently experiences significant lapses of memory. More than once his forgetfulness has led to an unfinished job, and unhappy clients have begun to whisper to Martha and Stew that they no longer want to work with George. He admits he is sometimes forgetful, but he insists that he is fit to continue working. But when they almost lose their biggest client, Stew and Martha face the truth that George is not mentally up to continuing to work. Since George is a general partner entitled to an annual share of the company profits, the only sensible way to stop him from receiving 1/3 of the company's profits is to ask him to sell out. But when confronted by Stew and Martha, George refuses, threatening to get a lawyer. Martha and Stew rue the day, ten years before, when they didn't insist on a buy-sell agreement dealing with disability as a condition of starting the business with George.

⚠ Not for silent investors. If your company is owned by both inactive, "silent" investors and actively participating owners, this buyout option may not suit your needs. (If an investor was not working in the first place, disability should not necessarily give him the right to force a buyout of his interest.) Again, since most of our advice is tailored to small businesses where the owners are active in the business, we don't deal in detail with the special needs of investors. If you face this situation, be sure to have an attorney look over your agreement. We cover finding expert help in Chapter 10.

As you can see from the example, a big issue you'll have to face and provide for in your agreement is when an owner is truly disabled. Normally, in this context, your agreement should specify that the owner must be "totally disabled"—unable to perform most or all of his duties in your company. In addition, your agreement should include a clear procedure to determine when an owner is considered disabled, such as employing the opinion of the owner's doctor. Or, if your agreement will require disability insurance to fund the buyout of a disabled owner (discussed briefly below and in more depth in Chapter 5), you may want to use your insurance company's definition of "total disability" and provide that the insurance company is the arbiter of whether the co-owner really is totally disabled. An added bonus of going that route is that the other owners will be relieved of the burden of supervising the disability claim and asking the disabled owner for medical evidence of a disability.

After you decide to adopt a disability provision, the next issue you'll want to consider is: Will the company or the nondisabled owners be able to come up with the money to buy a disabled owner out? After all, most small to mid-sized businesses need every penny they can scare up to maintain

or expand their business—they don't have a ready store of cash to fund a buyout. As you have probably guessed, one way to cope with this problem is to call for a long-term installment plan, allowing the company or continuing owners to make partial payments to a disabled owner over a number of years. But for larger companies, especially, there is a better way to cope with this issue that doesn't make the disabled owner wait many years to be paid off for her interest. Your buy-sell agreement can require the purchase of disability insurance for all co-owners. This way, if a disability occurs, the insurance policy proceeds will provide a source of funds to allow the company or the co-owners to buy back the interest of a disabled owner without diminishing company or personal cash reserves. If desired, additional financial benefits such as a wage continuation plan for the disabled owner can also be funded by disability policy proceeds. (We discuss using insurance to fund your agreement in more detail in Chapter 5.)

There are several additional issues you should consider to ensure that your disability clause has the maximum chance of working well:

- Your agreement should establish a period of time—a waiting period (or in insurance lingo, an elimination period)—over which an owner's disability must persist before a buyout can occur. This allows for the fact that the owner might recover. We recommend that your waiting period be at least six months, or perhaps as long as a year. A buyout attempted before it's really clear that the owner probably won't recover can result in bitterness and wasted time and money, especially if the former owner recovers. And it is also sensible to provide that time spent off work by an owner with a series of illnesses with the same or related causes can be added up to fulfill the waiting period requirement. Otherwise, requiring six months to a year of *continuous* inability to work might discourage an injured or ill individual from returning to work if he's feeling better (perhaps to test whether going back to work would be feasible). Of course, if your agreement will require the purchase of disability insurance policies to fund the agreement, your elimination period should coincide with that in the insurance policies.

- Your agreement should also specify how and when the buyout price will be determined. When it comes to determining the price, this is usually done following the same formula as if the co-owner quits, dies or retires (the standard buyout Agreement Price is discussed in Chapter 6). But "when" the price is determined is usually addressed as a separate issue in the disability provision.

Here's why: There may be a significant difference in the worth of the company in between the date the owner became unable to work and the date the disability waiting period is over. Most agreements use the date the owner stopped working as the date to value the business—since that is the date the owner stopped contributing to the company. This way, any changes in the worth of the company can be attributed to the remaining owners.

The clause included in our buy-sell agreement to cover a situation when an owner becomes unable to work is shown in Excerpt 4.

Scenario 2. When an Owner Becomes Disabled

☐ **Option 1: Option of Company and Continuing Owners to Purchase a Disabled Owner's Interest**

(a) When an owner becomes permanently and totally disabled, and such disability lasts at least _insert number of months, such as "six"_ months (the "waiting period"), either consecutively or cumulatively, he or she is deemed to have offered his or her ownership interest to the company and the continuing owners for sale. The company and the continuing owners shall then have an option, but not an obligation (unless otherwise stated in this agreement), to purchase all or part of the ownership interest within the time and according to the procedure in Section IV, Provision 1 of this agreement. The price to be paid, the manner of payments and other terms of the purchase shall be according to this section and Sections V and VI of this agreement.

An owner is considered disabled when he or she is unable to perform his or her regular duties. If disability insurance is used to fund a buyout under this provision, the insurance company shall establish whether an owner is disabled; without disability insurance, the owner's doctor will establish whether an owner is disabled. An owner who becomes disabled according to this section is referred to as a "disabled owner" below.

(b) Price

You must check either Option 1a or Option 1b below if you checked Option 1 above.

☐ **Option 1a: Date disabled owner stops working**

The Agreement Price as selected in Section VI of this agreement shall be established as of the date the disabled owner first stopped working.

☐ **Option 1b: Date of buyout**

The Agreement Price as selected in Section VI of this agreement shall be established as of the date of the proposed buyout of the disabled owner's interest.

Excerpt 4

 If you are interested in giving the company and the continuing owners the option to buy a disabled owner's interest, check Option 1 on your worksheet now (Section III, Scenario 2), and insert the amount of time an owner must be disabled before the company has the option of buying out his interest, at least six months to one year. If you check Option 1, either check Option 1a to establish the Agreement Price when the disabled owner first stops working, or check Option 1b to establish the Agreement Price as of the date of the buyout.

2. Right of Disabled Owner to Force a Sale

You may have noticed that we haven't mentioned the needs of the disabled owner himself. It's possible that a situation may arise where you or another owner becomes unable to work but the other owners don't jump to buy you out, most likely because they don't have the necessary funds. In this situation, a disabled owner without a salary and who does not automatically draw a percentage of profits from the company will probably be anxious to be bought out. (And even if the disabled owner is entitled to a percentage of profits after she stops working, that draw will no doubt decrease, as the profits of a small company will likely drop soon after one of the owners stops working for it.) To avoid being locked into a business in whose profits they can no longer participate, many owners want a buy-sell provision that guarantees a buyer for their ownership interest in case they become disabled.

EXAMPLE: Steve is a 10% owner and employee of FastShip, Inc., a small, family-run freight-forwarding corporation, where all owners participate in the heavy lifting. After he injures his back lifting boxes, Steve's doctor says he can never again do warehouse work. Since he can no longer work at FastShip, Steve stops getting a paycheck. (FastShip, like many corporations, doesn't pay stock dividends, with the result that except for a small weekly disability payment, Steve's income is zero.) Short of cash, Steve asks his co-owners to buy him out. While sympathetic, the other owners had just made a personal loan to the business (which has been struggling) to purchase new timesaving electrical lifting equipment. They tell Steve that neither they nor the company itself can afford to buy Steve out for at least two years. Steve can't find an outside buyer for his shares and is stuck keeping an interest in a company that produces no dividends and that he can no longer work for.

Steve would have been much better off if he and the other owners had formed a buy-sell agreement that required the company or co-owners to buy out a disabled owner, using policy proceeds from required disability insurance. Fortunately, your buy-sell agreement can do this with a Right-to-Force-a-Sale clause that's very similar to the one we discussed for retiring owners. The clause in our buy-sell agreement that provides some security for a disabled owner who no longer works for the company is shown in Excerpt 5.

☐ **Option 2: Right of Disabled Owner to Force a Sale**

(a) When an owner becomes permanently and totally disabled, and such disability lasts at least *[insert number of months, such as "six"]* months (the "waiting period"), either consecutively or cumulatively, he or she can require the company and the continuing owners to buy all, but not less than all, of his or her ownership interest by delivering to the company, within 30 days of the expiration of the waiting period, a notice of intention to force a sale ("Notice of Intent to Force a Sale") in writing. The notice shall include the name and address of the owner, a description and amount of the owner's interest in the company and a statement that the owner wishes to force a sale due to disability as provided in this provision. The procedure for purchase of the ownership interest shall be according to Section IV, Provision 2 of this agreement. The price to be paid, the manner of payments and other terms of the purchase shall be according to this section and Sections VI and VII of this agreement.

   An owner is considered disabled when he or she is unable to perform his or her regular duties. If disability insurance is used to fund a buyout under this provision, the insurance company shall establish whether an owner is disabled; without disability insurance, the owner's doctor will establish whether an owner is disabled. An owner who becomes disabled according to this section is referred to as a "disabled owner" below.

(b) Price

   You must check either Option 2a or Option 2b below if you checked Option 2 above.

   ☐ **Option 2a: Date disabled owner stops working**

   The Agreement Price as selected in Section VI of this agreement shall be established as of the date the disabled owner first stopped working.

   ☐ **Option 2b: Date of buyout**

   The Agreement Price as selected in Section VI of this agreement shall be established as of the date of the proposed buyout of the disabled owner's interest.

Excerpt 5

If you are interested in giving a disabled owner the right to force the company or continuing owners to buy her interest, check Option 2 on your worksheet now (Section III, Scenario 2), and insert the amount of time an owner must be disabled before the owner can force a sale. If you check Option 2, either check Option 2a to establish the Agreement Price when the disabled owner first stops working, or check Option 2b to establish the Agreement Price as of the date of the buyout.

All or nothing. Note that our Right-to-Force-a-Sale provision does not allow a disabled owner to require the company and the continuing owners to buy just a portion of his ownership interest.

Possible overlap between clauses is not a Problem. Of course, a person who becomes disabled may decide to retire. Thus there could be situations where, if you include in your buy-sell agreement a Right-to-Force-a-Sale clause for both retiring owners and disabled owners, a disabled owner could use either provision. Which one would he use? Undoubtedly, whichever clause has more generous terms. It follows that if you decide to include one or more buyout clauses, you'll want to be sure they fit well together. For instance, many companies choose to 1) give the company and continuing owners an option to purchase a retiring owner's interest, 2) give a disabled owner the right to force a sale and 3) allow a retiring owner's right to force a sale only if the owner has reached a certain age or has worked for the company for a minimum number of years.

D. What If an Owner Dies?

Do not skip this section. Even if you and your co-owners are all 28 and in radiant health, it's crucial to deal with the possibility that one of you will die. Put bluntly, what happens in case of an owner's death may be the most important scenario you can include in your buy-sell agreement.

The death of an owner, especially one who is an active manager or worker, is almost sure to be extremely traumatic for your business, both emotionally and economically. First, you will lose the services of a central player and worker. And if the owner was someone your customers highly regarded (common in a service business), you'll face the real possibility of a business meltdown. And, even if you keep your business together, you'll need to cope with the fundamental fact that someone else will have control over your former co-owner's interest after her death.

This raises the key question: Who will own the deceased owner's share? Right after an owner's death, her interest will be part of her estate (along with all other property she owned at death). If the deceased co-owner left her interest to an inheritor under the terms of a will, a personal representative (named by the will or by the court) will manage it through a lengthy probate process before it is eventually transferred to its new owner.

If the owner put the interest into a probate-avoiding living trust before she died, the interest will be promptly transferred to whoever is named to receive it in the trust (absent a buy-sell agreement).

 Probate-avoidance living trusts are discussed in Chapter 2, Section B3.

1. Business Succession

Whether an owner of a small business leaves her interest by will or is wise enough to use a probate-avoiding living trust, the end result is that the surviving owners are faced with the specter of sharing management duties and profits of the company with new owners—the inheritors of the deceased owner's interest. And if this isn't scary enough, realize that these people may be immature, inexperienced, uninterested or even destructive. Surviving owners who find themselves in this situation have several options. They can:

- welcome the deceased owner's inheritors into the company and share the work, control and profits with them
- accept the inheritors as silent, nonworking owners—potentially giving them a free ride if the business prospers
- negotiate with the inheritors to buy them out
- negotiate with the inheritors to sell the rest of the company to them, or
- liquidate the business.

If these options haven't been discussed—and a clear plan enshrined in a buy-sell agreement—beforehand, tensions can arise as the new owners and the old owners discuss the future of the company. If arguments turn nasty, resulting in business owners' losing focus on continuing operations, the company's business and reputation can suffer, sometimes even causing it to fail.

Why are conflicts so common during business ownership transitions? When an inheritor steps into a deceased owner's shoes, especially if she doesn't plan to take an active part in the company, it's likely that her view of the business will differ from that of the other owners. For example, the surviving owners may want to:

- keep control of the company to themselves
- share ownership only with those who actively work in the business
- maintain or increase salaries, and/or
- reinvest earnings and profits (rather than distributing them to the owners).

The new owners may want to:

- influence decision-making to protect their interests
- receive cash to pay out death taxes and administrative expenses
- not work due to lack of experience, age, ability or desire
- maximize the profits allocated to them as owners, and/or
- sell their interests to outsiders for cash.

In addition to all these potential problem areas, there is also the possibility that an inheritor and one or more of the surviving owners simply won't like each other (for example, the third wife of a deceased owner may despise one of the surviving owners who has snubbed her). And even if both sides have unselfish interests, there just may not be enough money to go around. Let's take a look at how problems can arise even in relatively amiable circumstances.

EXAMPLE: Joe and Chris, brothers and good friends, went into the sporting goods business years ago as partners of a retail store, sharing the profits equally. They put in long hours both in the store and behind the scenes, buying inventory and keeping the books. Joe married his highschool sweetheart and had three kids, while Chris never married.

One night as he is locking up, Joe suffers a stroke and dies. Luckily, Joe had some life insurance. But it's not even close to enough to support his family indefinitely. Joe's wife Pat imagines continuing to own Joe's share of the shop and tells Chris how much she'll need to draw against her share of the profits to take care of herself and her kids. Since this amount is almost as much as Joe was receiving in salary, Pat is essentially proposing that she receive close to 50% of the company's profits without doing any work. Chris, who is very close to his sister-in-law and nieces and nephew and wants to do right by them, nevertheless knows the company can't operate along the lines Pat proposes, given the fact that Chris will have to hire someone to take Joe's place.

Enough about problems! The point is that any owner who wants to give his business a decent chance to succeed after he dies should work with his co-owners to create and fund a sensible succession strategy. Decisions that are well thought out, made beforehand and recorded in a buy-sell agreement can really help avoid delays and conflicts.

2. Deciding What to Put in Your Buy-Sell Agreement

At bottom, you and your business partners have to decide who will continue the company when you or a co-owner dies: the surviving co-owners or the deceased owner's inheritors, or a combination of both.

Your first thought may be, "Well, of course my family will inherit my share of the business." Not so fast. This is an issue you should discuss in depth with your co-owners and your family. Co-owners should frankly talk about whose kids, if anyone's, will be welcome to work in the business when one of you retires or dies. You may well conclude that unless one of your kids already works in the business and has been fully accepted by your co-owners, it's best to provide that no owners' kids are guaranteed a spot. As part of having this discussion, here are some key questions you and each of your co-owners will want to answer:

- Do you want your spouse or children to be able to retain your business interest, or is it better to require that they sell it after your death?

- Who do you want to gain control and management of the company? The existing owners? Your inheritors?

- Do your adult children want to take over your position in the company? Have they shown any interest in the company? Do they have any knowledge of the business?

- If you want your inheritors to retain their interest in the company and succeed you, will they really be able to do the work you now do? When? If not now, who will run the company in the meantime, until your inheritors have the maturity and skills to take over?

- Do you want your business partners' inheritors to be able to fill their shoes? Do you want the right to say "yes, they can" or "no, they can't" or "only under these conditions"?

EXAMPLE: Mike and his co-owners discuss their company's future when Mike is 40 years old. Mike gets his co-owners to agree that his son, Greg, can take over his ownership interest and his management duties when he dies. But Mike dies suddenly of a heart attack at age 45, when Greg has just started college. Greg and his father's surviving co-owners agree that he is not ready to take over the business. But Greg wants to hold on to his interest until he graduates, at which point he'll join the company. The surviving owners, however, don't want to have to share profits with Greg while he finishes his education, and they aren't so sure they want him to take over his father's role with no real-life business experience. To try to head off the problem, they offer Greg a generous lump-sum payment to sell out. Greg says, "No way. I want to join the company." Without a buy-sell agreement, the surviving owners can't *force* Greg to sell. Eventually relations between Greg and the other owners deteriorate to the point where they decide to liquidate the company and go their separate ways.

Look at the situation from both sides. You usually have no way of knowing which owner will die first. You could be a surviving owner faced with the possibility of a deceased co-owner's unqualified son wanting to join the company. Or you could be the first co-owner to become critically ill and die, hoping the others will accept your capable daughter as a fully participating co-owner. So in drafting your agreement, try to balance the future needs of the owner whose circumstances will have changed against the interests of the company and the other owners as a whole.

Luckily, it's possible to use your buy-sell agreement to create appropriate tools to manage what happens when an owner dies. The idea is to have a plan in place that allows the surviving owners of the company to make sensible decisions fair to all at the time of an owner's death, because when an owner dies, the surviving owners of the company —not the inheritors—are probably best equipped to make a decision about the company's future.

Family Succession: Splitting Up the Pie

Let's expend a little ink looking at the special problems that ownership transition of family businesses often brings up. Although it's probably not of interest to most readers of this book (who no doubt will want to provide the company and continuing co-owners with the right to buy the interest of a deceased owner), some readers may be interested in the possibility that their inheritors will continue as co-owners, particularly if they own most of the company. If you are pretty sure that you do want your children to succeed you (perhaps you are the majority owner in a truly family business), you need to plan for the smooth transition of your ownership interest.

First, after you die, even if your heirs are ready and itching to take over, and the co-owners, if any, of your company are agreeable, you need to have made clear exactly what the plan is. Unfortunately, family members are often touchy about making formal agreements with each other—some families wrongly believe that a written agreement is a badge of dysfunction. As a result, family businesses are often run on the basis of oral promises and informal understandings that have never been formalized. But when the tension produced by the death of a key person arises, this is almost always a recipe for disaster! If an owner wants to have control over the future of his business to ensure its success even after he dies, he must put everything in writing.

Second, it is crucial that you select inheritors who are willing, and able, to succeed you. If there's any doubt that an inheritor won't be able to take over for you right away, you might want to choose an interim successor, such as a long-term employee or a trustee, who can keep the business running smoothly until your inheritor can take over.

If you have more than one child, it's important not to confuse your likely desire to split up your estate fairly with the fact that only one of them may be equipped to run the business. If so, you need to discuss this frankly with your children, and put into place a sound legal plan to carry out your wishes. It should go almost without saying that without an explicit and formal legal structure for business succession, siblings have been known to get into nasty battles over money and control.

Here's one possible approach: If you want to leave equal inheritances for your children, but not all of them are interested in working and running the business, consider leaving the business to the children who are active in it, and buying life insurance of equal value for the others. (You should buy insurance for this purpose early, rather than waiting until your 60s or 70s, when it might be too expensive.) Alternatively, your buy-sell agreement can provide for the business-minded child to buy the ownership interests from your other inheritors after your death—but for this to be enforceable, all of your inheritors must sign the agreement.

Probate Fees and Estate Costs Can Ruin a Successor's Chances

In some instances, you may have planned for your heirs to take over the company. Unfortunately, to make sure the eventual transition is a smooth one, there are additional issues to be dealt with. To mention a few, after your death, your estate may have to pay probate costs, funeral expenses, final illness bills and death taxes. Where will this money come from? Without advance planning, your heirs may even have to sell the business or take working capital from the company to pay for these expenses.

EXAMPLE: Hillary and her brother Mike run a bed and breakfast on the edge of town that provides them with a satisfying and fairly profitable living. They have a steady, seasonal clientele, who keep returning because of Hillary's gracious hospitality and Mike's gourmet cooking.

Mike dies unexpectedly and leaves his share of the business to his daughter Miriam, using a probate-avoiding living trust. Hillary welcomes Miriam to the B&B, since she and Miriam get along fine. So far, so good, but to pay death taxes, funeral expenses and several big debts that her father had left behind, Miriam must take out a mortgage on the build-

ing that houses the bed and breakfast. On top of the financial strain the mortgage causes, Miriam doesn't know how to cook, so they have to hire a third person to replace Mike. And still depressed by her brother's death, Hillary is in no mood to play the happy hostess much of the time. Eventually, when word spreads that the quality of the food and hospitality at the bed and breakfast has declined, bookings drop off. Before long, Miriam can't make her loan payments, and Hillary doesn't have the cash to buy her out. They end up hurriedly selling their B&B for less than its real value.

Although planning ahead won't deal with the sadness that accompanies the loss of a loved one, you can protect your heirs from a financial squeeze by planning ahead for money problems. One way to do this is by purchasing enough life insurance, to be paid to your inheritors upon your death, so that they can pay any debts, taxes and bills your estate may owe without having to take it out of the business you took so long to build up. Another way is to plan ahead to lower eventual estate taxes. We discuss estate taxes in detail in Chapter 9, Section B.

3. Option of Company and Surviving Owners to Purchase a Deceased Owner's Interest

For the reasons mentioned above, most savvy business owners have their buy-sell agreement provide the company and the surviving co-owners with the right to buy a deceased owner's interest from his estate or trust. Normally, such a provision states that, when an owner dies, the company and the surviving owners have the option to buy the interest from the executor or administrator of the

estate or the trustee of a trust that holds the ownership interest (this is often referred to as an "Option to Purchase a Deceased Owner's Interest"). Of course, under this type of agreement, the surviving owners have the discretion to decide not to buy the interest, if they feel they can work well with any inheritors who evince an interest in participating in the business.

EXAMPLE: Remember Joe and Chris, the two brothers who co-owned a sporting goods store before Joe died suddenly leaving a wife, Pat, and their children behind? Let's keep the facts the same except that Joe and Chris had the wisdom to adopt a buy-sell agreement. This time when Joe dies, Pat again says she needs an income to support herself and her kids. Chris —who realizes the company can't survive if it has to pay half the profits to a nonworking owner—invokes their buy-sell agreement's buyout clause, which provides that he can buy out Pat's interest by paying her $100,000 over three years. Combined with the payoff from a life insurance policy Joe had purchased, this is enough money to give Pat the time she needs to freshen up her skills as a paralegal and go back to work. And it allows Chris to search for a new partner to share work and profits with.

The owner who lives the longest gets the business. Understand that this common provision in small business buy-sell agreements, which allows surviving owners to buy out the interests of owners who die first, often results in the owner who remains alive the longest ending up with the whole business. This may be a reasonable outcome—especially if the buyout price is fair—since the last owner to die managed and/or worked for the company for the longest amount of time. Nevertheless, you should also understand how it can work against your survivors in some circumstances. Suppose your son works for the company and wants to succeed you as one of the owners, but you die before the other owners. If you've included an Option-to-Purchase clause and the company or the surviving owners force your son to sell out, his career could be over before it started.

 A fair price protects your inheritors. A reasonable buyout price protects your inheritors. You may not be crazy about the idea of giving the company and surviving owners the absolute right to buy your share from your estate, rather than letting it go to your inheritors. But as long as your agreement ensures that the price paid to your estate for your share is reasonable—and, of course, you can take pains to make sure that it will be—then at least you know your inheritors will be fairly compensated. We discuss how to set a fair price in Chapter 6.

The provision in our agreement is shown in Excerpt 6, below.

Scenario 3. When an Owner Dies

☐ **Option 1: Option of Company and Continuing Owners to Purchase a Deceased Owner's Interest**

(a) When an owner dies, he or she, and the executor or administrator of his or her estate or the trustee of a trust holding his or her ownership interest, are deemed to have offered the deceased owner's ownership interest to the company and the continuing owners for sale as of the date of the notice of death received orally or in writing by the company. The company and the continuing owners shall then have an option, but not an obligation (unless otherwise stated in this agreement), to purchase all or part of the ownership interest within the time and according to the procedure in Section IV, Provision 1 of this agreement. The price to be paid, the manner of payments and other terms of the purchase shall be according to Sections VI and VII of this agreement. An owner who has died is referred to as a "deceased owner" below.

Excerpt 6

If you are interested in giving the company and the continuing owners the option to buy a deceased owner's interest from his estate representative or trustee upon notice of death, check Option 1 on your worksheet now. (Section III, Scenario 3.)

Note that you must include this option if you want to use your agreement to try to set the value of the ownership interests for estate tax purposes. We discuss setting the value for estate tax purposes in Chapter 9, Section B.

For majority owners. Majority owners may want to change the death clause in a buy-sell agreement so that some provisions don't apply to them. To avoid being restricted under any provision of a buy-sell agreement, a majority owner simply needs to add a sentence at the end of the provision (the language of Option 1 as set out above, in this case), such as: "This section applies only to owners of less than 50% of the interests in the company." This might be appropriate in a situation in which the majority owner's spouse or child wants to continue the business. Note that if you do this, the Agreement Price will not set the value of the ownership interests for estate tax purposes. (We discuss setting the value for estate tax purposes in Chapter 9, Section B3.) This is another example of why a majority owner should consult a small business expert before signing a buy-sell agreement.

Making sure funds will be available to pay for a buyout is, of course, a key part to making sure an Option to Purchase is truly usable by the company and surviving owners. One excellent way to do this is for the company to take out an appropriate amount of life insurance on the life of each owner. The company pays the premiums on each policy and receives the benefits from them when an owner dies. The insurance policy payoff is then available to buy the interest of the deceased owner. (We discuss using insurance to fund buy-sell agreements in more detail in Chapter 5.)

4. Right of Estate, Trust or Inheritors to Force a Sale

Up until now we've talked about situations where the company or surviving owners *want* to buy out a deceased owner's interest from her estate. But what happens to a deceased owner's inheritors if the company or the surviving owners do not choose to buy the deceased owner's interest (for instance, because the company is short of funds)? There are many reasons inheritors might want to promptly sell their interest—for instance, they're not interested in working in the company; they're too young, too old or unqualified; or they may simply have other places to spend or invest the proceeds they could get from selling their interests. As we discussed in Chapter 1, it can be difficult to impossible to find an outside buyer for a partial interest in a small business.

EXAMPLE: Sam, Carla and Diane take out a large mortgage to buy a parking garage downtown. Sam dies suddenly in a car accident soon afterwards. His wife Rebecca inherits his interest in the garage. Unable to survive on her salary alone, Rebecca asks Carla and Diane to buy out her share of the garage. Carla and Diane, however, with no surplus funds to buy her out (the garage is already mortgaged to the hilt), say "not right now." Sam's wife looks for an outside buyer, but no one wants to purchase a minority interest in the business, since the business will continue to be controlled by Carla and Diane. Rebecca and her kids are stuck. She is eventually all but forced to sign over her share in the company to pay her bills, getting credit for far less than her share of the business was really worth.

To deal with this potential problem, you may want to include a clause in your agreement that makes sure the estate or trust of a deceased owner or her inheritors can sell the deceased owner's interest. Again, the purpose of this clause is to guard against the possibility that neither the company nor the surviving owners want to buy the deceased owner's share from the deceased owner's estate, trust or inheritors. To actually accomplish this, your agreement should contain a Right-to-Force-a-Sale clause that requires the company or the surviving owners to buy back the interest if the estate representative, trustee or inheritors want to sell it. For instance, if an owner dies and leaves his ownership interest to his wife and children, and they need cash for their expenses (to pay bills or to fund tuition), they have the power to force the company to buy back the interest.

EXAMPLE: Let's give Sam's wife and kids a better outcome with a buy-sell agreement. Remember that Sam, Carla and Diane owned a downtown parking garage when Sam died suddenly in a car accident. His wife Rebecca inherited his interest in the garage. Needing cash to pay for living expenses for herself and her children, Rebecca invokes the Right-to-Force-a-Sale clause in the company's buy-sell agreement to require Carla and Diane to buy out her share of the garage. Since their agreement required the purchase of life insurance policies on each owner, Carla and Diane have no problem buying out Rebecca at the price in their agreement with the proceeds from the life insurance policies. Now Rebecca and Diane and Carla can part on good terms, since all of them feel fairly treated.

The Right-to-Force-a-Sale clause in our buy-sell agreement is shown in Excerpt 7, below.

☐ **Option 2: Right of Estate, Trust or Inheritors to Force a Sale**

(a) When an owner dies, the executor or administrator of the deceased owner's estate, or the trustee of a trust holding the deceased owner's ownership interest, or the deceased owner's inheritors can require the company and the continuing owners to buy all, but not less than all, of the deceased owner's ownership interest by delivering to the company within 60 days a notice of intention to force a sale ("Notice of Intent to Force a Sale") in writing. The notice shall include the name and address of the deceased owner, the date of death, a description and amount of the owner's interest in the company, the name and address of the person exercising the right to force the sale and a statement that this person wishes to force a sale of the interest due to the owner's death as provided in this provision. The procedure for purchase of the ownership interest shall be according to Section IV, Provision 2 of this agreement. The price to be paid, the manner of payments and other terms of the purchase shall be according to Sections VI and VII of this agreement. An owner who has died is referred to as a "deceased owner" below.

Excerpt 7

If you are interested in giving a deceased owner's estate, trust or inheritors the right to force the company or the remaining owners to buy her interest, check Option 2 on your worksheet now. (Section III, Scenario 3.)

All or nothing. Note that our Right-to-Force a-Sale provision does not allow the holder of a deceased owner's interest to require the company and the continuing owners to buy just a portion of the deceased owner's interest.

You Can Customize Any Buyout Option to Make It Mandatory

Another way to plan ahead for the death of a co-owner is to adopt a buy-sell agreement that *requires* the company or the remaining owners to buy the interest of the deceased owner from his estate. In other words, after an owner dies, the company or the surviving owners would have no choice but to buy the deceased owner's share. This clause, however—often called a mandatory purchase provision—takes away much of the surviving owners' discretion and doesn't provide much flexibility for either side.

We believe it should be used only in limited circumstances, and only after consultation with a small business lawyer. If you do decide to *require* the company or the continuing owners to purchase a deceased owner's interest, in subsection (a) of Option 1, simply cross out the words "an option, but not an obligation (unless otherwise stated in this agreement)," and write in "an obligation."

Any of the Options to Purchase in our buy-sell agreement can be made mandatory—but we don't see the need for this in most cases. We think it's better to let the parties decide at the time of the business-changing event, when they have more information than the drafters of the buy-sell agreement do today.

E. What If an Owner Divorces?

If you don't cover the possibility of divorce in your buy-sell agreement, you'll have to face the possibility that if a co-owner gets divorced, her ex could become your new business partner! And, of course, the co-owner who is getting a divorce may have no power to stop this in a situation where, under state law, a judge has the power to divide marital property. And we hope you don't need us to tell you that, at a time when one in two marriages end in divorce, it's just plain silly to overlook this possibility.

Dividing Property at Divorce

Absent a bulletproof premarital agreement (an oxymoron if there ever was one) in which spouses agree to keep their property separate, chances are good that your business partner's ex-spouse has a legal interest in your company. This is certainly true in community property states (Arizona, California, Idaho, Nevada, New Mexico, Texas, Washington and Wisconsin), where each spouse owns one-half of all the couple's community property (which includes most property earned or accumulated after the wedding but before permanent separation). And practically speaking, it's likely to be true in the other states as well, where equitable distribution laws require that marital property be divided fairly during divorce (and inheritance laws normally require that a surviving spouse receive at least one-third to one-half of a deceased spouse's estate).

Perhaps the most troublesome prospect of becoming co-owner with an owner's ex-spouse involves a situation where the original owner (the owner who gets a divorce) is still involved in the business. But even if this isn't true, an inexperienced, angry or mistrustful ex-spouse may want to get as much money as he or she can out of the company in the short term, even at the risk of damaging the company's long-term prospects.

EXAMPLE: Mike and Marti, friends from college, start a medical supply company while Mike is married to Betsy. A few years later, Mike and Betsy file for divorce. Betsy's lawyer demands half of Mike's interest in the company. Mike, having few other assets, has no choice but to sign it over as part of a property settlement agreement. Mike and Marti dread being in business with Mike's ex-wife, Betsy, who has a dozen reasons to be mad at Mike and, by extension, his friends. Without a buy-sell agreement, Mike and Marti have no way to force her to sell her interest and, as a result, eventually disband the company.

A well-drafted "contemplation-of-divorce" buy-sell provision—sometimes drawn up as a separate spousal agreement—protects the owners of the company from having to work with potentially undesirable ex-spouses. Under such a provision, the company and the other owners can buy the interest received by a former spouse if they choose, at the price in the agreement. (Only the interest transferred to an ex-spouse as part of a divorce is subject to buyback; any interest kept by the original owner stays with the original owner.) However, and this is a big however, an ex-spouse cannot be required to sell back his interest if he did not sign the buy-sell agreement.

To avoid this prospect, all of the married owners should have their spouses read and sign the buy-sell agreement. By signing, the spouse explicitly agrees to abide by the agreement's provisions for buybacks of spousal interests. In our agreement, spouses agree to sell any interest received in a divorce settlement back to the company or to the other owners for the Agreement Price or to abide by the terms of the buy-sell agreement that are applicable to all owners (if the company decides not to buy back the interest from the ex-spouse).

Make Sure the Spouse Understands What He's Signing

In at least one case, the court refused to enforce a provision in a buy-sell agreement requiring an ex-spouse to sell back an interest received as part of a divorce, even though the ex-spouse had signed the agreement. The ex-spouse, who didn't work in the business or have a financial background, successfully argued that she never understood the agreement (and that she wasn't represented by a lawyer). To avoid the possibility of this happening, it's a good idea to add to your spousal provision an acknowledgment for the spouse to sign agreeing that she has received a copy of your company's financial report, has reviewed the agreement with a lawyer of her own choosing and fully expects the agreement to be binding in case of divorce. And if spouses also prepare a pre- or post-marital contract defining their property ownership vis-à-vis each other, make sure it contains the same provisions as the buy-sell agreement regarding business ownership.

Don't use a different price in your spousal provision. Don't set an extra low price for a buyback from ex-spouses of owners, or your agreement may be ruled invalid in court. There are other ways to differentiate between the price paid to an ex-spouse for her interest and the amount paid by a company to a retiring owner. For instance, generous severance packages and retirement plans that are offered to other departing owners do not have to be offered to an ex-spouse, who, after all, has probably never worked for the company.

Again, remember, contractual provisions contained in a buy-sell agreement don't have to be binding if none of the parties want them to be. Owners have flexible buy-sell agreements to protect and define their rights, not to freeze them in legal straitjackets. For example, suppose that, despite a mandatory buyout provision, the remaining owners actually like the ex-spouse—perhaps even better than they ever liked their old business partner—and want her to join the business. As long as she agrees, this is no problem since when all parties agree, any agreement can be changed.

The language of the "contemplation of divorce" clause contained in our buy-sell agreement, which includes the options mentioned above, is shown in Excerpt 8. Note that it gives the divorced owner the first chance to buy back the interest awarded by a court to his former spouse, then gives the company and all owners (including the divorced owner) a chance to buy the interest. We think this makes sense—it allows the divorced owner to return to his status quo ownership position in the company by buying the entire interest awarded by the court back from his former spouse.

Scenario 4. When an Owner's Interest Is Transferred to His or Her Former Spouse

☐ **Option 1: Option of Company and Continuing Owners to Purchase Former Spouse's Interest**

(a) If, in connection with the divorce or dissolution of the marriage of an owner, a court issues a decree or order that transfers, confirms or awards part or all of an ownership interest to a divorced owner's former spouse, the former spouse is deemed to have offered his or her newly acquired ownership interest to the divorced owner for purchase on the date of the court award or settlement, according to the terms of this agreement. If the divorced owner does not elect to make such purchase within 30 days of the date of the court award or settlement, the former spouse of the divorced owner is deemed to have offered his or her newly acquired ownership interest to the company and the co-owners (including the divorced owner) for purchase, according to the terms of this agreement. The divorced owner must send notice to the company, in writing, that his or her former spouse now owns an ownership interest in the company. The notice shall state the name and address of the owner, the name and address of the divorced owner's former spouse, a description and amount of the interest awarded to the former spouse and the date of the court award. If no notice is received by the company from the divorced owner, an offer to the company and the co-owners is deemed to have occurred when the company actually receives notice orally or in writing of the court award or settlement transferring the divorced owner's interest to the owner's former spouse. The company and the co-owners (including the divorced owner) shall then have an option, but not an obligation (unless otherwise stated in this agreement), to purchase all or part of the ownership interest within the time and according to the procedure in Section IV, Provision 1 of this agreement. The price to be paid, the manner of payments and other terms of the purchase shall be according to Sections VI and VII of this agreement.

(b) A former spouse who sells his or her ownership interest back to the company or continuing owners agrees to be responsible for any taxes owed on his or her sales proceeds.

Excerpt 8

 If you are interested in giving the company and the continuing owners the option to buy a former spouse's ownership interest, check Option 1 on your worksheet now. (Section III, Scenario 4.)

F. What If an Owner Loses His or Her Professional License?

So far we have covered the most common scenarios that happen to the owners of small businesses. In the rest of this chapter we deal with a few less likely scenarios: loss of a professional license, personal bankruptcy of an owner, default on a personal loan and expulsion. First, let's look at what happens if an owner loses his professional or vocational license.

An owner can be prevented from working if he loses a license that he needs to do his job. For example, a veterinarian cannot legally treat animals without a veterinarian's license. What happens if your co-owner loses his professional or vocational license, preventing him from doing his job? Does he have to offer his interest for sale back to the company or to the still-licensed owners? Even absent a buy-sell agreement, the law of many states requires this for some professions (in California, for example, you can't be a partner in a law firm without being a licensed lawyer). But even where this is true, the issues of placing a value on the departing owner's interest and deciding on a mutually agreed method for payment still need to be dealt with.

EXAMPLE: Carol and Mike, friends from school, start a professional corporation to engage in the practice of architecture. After he starts to drink heavily, Mike is found to have improperly used a client's funds. After a hearing, his license is revoked by the state board. No longer able to work, Mike demands that Carol pay him for his interest in the firm. When Carol refuses to pay Mike's asking price for his ownership share, Mike files a lawsuit. Carol countersues, claiming Mike doesn't deserve anything, since his own wrongdoing greatly harmed the practice's reputation. While the likely outcome is hard to call, one thing that's sure is both parties will rack up attorneys' fees.

If you find this little scenario sobering, it's likely you'll want to include loss of license in your buyback scenarios, to require a co-owner who has his license suspended or revoked to relinquish his duties and sell his ownership interest back to the company or to the other owners. This protects the owners of the company from having to share profits with someone who can no longer practice and may be in disrepute.

In addition, you may want to provide that the company or the continuing owners can repurchase the interest of an owner who has lost his license at a discount. For instance, your agreement can allow the company or the remaining owners to purchase the owner's share at 40% to 50% of the full agreement price. Or to allow for the possibility that the conduct that caused the co-owner to lose his license may have hurt the reputation of your business, you may simply want to provide for a new appraisal of the company to establish its current worth. (We discuss the procedure for getting an appraisal in Chapter 6.)

The language of the loss of license provision in our agreement, with the price options we discussed, is shown in Excerpt 9.

Scenario 5. When an Owner Loses His or Her Professional License

☐ **Option 1: Option of Company and Continuing Owners to Purchase Interest of an Owner Who Has Lost His or Her Professional License**

(a) If an owner suffers the surrender, revocation or suspension, which will stand for at least three months, of his or her license to perform services essential to the business purposes of the company, that surrender, revocation or suspension of the license shall be deemed to constitute an offer by the owner to sell his or her interest to the company or the other owners. The owner shall notify the company in writing of such surrender, revocation or suspension. The notice shall include the name and address of the owner, a description and amount of the owner's interest in the company and a description and effective date of the decision that resulted in the surrender, revocation or suspension of the owner's license. If no notice is received by the company, an offer is deemed to have occurred when the company actually learns of the decision to surrender, revoke or suspend the owner's license. The company and the continuing owners shall then have an option, but not an obligation (unless otherwise stated in this agreement), to purchase all or part of the ownership interest within the time and according to the procedure in Section IV, Provision 1 of this agreement. The price to be paid shall be as specified in this section; if not so specified, then according to Section VI of this agreement. The manner of payments and other terms of the purchase shall be according to Section VII of this agreement.

(b) If an owner's license is surrendered, revoked or suspended, the price that the company and/or the continuing owners will pay for the expelled owner's ownership interest will be:

☐ **Option 1a: The full Agreement Price according to Section VI of this agreement**

☐ **Option 1b: Decided by an independent appraisal, according to the Appraised Value Method in Section VI of this agreement**

☐ **Option 1c: The Agreement Price as established in Section VI of this agreement, decreased by** _[insert percentage, such as "50"]_ .

Excerpt 9

a waiting document

If you are interested in giving the company and the continuing owners the option to buy the interest of an owner who has lost a required professional license, check Option 1 on your worksheet now. (Section III, Scenario 5.) If you check Option 1, also:

- check Option 1a, 1b or 1c to establish what price will be paid to an owner who has lost his license. If you check Option 1c, fill in the amount of the discount to be taken off the Agreement Price.

G. What If an Owner Files for Personal Bankruptcy?

When an owner can't pay his bills and files for bankruptcy protection, it affects not only *his* future, but the company's as well. That's because a bankruptcy trustee (a clerk of the bankruptcy court) has the right to gather and sell all of the debtor's nonexempt property, including her stake in a co-owned business. It follows that the company and the remaining owners will want at their disposal the means to prevent others from getting hold of an ownership interest.

Depending on state law, there can be three ways a bankruptcy trustee could take the ownership interest to pay off creditors, including:

- selling the ownership interest
- selling a proportional share of the business's assets, such as business equipment and inventory, or
- forcing the entire company to be liquidated.

In reality, however, circumstances rarely require these drastic measures (and in fact, in many states, the trustee is only allowed to try to sell the ownership interest as is, not any equipment or inventory). As long as the company or the co-owners are willing to pay a reasonable amount for the ownership interest in question, the bankruptcy trustee will usually be willing to sell it back to them. But while the bankruptcy trustee is trying to sort things out, your company can end up in legal and ownership limbo—a situation

banks and other creditors would not take kindly to.

No question, it pays to plan to avoid any possibility that an ownership interest in your business might be tied up in bankruptcy court or, in a worst case scenario, that your company might be liquidated. To do this, your agreement should require an owner to give the company 30 or 60 days notice before filing for bankruptcy, to give the company time to structure a purchase. It should also state that that owner's notice is considered an automatic offer to sell his ownership interest back to the company or to the other owners immediately, at which point the company and the co-owners can purchase it if they choose to.

Pay a fair price for a bankrupt owner's shares. Even if a co-owner sells his interest and *then* files for bankruptcy, a bankruptcy trustee has the power to examine and possibly disallow the transaction (and may well do so if it looks like a phony or underpriced transaction). To reduce the likelihood of this happening, don't use an extra low buyout price for your bankruptcy clause. Far better to provide that the price paid to a co-owner who faces bankruptcy is the same as if she announced her retirement (the full Agreement Price).

Should a co-owner get into serious financial problems, step one should be for everyone involved to consult with an experienced bankruptcy lawyer.

Of course, people don't always follow their buy-sell agreement, especially when they have little to lose. If an owner violates the agreement by filing for bankruptcy without first giving notice to his co-owners, your buy-sell agreement can still help to remedy the situation. That's because a bankruptcy clause can allow the company or the other owners to buy the interest back from a bankruptcy trustee, at the buyout price and terms in the agreement. And as we mentioned above, as long as this price seems fair, the trustee will likely accept it (though she may not be legally bound to do so), since the trustee may not have much luck selling the debtor's partial interest in the business to an outsider.

⚠️ **Partnerships and LLCs beware.** The Uniform Partnership Act, which has been adopted in substantially similar form by all states, says that a partner who files for personal bankruptcy will cause an automatic dissolution (termination) of the partnership! Same goes for LLCs in some states. So if you don't have a buy-sell clause in your partnership or LLC operating agreement (or in a separate document) that deals with bankruptcy, an owner who declares personal bankruptcy may terminate your partnership or LLC! (But for LLCs, most states allow the remaining members 90 days after the bankruptcy of an LLC member to vote to continue the LLC. And, of course, most companies with a bankrupt owner will vote to continue.)

To be safe, in case an owner who files for bankruptcy does not provide notice to the company (in which case he can't be bought out before the filing can take place), your agreement should provide that an owner who obtains or becomes subject to a bankruptcy order is automatically subject to the buyback provisions contained in your buy-sell agreement. (We include this in our bankruptcy clause below.)

The clause in our agreement that contains the bankruptcy filing scenario we discussed is shown in Excerpt 10.

✏️ If you are interested in giving the company and the continuing owners the option to buy a bankrupt owner's interest, check Option 1 on your worksheet now. (Section III, Scenario 6.) If you check Option 1, also insert the number of days' notice an owner must give to the company before filing for bankruptcy.

Scenario 6. When an Owner Files for Personal Bankruptcy

☐ **Option 1: Option of Company and Continuing Owners to Purchase Interest of an Owner Who Has Filed for Bankruptcy**

(a) When an owner is planning to file for bankruptcy, he or she must give notice to the company, in writing, *[insert number of days, such as "30" or "60"]* days before he or she files for bankruptcy. The notice shall state the name and address of the owner, a description and amount of the owner's interest and the expected date of filing by the owner for bankruptcy. This notice shall be deemed to constitute an offer by the owner to sell his or her interest to the company or the other owners. If an owner files for bankruptcy without giving notice, the date when the company learns of the filing for bankruptcy will be deemed to be the date of this notice. The company and the continuing owners shall then have an option, but not an obligation (unless otherwise stated in this agreement), to purchase all or part of the ownership interest within the time and according to the procedure in Section IV, Provision 1 of this agreement. The price to be paid, the manner of payments and other terms of the purchase shall be according to Sections VI and VII of this agreement. An owner who has filed for bankruptcy is referred to as a "bankrupt owner" below.

Excerpt 10

H. What If an Owner Defaults on a Personal Loan?

First, you and your co-owners should decide whether owners will have the right to offer their ownership interests as collateral for personal loans—called "encumbering their interest." Buy-sell provisions can restrict owners from using their ownership interest in this way. Our buy-sell agreement provides two options: one that prohibits encumbering an ownership interest, and another that allows encumbrances, but only with added precautions in case of default.

1. Encumbrances Allowed Subject to Buyout on Default by Owner

After reflection, many owners decide not to prohibit owners from using their interest in the company as collateral for borrowing money, since it means you and your business partners may have a greatly reduced ability to qualify for getting personal loans. Especially for owners who have most of their net worth tied up in the business, it can be overly harsh to prevent owners from borrowing against it and may even result in their being unable to reinvest their profits in the company because of a personal shortage of cash.

If encumbrances are allowed, you may want to add a provision to your buy-sell agreement to handle the situation where an owner defaults on a personal loan and a creditor seeks foreclosure of the interest. The key issue to be dealt with is simple: If the owner defaults on the loan and the creditor threatens to foreclose and take title to the interest, should the company (and the remaining owners) have the right to cure the default? (That is, pay off the loan and take back the interest from the creditor?) The answer should usually be yes; a good buy-sell agreement provides the company and remaining owners with this right. After all, foreclosure of an owner's interest could allow an outside creditor (or the person or entity to whom the creditor sells the interest) to gain a

share of the company and possibly a say in management—the main predicament your buy-sell agreement is meant to avoid. If a foreclosure is imminent, the company or the remaining owners would probably want to pay off the debt, essentially buying the interest in question, instead of allowing the foreclosure to take place.

EXAMPLE: Chris and Lisa run a medical supply corporation together. They have a buy-sell agreement with a Right-of-First-Refusal clause in case of foreclosure. Chris comes up with an idea for reducing inflammation for patients with arm or elbow injuries. It consists of a sleeve filled with a gelatinous substance that can be thrown in the freezer and then pulled over the arm, icing the whole arm at once. Lisa doesn't want any part of funding the development and sale of this new product, because she doesn't think the product will sell. Undaunted by Lisa's lack of enthusiasm, Chris sets up a separate sole proprietorship and applies for a patent. Then, to finance development costs, he gets a loan from the bank by offering his one-half interest in the medical supply company as collateral. He buys enough material to make 5,000 sleeves and hires an outside manufacturer to produce them, making a big, up-front investment. The manufacturer screws up the sleeves, but blames it on Chris's design. Chris, who has no product to sell, misses his first three loan payments, with the result that the bank starts to foreclose on his share of the company.

Lisa reads the buy-sell agreement and finds out she can pay off Chris's loan to the bank and, in exchange, take control of Chris's shares. Fortunately, Lisa is able to quickly gather financing and savings to repay Chris's debt. The creditor accepts Lisa's payment for the interest and stops foreclosure proceedings because he's happy just to close out the loan.

A way to give owners the chance to avoid foreclosure on a defaulting owner's interest is to include an "Option-to-Purchase-an-Owner's-Interest" provision in your agreement. This provision provides that the company and the other owners can elect to buy an owner's encumbered property if it is subject to imminent foreclosure. Depending on the situation, the company or the co-owners could allow the creditor to take ownership of the interest or decide to pay off the creditor. If they choose to "cure" the default, whoever paid off the creditor—the company and/or the co-owners—would then own the interest that had acted as collateral for the loan.

Of course, the amount the company or continuing owners (whoever buys the interest) pay to the creditor to pay off the loan is likely to be higher or lower than the Agreement Price for the interest. In that case, if the amount paid to the creditor is less than the Agreement Price, the buyer should be required to pay the remainder of the Agreement Price to the defaulting owner. If the amount paid to the creditor is more than the Agreement Price, the defaulting owner should owe the difference to the buyer of his or her ownership interest.

The language in our buy-sell agreement that allows encumbrances and includes the buy back option discussed above, in case of default by the owner of the encumbered interest, is shown in Excerpt 11.

☐ **Option 1: Encumbrances Allowed Subject to Option of Company and Continuing Owners to Purchase Interest**

(a) Any owner may encumber any or all of his ownership interest in the company in connection with any debt, but any such encumbrance is subject to the following condition:

(b) If an owner defaults on a debt secured by his or her ownership interest, he or she must promptly give notice in writing to the company. The notice shall include the name and address of the owner, a description and amount of the owner's interest in the company, the date and description of the encumbrance on the owner's interest and the date and description of any action taken by creditors as a result of the default. If no notice is provided by the owner, notice shall be considered given to the company on the date the company learns of the owner's default or of any action by a creditor as a result of the default. (An owner who defaults on a debt secured by his or her ownership interest is referred to as a "defaulting owner" below.) The company and the continuing owners shall then have an option, but not an obligation (unless otherwise stated in this agreement), to pay off the debt and to take title to the interest.

(c) If the amount paid to the creditor (debt plus any interest) is less than the Agreement Price selected in Section VI of this agreement, the remainder of the Agreement Price shall be paid to the defaulting owner by the buyer of his or her ownership interest. If the amount paid to the creditor (debt plus any interest) is more than the Agreement Price selected in Section VI of this agreement, the defaulting owner shall owe the difference to the buyer of his or her ownership interest.

(d) If the company and/or the other owners do not cure the default as provided in subsection (b) above, the creditor may pursue any and all legal and equitable remedies.

Excerpt 11

If you do wish to allow the owners of your company to use their ownership interests as collateral for personal loans, but want to give the company and the remaining owners to right to cure a default by buying back an owner's interest, check Option 2 on your worksheet now. (Section III, Scenario 7.)

If you do allow owners to encumber their ownership interests, you should place a legend on any certificates of ownership (which usually only exist for stock in a corporation) to remind owners and give notice to others who lend money based on ownership interests that the interest cannot be freely disposed of, but must be sold to the company or co-owners under the terms of your buy-sell agreement. We show you how to do this in Chapter 8, Section B.

Regardless of your type of business, if you adopt this provision, try to keep tabs on any personal pledges of ownership interests by owners to secure loans. If you learn of a default by an owner on a loan secured by an ownership interest, notify creditors immediately of the company's and the co-owners' buyback rights under your agreement.

2. Encumbrances Not Allowed

The provision in our agreement that forbids owners from pledging their ownership interests for loans is shown in Excerpt 12.

If you do not want to allow the owners of your company to use their ownership interests as collateral for personal loans, check Option 2 on your worksheet now. (Section III, Scenario 7.)

I. What If an Owner Is Expelled?

Expelling a co-owner from your business can be a wrenching experience, one you surely hope you never have to encounter. Certainly many new business owners find it very difficult to even consider this possibility. But putting your head in the sand and pretending you'll never have to deal with a co-owner who fails to adequately perform her job-related duties is a serious mistake. When bad things happen to the owners of good companies, you need to be able to deal with them. Here is a short list of some of the unhappy possibilities you may have to cope with:

- An owner becomes seriously alcohol or drug dependent.
- An owner loses interest in the business.
- An owner exhibits disturbing personal behavior patterns such as extreme anger or depression.
- An owner steals from the business or is dishonest.
- An owner engages in unacceptable conduct at work, such as harassing co-workers.

To cope with an owner who is irresponsible, untrustworthy or just not performing up to the company's standards, it can make sense to include in your buy-sell agreement a provision that

---

Scenario 7. Encumbrance of Interest

☐ **Option 2: No Encumbrance Allowed**

No owner may encumber any or all of his ownership interest in the company in connection with any debt, guarantee or other personal undertaking.

Excerpt 12

requires such an owner to relinquish his duties and sell his ownership interest to the company or the other owners. Sounds good, but actually implementing such a clause can be tricky, since whether an owner really is underperforming or acting badly is usually a matter of opinion. That's why it's a good idea to put reasons for expelling an owner into your buy-sell agreement if you want your agreement to cover this scenario. Then an owner who signs the agreement can't later claim that it's unfair. It follows that if you are interested in including such a provision, you'll also want to include a list of specific grounds that constitute "adequate cause" for expulsion. In real life, people can and do challenge "adequate cause" in wrongful termination suits, but at least if you've set out some standards to measure against, you'll be ahead of the game.

In order to avoid more bitterness than is already likely to surround any expulsion, you may want to provide that the company or the continuing owners will repurchase an expelled owner's interest at the full agreement price, not at a discounted price, except possibly in a few situations where the co-owner's failure to meet her obligations is objective and clear. In those cases, you may want to provide a method for discounting the buyout price according to possible impairment of your company's reputation. For instance, your agreement can allow the company or the remaining owners to purchase the share of an expelled owner who embezzles from the company at 40% to 60% of the full Agreement Price that would be paid to a co-owner's estate if he died. Or to allow for the possibility that the bad-acting co-owner's conduct may have resulted in the business's doing poorly, you may simply want to provide for a new appraisal of the company to establish its current worth. (We discuss the procedure for getting an appraisal in Chapter 6.)

 Expulsion may be one area where you do not want to allow binding arbitration. Arbitration is a method of settling a conflict where a neutral third party makes a decision rather than a judge (discussed in Chapter 8). For many people, it's usually a better choice than going to court, but in this situation, an arbitrator might decide you can't expel a partner or other co-owner when you think it is absolutely necessary for your business's survival. So if you have an arbitration clause in your contract (our buy-sell agreement does—see Chapter 8), you may want to specifically rule it out for expulsion. To accomplish this, at the end of your expulsion clause, add a declaration that any expulsion decision is absolutely final and is not subject to arbitration or other review, including review by any court. (This will make any later arbitration clause you have not apply, since the arbitration clause we suggest in Chapter 8 starts with the phrase, "Except as otherwise provided in this agreement.")

The expulsion clause included in our buy-sell agreement is shown in Excerpt 13.

If you are interested in giving the company and the continuing owners the option to buy an expelled owner's interest, check Option 1 on your worksheet now. (Section III, Scenario 8.) If you check Option 1, also:

- check Option 1a, 1b and/or 1c to establish instances of adequate cause. If you check Option 1c, fill in additional reasons for expulsion. If you do not check any of the boxes, adequate cause will be determined at the time of expulsion.
- if you checked 1a, 1b or 1c, check Option 1d, 1e or 1f to establish what price will be paid to an owner expelled for one of the enumerated instances of adequate cause. If you check Option 1f, fill in the amount of the discount to be taken off the agreement price.

You can change the voting procedure. As you can see, our agreement provides that an owner can be expelled only by unanimous vote of all other owners. (But if your business only has two owners, neither one can expel the other.) If

Scenario 8. Expulsion of Owner

☐ **Option 1: Option of Company and Continuing Owners to Purchase an Expelled Owner's Interest**

  (a) At a time when the company has three or more owners, situations may arise in which a group of owners wish to expel another owner. An owner may be expelled upon a unanimous vote of all other owners for adequate cause. Upon such expulsion, the expelled owner is deemed to have offered to sell all of his or her interest to the company and the continuing owners. The company and the continuing owners shall then have an option, but not an obligation (unless otherwise stated in this agreement), to purchase all or part of the ownership interest within the time and according to the procedure in Section IV, Provision 1 of this agreement. The price to be paid shall be as specified in this section; if not so specified, then according to Section VI of this agreement. The manner of payments and other terms of the purchase shall be according to Section VII of this agreement. An owner who has been expelled is referred to as an "expelled owner" below.

  (b) Adequate cause includes, but is not limited to:

    ☐ **Option 1a: Any criminal conduct against the company (such as embezzlement)**
    ☐ **Option 1b: A serious breach of the owner's duties or of any written policy of the company, or**
    ☐ **Option 1c** _____ *[insert reasons]* _____

  (c) If an owner is expelled for a reason listed in subsection (b), the price that the company and/or the continuing owners will pay for the expelled owner's ownership interest will be:

    ☐ **Option 1d: The full Agreement Price according to Section VI of this agreement**
    ☐ **Option 1e: Decided by an independent appraisal, according to the Appraised Value Method in Section VI of this agreement**
    ☐ **Option 1f: The Agreement Price as established in Section VI of this agreement, decreased by** ___*[insert percentage, such as "50"]*___ %

Excerpt 13

you want to provide for expulsion upon a less than unanimous vote, your agreement should also set out a voting mechanism for owners to expel a co-owner. For example, you may want to provide that an owner can be expelled by a vote of ⅔ or more of the voting owners (per capita), or by agreement of the owners who hold 60% or more of the company's capital (percentage of ownership).

This provision only applies to businesses with more than two owners. If you own your business with one other person, you will not be able to expel that person under a provision that requires a unanimous or majority vote, and vice versa. So if your co-owner is acting badly or not working up to par, unless you convince her to sell out, your only other option might be to disband the company. ■

CHAPTER

4

Structuring Buyouts

In Chapters 2 and 3, we discussed how you can use buy-sell provisions—including the Right of First Refusal, the Option to Purchase an Owner's Interest and the Right to Force a Sale—to control who owns your company and to give departing owners a mechanism to cash out. If you include any of these provisions in your buy-sell agreement, it's almost sure that at some point during your company's life, the company or the continuing owners will purchase a departing owner's interest. To ensure that all buyout situations are handled smoothly, your buy-sell agreement should provide *how* a future buyout will be carried out.

A good, clear buyout procedure should include details like:

- how and when the company and the continuing owners decide who will buy the interest of the selling, departing or deceased owner (we'll call that owner the "transferring" owner, and the interest the "available interest"). In other words, will the company itself or the owners who will remain in the company (we'll call them the "continuing owners") buy the available interest?
- how and when the company and continuing owners must notify the transferring owner that they will purchase his or her interest (with a Notice of Intent to Purchase an Owner's Interest).

We show you how our buy-sell agreement handles these items below.

A. Types of Buyout Procedures

The first thing you need to do is decide which of three broad approaches you'll adopt to implement your buyout. The main difference between these methods involves who will buy the transferring owner's interest—the company or the continuing owners, or a combination of the two. Following are the three common methods of buying back interests. (Our agreement uses the third method, for the reasons explained below.)

1. Entity-Purchase Buyback (Called a Redemption Buyback for Corporations)

In this first type of buyback procedure, called an "entity-purchase buyback," when an owner retires, dies or wants to sell out, only the company (the "entity") has the option, or sometimes the obligation—depending on what clauses you choose to include in your buy-sell agreement—to buy the transferring owner's interest in the company.

What happens after the company buys the available interest depends on how your business is organized. In a corporation, the company simply cancels the redeemed shares after a buyback, and the continuing shareholders' ownership percentages in the company increase accordingly (though the amount of shares they own will not change). Similarly, in a partnership or an LLC, after the company buys an owner's interest, the interest is "liquidated," and the continuing partners' or members' ownership percentages increase.

The entity-purchase method is popular because it allows company funds rather than personal funds or personal loans to complete a buyout. But the main advantage of this method is its simplicity. By deciding who will buy the transferring owner's interest far in advance of the actual buyback, this method eliminates the need to decide who will make the buyback at the time of the buyout. But precisely because it's so simple, it lacks flexibility. For example, it doesn't give one or more continuing owners the option of buying the ownership interest themselves, an approach that can sometimes result in significant income and capital gains tax advantages to both the continuing owners and the transferring owner. In short, since rapidly changing tax laws as well as constant changes in companies' and owners' situations make it impossible to know years in advance whether it would be best have the company or the continuing owners buy the interest in question, a much more informed decision can be made at the time of the buyout.

We discuss the income tax disadvantages of company-sponsored buyouts briefly in Chapter 9, Section A. Note, however, that this is a very complicated area, and you will no doubt want to get a tax expert's opinion before having your company or the continuing owners buy out an owner's interest.

Corporations and LLCs can't always buy out a departing owner. In most states, corporations and LLCs cannot absolutely bind themselves to a plan to buy back the interest of a departing owner. That's because, to legally do this, the company is required to be in good financial shape—in other words, to have sufficient surplus funds available before purchasing a transferring owner's interest. (See sidebar, "Your Company Should Remain Solvent After a Buyback.")

Your Company Should Remain Solvent After a Buyback

As a rule, state corporation and LLC laws prevent a corporation or LLC from buying back an owner's interest if specific financial solvency tests cannot be met. Generally, state law requires that, after the buyback, the company's assets must exceed its liabilities (sometimes by a specified amount)—for example, a state may say that a company's assets must be at least one and one-half times its liabilities after the buyback. And, almost as a universal rule, to participate in a buyback, the corporation or LLC must be able to pay its debts as they become due after the buyback (that is, the company must remain solvent after the purchase of the owner's interest). Rather than worry too much about these restrictions now, just realize that in the future, if your corporation or LLC would have to use most or all of its cash reserves to buy back a departing owner's shares, it may be illegal to go forward with the deal. But this doesn't mean there would be a legal impediment to one or more co-owners individually buying back shares. Which, of course, is another way of saying that it's important to have a buy-sell agreement procedure that lets you decide at the time of the buyout who should buy the shares of a transferring owner.

Partnerships should follow this solvency test, too. While not normally required under state partnership laws, it also makes sense for partnerships to make sure that they remain solvent after a company buyback of a partner's interest. Even if your partnership agreement and state law allow your company to pay more than it can afford to buy back an owner's interest, obviously, it would be foolhardy for it to do so.

2. Cross-Purchase Buyback

The second common type of buyback procedure is called a "cross-purchase buyback." Under this approach, when an owner retires, dies or wants to sell out, only the continuing owners—not the business itself—have an option (or sometimes an obligation, depending on what you choose to include in your agreement) to purchase that owner's interest. Usually this means each continuing owner can purchase a share of the departing owner's interest in proportion to their current holdings (for instance, a 10% owner—that is, a person holding 10% of the total interests held by all continuing owners, not counting the interest owned by the departing owner—can purchase 10% of the ownership interest in question). Again, since the company itself is not a party to this type of agreement, it cannot purchase the transferring owner's interest itself.

One problem with co-owners individually buying out a departing owner is that when a company has more than two or three owners, this method can get complicated in terms of notice requirements (using insurance funding also becomes harder to deal with; see Chapter 5, Section C). And like the entity-purchase buyback, this procedure does not allow the flexibility of deciding at the time of the buyout who should buy the ownership interest, the company or the continuing owners. Again, when you're forming your buy-sell agreement, you probably won't have the necessary information you need to make the best decision as to who should perform the buyback.

 We discuss the income tax advantages of owner-sponsored buyouts briefly in Chapter 9, Section A. Note, however, that this is a very complicated area, and you will no doubt want to get a tax expert's opinion before deciding to buy out an owner's interest.

3. Combination of Entity-Purchase and Cross-Purchase Buyback

As you probably guessed, this third type of buyback procedure, called a "combination of entity-purchase and cross-purchase buyback," usually works best for most buyout situations. That's because it affords both the company and the continuing owners an option to purchase an owner's interest when a buyout situation presents itself. Usually, the company gets the first opportunity to purchase the interest in question, and then the continuing owners are allowed to purchase any of the transferring owner's interest not purchased by the company, usually in proportion to their current holdings.

Probably the biggest advantage of this method is its flexibility. It allows the company and the continuing owners to wait until a buyout situation comes up, at which point they can decide—considering tax consequences and the company's and owners' circumstances—who will buy a transferring owner's interest.

For these reasons, in our agreement we use this third "wait and see" approach. Almost always we believe it is best to allow the company and the continuing owners to decide at the time of the buyout—and not when the buy-sell agreement is drafted—who will buy a departing owner's interest.

📁 **See a lawyer if you are interested in using a different procedure.** Though we see few situations in which they are preferable, if you think a straight entity-purchase procedure or a cross-purchase procedure would best suit your company, see a lawyer for help in changing your agreement. We discuss finding and working with lawyers in Chapter 10.

While the "wait and see" buyback procedure works similarly for all three types of buyout provisions discussed in Chapters 2 and 3 (the Right of First Refusal, the Option to Purchase and the

Right to Force a Sale), a few different steps must be followed to implement it in each situation. Let's take a brief look at each type of buyout situation.

B. How Our Buyback Procedure Works

By choosing the buy-sell provisions discussed in Chapter 2 and 3, you've already handled the details of *when* a buyout right or obligation is triggered. As a short review, this happens:

- upon receipt of a Notice of Intent to Transfer (in a Right-of-First-Refusal buyout situation)
- upon the happening of an event that triggers a buyout right, such as an owner's retirement, disability, death, divorce, bankruptcy, loss of license or default (in an Option to Purchase an Owner's Interest), and
- upon receipt of a Notice of Intent to Force a Sale (in a Right-to-Force-a-Sale situation).

You still need to deal with what happens after the buyout right or obligation is triggered. Let's look at each type of buyout situation to see what happens next.

1. How Our Buyback Procedure Works With a Right of First Refusal

As we discussed in Chapter 2, when an owner whose buy-sell agreement contains a Right-of-First-Refusal clause receives an offer from an outsider or a current owner to buy her ownership interest (or considers giving it away), the Right-of-First-Refusal clause is triggered. The clause says that, before making a sale or transfer, the owner considering a transfer must offer her interest to the company and to her co-owners for purchase by delivering notice to the company of the terms of the intended transfer.

At that point, the transaction unwinds just as if it arose under an Option-to-Purchase clause—the

company and the continuing owners now have an option to purchase the transferring owner's interest if they choose. Since this part of the buyback procedure is the same under the Right-of-First-Refusal provision as it is under an Option-to-Purchase provision, we avoid repetition by explaining how the option part of the procedure works just once, immediately below, in Section 2.

The only significant difference between a regular Option to Purchase and an option following a Right of First Refusal is in what happens after the option periods are up. In a Right-of-First-Refusal situation, if the company or the continuing owners buy *all* of the transferring owner's interest, the outsider or potential transferee is essentially shut out of the company. But if the company and the continuing owners *decline* to buy *all* of the transferring owner's interest, the transferring owner is then free to sell her entire interest to the outsider or current owner (or give her interest to a relative, if that's what she was after) within 60 days, at the same price and terms in her Notice of Intent to Transfer. By contrast, the procedure for the regular Option-to-Purchase clause simply ends if neither the company nor the owners elect to purchase the departing owner's interest. In that case, the departing owner or his family members are free to hold on to their interest.

2. How Our Buyback Procedure Works With an Option to Purchase

The Option to Purchase an Owner's Interest procedure (Section IV, (1) in our agreement) is triggered whenever notice is received by the company of an option to purchase, whether it's by a Notice of Intent to Transfer the Interest according to a Right of First Refusal (Chapter 2) or notice of a business-disrupting event such as the retirement, divorce, disability or death of an owner (Chapter 3). Of course, in a small company, informal notice of departure or death happens almost automatically and immediately, but notice of a divorce or bankruptcy may not occur until the ex-spouse of an owner or the bankruptcy trustee wishes to cash in their newly gained interest. But no matter how informally notice may be given, it's important to understand that our option periods start only after the company knows that the triggering event has occurred. (For example, if the company does not receive formal notice that an owner has filed for bankruptcy, when the company becomes aware of this, the buyback right is triggered, and the option period starts to run.)

After the company receives notice, the company's owners (or in a corporation, its board of directors) should meet with their tax advisors and each other to decide if it's in their best interest for the company itself to buy the available interest.

What does the term "available interest" mean? The "available interest" is the ownership interest that is up for sale—it may be owned and held by a transferring, retiring, disabled, expelled or bankrupt owner or by an ex-spouse or creditor, or it may be owned by a deceased or disabled owner and controlled by the deceased owner's estate or guardian. In our discussions below and in the language of the buy-sell agreement, we refer to the interest that is subject to buyback as the "available interest."

It is up to you to decide on what a fair amount of time is for the company to make its decision, but we think 30 or 60 days is reasonable. (Remember, the continuing owners of the company then have another period to decide individually whether they want to purchase the available interest.) Of course, you can insert a longer time limit for the company to decide to buy back the interest.

Allow adequate time for a buyback decision. For a high-stakes buyout, less than 30 or 60 days can be too short a time for a company to make an informed decision with the help of a tax advisor.

Excerpt 1 shows the language taken from the Option-to-Purchase provision in our buy-sell agreement that covers this part of the procedure (see Section IV, (1) of the agreement).

All readers should include Section IV in their buy-sell agreement. Add to your worksheet the number of days that you want your company to have—after receiving notice or becoming aware of the event triggering the Option to Purchase—to make its buyback decision under an Option to Purchase. (Section IV, (1), (b).)

Section IV: Buyout Procedure

(1) Option of Company and Continuing Owners to Purchase an Interest

    (a) This provision is triggered upon receipt of notice by the company according to Section II or the notification of any of the events checked in Section III where the company and/or the continuing owners have an option, but not an obligation (unless otherwise stated in this agreement), to purchase the interest that is the subject of the notice (called the "available interest").

    (b) The company shall have an option to purchase any or all of the available interest within _[insert number of days, such as "30"]_ days after the date on which the company receives notice or becomes aware of the event triggering the Option to Purchase.

Excerpt 1

If the owners or directors decide that the company should buy all of the available interest, the company must exercise its option by delivering a written Notice of Intent to Purchase to the transferring owner (or the current holder of the interest) within the option period. In other words, this Notice of Intent to Purchase is sent to the transferring, retiring, disabled, expelled, bankrupt or defaulting owner if the interest is still in the owner's hands, or to the person who now has ownership or control of the interest, such as a creditor, a bankruptcy trustee, an estate representative or the ex-spouse of an owner. The contents of the notice are covered below.

If the company does not decide to purchase all of the available interest, the company must immediately let each of the continuing owners know that some or all of the interest is available for purchase by them (the part of the interest not purchased by the company). Our provision gives the continuing owners another time period (usually 30 or 60 days) following the expiration of the company's option period to decide individually whether they want to purchase any of the interest not purchased by the company. Again, it is up to you and your co-owners to decide on what you think is a fair amount of time for the continuing owners to reach their decisions.

Excerpt 2 shows the language that covers this part of the procedure, taken from the Option-to-Purchase provision in our buy-sell agreement. (Section IV, (1).)

Add to your worksheet the number of days that you want the continuing owners to have (immediately after the expiration of the company's period for making its purchase option decision) to make their individual buyback decisions under an Option to Purchase. (Section IV, (1), (c).)

Within this second time period, each owner who wishes to purchase any of the available interest must submit to the company a notice of how much of the interest he wants to buy.

(c) If the company does not decide to purchase all of the available interest within the time allowed, it shall immediately, and, in all cases, no later than the date of expiration of the company's right to exercise its purchase option of the available interest, notify the continuing owners of their right to purchase the available interest not purchased by the company. This notice by the company to the continuing owners shall state:

1) the amount and description of the interest available for purchase by the continuing owners

2) the date by which the continuing owner must respond in writing to the company that he or she wishes to purchase any or all of the available interest, which date shall be _[insert number of days, such as "30"]_ days after the date of the expiration of the company's purchase option, and

3) that any purchase by a continuing owner must be according to the terms of this buy-sell agreement.

A copy of this buy-sell agreement shall be immediately furnished to any continuing owner who requests a copy.

Excerpt 2

Excerpt 3 shows the language that covers this part of the procedure, taken from the Option-to-Purchase provision in our buy-sell agreement. (Section IV, (1).)

If only one continuing owner wants to individually purchase the available interest, it's simple —that party simply purchases the interest in its entirety. The purchasing procedure can become a bit more involved if more than one of the continuing owners want to buy the available interest. Problems develop when two or more continuing owners together wish to buy an amount larger than the available interest being offered to the continuing owners. When this occurs, the available interest must be split up according to the terms set out in the buy-sell agreement. Usually, the owner who currently owns the largest percentage of the company gets to buy the lion's share of the available interest.

Our agreement allows the owners who wish to purchase the available interest to buy in an amount relative to their ownership percentages within the group of owners who elect to buy the interest (let's call them "the purchasing group"). In other words, an owner who wishes to purchase the available interest can buy as much of the interest as the percentage she owns of the total amount of interest currently owned by the purchasing group. Note that this purchasing group excludes the transferring owner's interest or the interests of any owners who don't want to buy

the newly available interest. The available interest is then divvied up to the purchasing owners based on those percentages.

Confused by all this gobbledygook? Here are a couple of examples that should help. First, one that illustrates the allocation of the available interest among shareholders:

EXAMPLE 1: In Chapter 2 we introduced you to a travel-adventure company called Run-a-Muck, owned by Jason, Tim, Chris and Bart. You may remember that each of the four owners owns 250 shares of the corporation. Jason (the transferring owner) gives the company notice of his intent to sell the shares to an outsider (Kacey). The company, itself, declines to exercise its buyback option. Out of the three continuing owners of the company, only Tim and Chris decide to purchase Jason's shares individually. Together Tim and Chris (whose interests are pooled in computing the total interests owned by the purchasing group) already own 500 shares. Since each of them owns half (250) of the total shares (500) owned by the purchasing group, each is entitled to purchase half of Jason's shares, or 125 shares apiece. (Note that before purchasing Jason's shares, Tim and Chris were both 25% owners of the company —but they nevertheless each were able to purchase 50% of Jason's shares.)

(d) Each continuing owner may exercise his or her option to purchase any or all of the available interest in writing by delivering or mailing to the company an individual Notice of Intent to Purchase. This notice shall be sent to the secretary or equivalent officer of the company, and shall show the name and address of the continuing owner who wishes to purchase part or all of the available interest and the amount and a description of the interest that the continuing owner wishes to purchase.

Excerpt 3

Second, here is an example that illustrates the allocation of the available interest among the owners of an LLC or partnership:

EXAMPLE 2: Janet, Spencer, Patti and Stephen own a limited liability company called Megasoft. Patti Elias owns 45% of the company, Janet Gima owns 25%, Spencer Portman owns 15% and Stephen Stewart owns 15%. Patti gets an offer from an outsider to buy her 45% of the company, and she notifies the company of her intention to sell, attaching a copy of the offer to purchase her shares. The directors of the corporation decide the corporation, itself, isn't interested, but Janet and Sherman, using their Right of First Refusal, want to buy as much of Patti's interest as they are allowed; Stephen, who needs every penny to put his son, Ruben, through medical school, opts not to buy any. Here's how Janet and Spencer divide up the interest: Together, Janet and Spencer (the purchasing group) own 40% (25% + 15%) of the company. Janet determines her ownership percentage of that total by dividing her individual ownership percentage (25%) by the total owned by the group (40%) to arrive at a percentage of 62.5%. Spencer divides his individual ownership percentage (15%) by the total (40%) to arrive at 37.5%. Therefore, Janet will get 62.5% of Patti's interest, and Spencer will get 37.5%. (If you're interested, after the buyout Janet ends up owning 53.125% of the company, Spencer 31.875%, and Stephen 15%.)

Excerpt 4 shows the language that covers this part of the procedure, taken from the Option-to-Purchase provision in our buy-sell agreement. (Section IV, (1).)

Now, let's look at the rest of the buyback procedure contained in this section of the buy-sell agreement. If the company or any of the continuing owners exercise their option to buy the available interest, the company sends out a collective notice to the transferring owner, or current holder of the interest, of the company's and/or continuing owners' intent to purchase a part or all the available interest.

Whom should the Notice of Intent to Purchase be sent to? Generally, the Notice of Intent to Purchase should be sent to the person who provided the original notice to the company of a proposed transfer or the occurrence of any of the triggering events that give rise to a buyback (the death, disability or expulsion of an owner and the like). For example, a Notice of Intent to Purchase the interest of a transferring owner will go to that owner, while the Notice of Intent to Purchase the interest of a deceased owner will go to the representative of the deceased owner's estate.

(e) If the total amount of interest specified in the notices by the continuing owners to the company exceeds the amount of the interest available for purchase by them, each continuing owner shall be entitled, up to the amount of interest specified in his or her individual Notice of Intent to Purchase, to purchase a fraction of the available interest, in the same proportion that the amount of the interest he or she currently owns bears to the total amount of the company's interest owned by all continuing owners electing to purchase.

Excerpt 4

The notice of Intent to Purchase should include the following information:

- the name and address of the company, and the name and title of the officer or employee who can be contacted at the company regarding the Notice of Intent to Purchase

- a description and the amount of ownership interest to be purchased by the company and/or each of the continuing owners, and the name and address of each such continuing owner

- the total amount of the available interest to be purchased by the company and the continuing owners

- the terms of the purchase according to the buy-sell agreement

- a copy of the buy-sell agreement, and

- if the interest to be purchased is represented by certificates, such as share certificates, a request for the surrender of the share certificates to the company.

Here's an example of a straightforward Notice of Intent to Purchase, in letter format:

Babak Pakroo
1500 West Covina Ave.
Covina Cove, CA 94560

Notice of Intent to Purchase Shares

Dear Babak,

ADC Data Corp has decided to exercise its right to purchase 500 shares of Class A voting stock owned by you for $5000.00, as provided in the buy-sell agreement dated 4/15/98 and on file with the company. A copy of the agreement is attached. Terms for payment shall be according to Section VII of the buy-sell agreement. The first payment, according to these terms, will be mailed to you on or by 5/30/2001. Please surrender the share certificates representing these shares to me at the address listed below, prior to this date. If you have any additional questions, please contact me at the address or telephone number shown below.

Sincerely,

Ali Hayward

Ali Hayward, Secretary
ADC Data Corp
800 Main Street
Oakland Beach, CA
Telephone: 555-555-5555

Excerpt 5 shows the language of our buy-sell agreement that covers the Notice of Intent to Purchase, taken from the Option to Purchase procedure. (Section IV, (1).)

After mailing the notice of intent, the company and/or the continuing owners buy back the interest according to the price and payment terms in the agreement.

What if the company and continuing owners don't buy the entire interest? As a practical matter, if there is a buyback option, either the company or the continuing owners will decide to buy back the available interest if company or personal finances permit. (Though sometimes they will allow a sale to an appropriate outsider under a Right-of-First-Refusal provision.) Further, they usually buy back the entire interest, not just part of it. But our agreement contains the flexibility to allow both the company and the continuing owners to participate in a full or partial buyback, so remember these basic rules:

- If the Option to Purchase arose under a Right of First Refusal, and the company and the owners decide not to purchase the entire interest, the buyback does not occur and the owner is free to sell, give away or otherwise transfer the entire interest (see Chapter 2).
- If the buyback arises due to an option by the company and continuing owners to buy the interest of a retiring, disabled, expelled, unlicensed, bankrupt or defaulting owner or the interest of an owner held by a divorced owner's ex-spouses or a deceased owner's estate, trust or inheritors, the company and/or the continuing owners are allowed to buy less than all of the interest. The owner or her ex-spouse, estate, trust, inheritors or creditors keep the amount of the interest not bought by the company and the continuing owners (see Chapter 3).
- If the buyback arises as part of a forced sale demanded by a retiring or disabled owner

---

(f) If the company or any continuing owner exercises their option to purchase a part or all of the available interest, the company shall deliver or mail to the current owner or, if different, the current holder of the available interest, no later than five business days after the expiration of the period to exercise their option to purchase the available interest, a Notice of Intent to Purchase, that includes the following information:
- the name and address of the company, and the name and title of the officer or employee who can be contacted at the company
- a description and the amount of ownership interest to be purchased by the company and/or each of the continuing owners, and the name and address of each such continuing owner
- the total amount of the interest to be purchased by the company and the continuing owners
- the terms of the purchase according to Section VII of this agreement
- a copy of the buy-sell agreement, and
- if the interest to be purchased is represented by certificates, such as share certificates, a request for the surrender of the share certificates to the company.

Excerpt 5

or a deceased owner's estate, trust or inheritors, the entire interest must be bought back by the company and/or the continuing owners (see Chapter 3).

Excerpt 6 shows the language that covers the final part of the procedure, taken from the Option-to-Purchase provision in our buy-sell agreement. (Section IV, (1).)

3. How Our Buyout Procedure Works With a Right to Force a Sale

Right to Force a Sale only. If you did not check an option on your worksheet to give a retired or disabled owner, or the estate, trust or inheritors of a deceased owner, the Right to Force a Sale (any of the Options 2's in Section III of the agreement), this section won't apply to you. Skip ahead to Chapter 5.

The procedural details and agreement clauses that handle a Right-to-Force-a-Sale scenario, where the company and continuing owners are *required* to buy back an owner's interest (discussed in Chapter 3), are almost entirely the same as those discussed above for the Option to Purchase an Interest procedure by the company and continuing owners. We won't explain each clause individually here; we just point out the few differences between the two procedures and the portions of the agreement that need to be completed (reread Section 2, above, if you have any additional questions about the forced sale procedure or agreement language).

First, forced sales may occur only in a few instances under our agreement: in the case of the retirement, the disability or the death of an owner. In these instances, if the forced-sale option is checked in the appropriate section of the agreement (see Chapter 3), the retiring or disabled owner or, if an owner has died, his family member, estate representative or trustee, can force a buyout of the owner's interest by submitting a Notice of Intent to Force a Sale. The contents of this notice under Section III of the agreement vary depending on the nature of the forced sale event (death, disability or retirement), but here's a sample notice based upon an owner's retirement:

> Niall Carnahan demands that Olympic Parking, LLC purchase all of his 50% capital interest in Olympic Parking, LLC, due to his retirement from the company, effective October,10, 2010. Price and terms for payment shall be according to Sections VI and VII of the buy-sell agreement, dated 4/15/98 and on file with the company, a copy of which is attached.

(g) The company and the continuing owners shall purchase the portion or all of the available interest each has exercised an option to purchase in the Notice of Intent to Purchase, according to the terms specified in Section VII of this agreement, each making payment for the interest to be purchased and complying with other terms as appropriate. The sale shall be considered final when the company and the continuing owners make payment to the owner or holder of the interest or, if payment is made over time, when all paperwork necessary to the sale has been executed by the company, the continuing owners and the owner or holder of the interest to be purchased.

Excerpt 6

Once this notice is received by the company, the company and then the continuing owners have a chance to buy all or a part of the interest of the retiring, disabled or deceased owner under the same procedure as that discussed in Section 2, above ("Option to Purchase an Owner's Interest").

As with the Option-to-Purchase clause, you must decide how much time to give the company and continuing owners to make their buyback decisions. Again, we think 30 or 60 days for each period is reasonable.

Excerpt 7 shows the language that covers the first part of the procedure, taken from the Right-to-Force-a-Sale procedure in our buy-sell agreement. (Section IV, (2).)

All readers should include Section IV in their buy-sell agreement. Insert in your worksheet the number of days that you want your company to have—after receipt of a Notice of Intent to Force a Sale—to make its buyback decision under a Right to Force a Sale. (Section IV, (2), (b).)

---

(2) Right to Force a Sale
   (a) This provision is triggered upon receipt by the company of a Notice of Intent to Force a Sale according to Section III, where the company and the continuing owners have an obligation to purchase the interest that is the subject of the notice (called the "available interest").
   (b) The company shall have an option to purchase any or all of the available interest within _[insert number of days, such as "30"]_ days after the date on which the company receives the Notice of Intent to Force a Sale.

Excerpt 7

If the company decides to buy back the entire interest, the process is complete. But if the company does not decide to buy all of the interest, the continuing owners get a chance to buy any part not picked up by the company. As in the Option-to-Purchase procedure, a continuing owner who wants to purchase any or all of the available interest must submit a Notice of Intent to Purchase the interest within a specified time period (see agreement subsection (1)(b), above, for details). Again, you must specify the period the continuing owners have to make their buyback decision.

Excerpt 8 shows the language in our agreement that covers this part of the procedure, taken from the Right-to-Force-a-Sale procedure in our buy-sell agreement. (Section IV, (2).)

Add to your worksheet the number of days that you want the continuing owners to have (immediately after the expiration of the company's period for making its purchase decision) to make their individual buyback decisions under a Right to Force a Sale. (Section IV, (2).)

If more than one continuing owner is interested in purchasing the available interest, the continuing owners get to purchase the available interest in proportion to their current ownership holdings (see Section 2, above, for the mechanics of how this allocation works among the continuing owners). If the continuing owners do not decide to buy all of the remaining interest available for purchase by them, the Right-to-Force-a-Sale procedure takes one very important extra step. In this case, the company *must* purchase all 100% of the available interest not bought by the continuing owners, according to the price and payment terms in the agreement. Why is this so? Because in any forced sale scenario under Section III of the agreement, the company and remaining owners are *required* to buy all of the retiring, disabled or deceased owner's interest if a forced sale is requested.

Excerpt 9 shows the language that covers this last part of the procedure, taken from the Right-to-Force-a-Sale provision in our buy-sell agreement. (Section IV, (2).)

(c) If the company does not decide to purchase all of the available interest within the time allowed, it shall immediately, and, in all cases, no later than the date of expiration of the company's right to exercise its purchase option of the available interest, notify the continuing owners of their right to purchase the available interest not purchased by the company. This notice by the company to the continuing owners shall state:

1) the amount and description of the interest available for purchase by the continuing owners

2) the date by which the continuing owner must respond in writing to the company that he or she wishes to purchase any or all of the available interest, which date shall be   _[insert number of days, such as "30"]_   days after the date of the expiration of the company's purchase option, and

3) that any purchase by a continuing owner must be according to the terms of this buy-sell agreement.

A copy of this buy-sell agreement shall be immediately furnished to any continuing owner who requests a copy.

Excerpt 8

(f) If the continuing owners decline to purchase all of the available interest that remains, the company *shall* purchase the amount of available interest not purchased by the continuing owners.

Excerpt 9

Don't change the purchasing order of this procedure without a tax expert's help. The order of the purchasing options is important for tax purposes—first the company has an option to purchase the transferring owner's interest, then the continuing owners, and if the total interest has not been purchased or subscribed to at that point, the company must buy whatever remains to be purchased.

The remainder of the procedure for forced sales is the same as that which applies to options to purchase covered in Section 2 above. That is, the company sends out a consolidated Notice of Intent to Purchase the interest (in this case, the entire interest) by the company and/or the continuing owners to the owner or the owner's estate, inheritors, guardian or whoever is forcing the sale. The entire interest is then purchased by the company and/or continuing owners according to the terms in Section VII of the agreement. ∎

Funding Buyouts

In Chapter 4, we discussed how to structure a buyout that will take place in the future. But if you don't adopt a sensible plan to provide the company or continuing owners with funds to carry out a future buyout, your buy-sell provisions may turn out to be worthless (for example, if your company or co-owners can't come up with the money to buy out an owner's estate after he has died, his inheritors will have an ownership interest in the company and may start to interfere). It is key to plan to fund a future buyout now, since some types of funding require long-term planning and accrual. In this chapter we briefly discuss several common ways to fund a buyback under your buy-sell agreement.

A. Cash

The most obvious way to pay for a buyout is with cash. Funding with cash is simple and has no immediate expense (unlike paying up-front premiums for life insurance, which we discuss in Section C, below). But unless your company or its owners are solidly solvent, planning to buy back an owner's interest with cash has a big downside. It requires that your company or the continuing owners keep a large cash reserve available at all times. And, of course, this ties up money (or the ability to borrow it) that could better be used for other purposes.

If the co-owners have decided on using cash to fund a buyout, but neither the company nor the continuing owners have adequate cash reserves when the time comes to buy out an owner or his family members, the capital or current income of the company or the continuing owners' personal savings could be seriously depleted (or in the worst case scenario, the buyback might not even happen).

Corporations: Watch out for the accumulated earnings tax. For corporations, it's even possible that holding a large cash reserve to fund a future buyout could trigger an accumulated earnings tax. This tax is assessed when corporations hold on to cash that the IRS decides is not needed for normal business expansion or growth purposes (although most corporations get an automatic allowance to accumulate $250,000).

If you plan on funding a future buyout with cash only, you do not need to check anything in Section V on your worksheet or in our buy-sell agreement.

B. Borrowing

Borrowing money to fund a buyout is also fairly simple and does not require an immediate outlay of cash, but this method has its obvious problems. At the time of a buyout, the company or continuing owners might have trouble getting a loan, especially if a co-owner has just died (since the business has probably just lost an important asset). And, of course, there are other problems with borrowing. The company may have already exhausted its ability to borrow, or high interest rates may make getting a loan unaffordable.

Private Annuities

Here's a creative way to structure and fund a buyout. The seller of an ownership interest, such as a retiring owner or a deceased owner's heirs, can opt to receive a "private annuity" in exchange for giving the company or continuing owners her ownership interest. A private annuity means that the buyer itself (the company or continuing owners; no insurance company is involved) will pay a fixed amount each year directly to the seller for the remainder of her life. This comes with two tax advantages: The ownership interest will not appreciate during the seller's lifetime, and the seller can spread her capital gain out over her lifetime. When the seller and buyer are longtime friends and the business is in excellent financial shape, this approach can make sense. But in other circumstances, a private annuity can be risky, since if the business goes belly up, the seller probably won't get paid. Recognizing this, many sellers will be tempted to require that the buyer post valuable property as security for the annuity. Unfortunately, if collateral is required to secure the private annuity, it loses its two main advantages—the ownership interest will continue to appreciate, and the gain cannot be spread out over the seller's lifetime. If you're interested in funding a future buyout with a private annuity, see a lawyer or tax specialist. (We cover finding and working with lawyers in Chapter 10.)

Consider installment plans. As we discuss in Chapter 7, Choosing Payment Terms for Buyouts, one way to handle the problem of having to suddenly come up with a chunk of cash to fund a buyout is to provide that payment for an owner's interest will be made by the company or the continuing owners in installments, perhaps over three to five years. But receiving payments in dribs and drabs can be inconvenient for the owner or his family members, especially if they don't have confidence in the abilities of the remaining owners to successfully continue to operate the business in the meantime. And, depending on the purchase price, and the length of the installment period, paying for an owner's share over time may not ease the burden of the buyout enough to allow the company or continuing owners to maintain their business comfortably. For these reasons, you may want to combine installment plans with the purchase of insurance, discussed below.

If you plan on funding a future buyout through company or personal loans, you do not need to check anything in Section V on your worksheet or in our buy-sell agreement.

C. Insurance

Life insurance and disability insurance can play a big part in funding buyouts. Not only can they fund buyouts in situations of the death or disability of an owner, in some cases they can also provide some monies for the buyout of a retired owner (see subsection 1b, below).

Here's how insurance funding works. The company or all the co-owners take out insurance policies on each owner. When an owner dies or becomes disabled, the insurance payoff is used to buy the owner's interest.

Of course, some business owners do not like paying dollars up-front for a need that may be years away. But insurance premiums are much cheaper than either saving or borrowing money. And having insurance guarantees that cash will be available to purchase an owner's interest. Insurance, however, cannot usually be used to fund a buyout that is triggered when an owner gets divorced, files for personal bankruptcy, loses a professional license or defaults on a personal loan. For those buyout scenarios, cash, loans or other types of funding must be used.

Under a traditional entity-purchase procedure, the company pays the premiums on an insurance policy for each owner and is the owner and beneficiary of each policy. When an owner dies or becomes disabled, the company uses the insurance policy payoff to buy the ownership interest of the owner. This is called "entity-purchase," or "company-purchased," life insurance.

> EXAMPLE: A company has three owners. They adopt a buy-sell agreement calling for the company to buy out the estate of a deceased owner (forced sale on death of owner), under an entity-purchase arrangement. The company buys three insurance policies, which insure the lives of each of the three owners. The face amount of each policy should be at least enough to add up to the full Agreement Price for the entire company (or at least should come close enough to the full purchase price set in the agreement so that the company does not need to raise substantial cash to complete the buyout).

This approach is simple and cheap—only one policy is needed on each owner (rather than several, as is necessary when the owners purchase the policies themselves—discussed immediately below).

Another approach is for each of the owners to individually purchase and pay for insurance policies on the lives of each of the other owners —this is called "cross-purchase," or "owner-purchased," life insurance. The individual owners pay the premiums, own the policies and receive the insurance benefits if there's a payout.

In a three-owner company, the face amount of a policy on another owner should be high enough to pay for half of the purchase price of the owner's interest.

> EXAMPLE: Jackie, Elizabeth and Graciela open a photography studio, to be operated as a partnership. They adopt a buy-sell agreement calling for the company to buy out a disabled

owner with disability insurance, under a cross-purchase arrangement. Under the buy-sell agreement, each person's share of the company is worth approximately $100,000. Jackie buys two disability insurance policies: one on Elizabeth for $50,000 and one on Graciela for $50,000. Elizabeth also buys two policies for $50,000: one on Jackie and one on Graciela. And, of course, Graciela buys two policies for the same amount: one on Jackie and one on Elizabeth. Jackie suffers a chronic disability from long-term exposure to developing chemicals, and the insurance company rules that she is permanently and totally disabled. After the required six-month waiting period goes by, Elizabeth and Graciela each purchase half of Jackie's interest with the $50,000 they each receive from the insurance company.

Cross-purchase arrangements require more paperwork and more premiums (more policies), and are more difficult to maintain, than a company-purchased insurance arrangement, especially for companies with more than a few owners. Also, paying several smaller policies (required by a cross-purchase insurance plan) is sometimes more expensive than paying for one larger policy (under an entity-purchase plan). Therefore, in businesses with more than two or three owners, entity-purchased insurance may be the way to go.

There are many factors involved in choosing between entity-purchase and cross-purchase insurance, but we can make a few observations here. If you expect your company, not the continuing owners, to exercise buyback rights when it comes time to buy out an owner under your agreement, it makes sense to opt for entity-purchase insurance in your agreement. On the other hand, if you expect the continuing owners to buy out ownership interests under your agreement, you would probably be best choosing the cross-purchase insurance option. Of course, if you expect both the company and continuing owners to effectuate buyouts under your agreement when the time comes, either type may make sense. But in this case, we believe it's often best to choose the entity-purchase option. Again, having the company purchase one policy on each owner can be simpler and less expensive than having three, four or more owners purchase a policy on each of their co-owners. If an owner dies or becomes disabled, and the company decides to buy a deceased owner's interest, it uses the life or disability insurance proceeds from the policy it owned.

But what happens if the continuing owners want to exercise their option to buy a deceased owner's interest, and your agreement calls for company-purchased insurance? In small businesses where all the owners participate, the company can always make loans to the continuing owners to purchase the available interest, and then use the cash from its insurance payout to increase the owners' bonuses and salaries to allow them to make their loan payments.

1. Life Insurance

In this section, we touch on a few things you should understand if you're interested in funding your buy-sell agreement with life insurance, but most of your planning in this area will be done with an insurance agent or broker (one who must be familiar with buy-sell agreements and small businesses) and/or a qualified financial planner or CPA.

⚠️ **Not everyone can get life insurance.** Life insurance may not be available to owners of advancing years or who have ill health. If this describes you or your co-owners, you'll have to consider other funding methods, such as accumulating cash reserves and borrowing money.

Life Insurance Funding for Sole Proprietorships

When a sole proprietor dies, her business may die with her unless other steps are taken. If there is a family member who is willing and able to take over, the sole proprietor can leave the business to that person as a gift. But often an owner doesn't have the option of giving the business to family members or relatives. Rather than selling the business to strangers, which could be risky if the owner is relying on the continuing operations of the company for his retirement income, the business can be sold to an employee who is willing and able to take over.

To fund an employee buyout of a sole proprietor, the employee must purchase an insurance policy on the life of the sole proprietor. The employee is the owner, the payer of premiums and the beneficiary of the policy. When the sole proprietor dies, the insurance proceeds will be used to buy the business from the owner's estate (and the proceeds will then go to the sole proprietor's inheritors). In case an owner retires (instead of dying), the cash value of the insurance (if a whole life policy is purchased) can also be used by the employee to make a down payment toward purchase of the retiring owner's interest.

a. Life Insurance Arrangements

As we mentioned in our initial discussion of insurance above, you need to choose an entity-purchase or a cross-purchase arrangement for life insurance when you're forming a buy-sell agreement. However, this is a very complicated area of buy-sell agreements, so you should always consult your insurance agent or broker as well as a tax expert before deciding on entity-purchase or cross-purchase life insurance.

The language of the provision in our buy-sell agreement that calls for company-purchased life insurance (Section V, (1) of the agreement) is shown in Excerpt 1.

Check Option 1 for this provision on your worksheet if you wish to provide for company-purchased life insurance. (Section V, (1).)

There are several disadvantages to entity-purchase life insurance. One, since the policies are company assets under this scheme, they are subject to the claims of business creditors. (The cash values of the policies are considered assets of the company.) Two, for corporations,

the corporate alternative minimum tax (AMT) may trigger an indirect income tax when proceeds are paid out. To avoid tax problems, you should see a tax advisor to discuss these issues before having your company purchase life insurance policies on the owners' lives.

The language calling for owner-purchased life insurance contained in our agreement (Section V, (1)) is shown in Excerpt 2.

Check Option 2 for this provision on your worksheet if you wish to provide for owner-purchased life insurance; this option is an alternative to Option 1 covered just above (do not check both Options 1 and 2). (Section V, (1).)

Section V: Funding

(1) Life Insurance

☐ **Option 1:   Company-purchased life insurance**

The company will apply for, own and be the beneficiary of life insurance policies on the life of each owner. The company will take any actions necessary to maintain in force all of the insurance policies it is required to maintain under this section, including paying all premiums, and will not cancel them or allow them to lapse. The policy benefits shall be applied to the purchase price in a buyout of a deceased owner.

Excerpt 1

☐ **Option 2:   Owner-purchased life insurance**

Each owner will apply for, own and be the beneficiary of life insurance policies on the life of each other owner. Each owner will take any actions necessary to maintain in force all of the insurance policies it is required to maintain under this section, including paying all premiums, and will not cancel them or allow them to lapse. The policy benefits shall be applied to the purchase price in a buyout of a deceased owner.

Excerpt 2

There are also disadvantages to cross-purchase life insurance. There are disadvantages to cross-purchase insurance that apply to any size company. Younger owners, who are usually in the weakest financial position to pay high life insurance premiums, bear the burden of paying higher premiums for older owners. In addition, cross-purchase insurance may not be the ideal choice for corporations. If the corporate tax rate is lower than the individual owners' tax rates, it will be cheaper for the company to purchase premiums than for the individual owners (the after-tax cost will be lower). Investigate these financial issue, with your insurance agent or broker and your tax advisor before going ahead with a cross-purchase insurance plan.

b. Buying Life Insurance Policies

Here are some key points you should know when shopping for life insurance:

- Ideally, life insurance policies should be purchased at the same time you create a buy-sell agreement. That's because the cost of premiums will only go up as owners get older. You should estimate the amount you'll need for a buyout, and then get life insurance policies for a little more than that amount. Also, the face amounts of life insurance policies should be scheduled to keep up with the value of the owners' interests.

- In particular, after the buyout of another owner, the value of the remaining owners' interests, will increase. Unfortunately, increasing the policy amounts at that point could be costly. But with some policies, policy dividends can be applied to purchase additional one-year term insurance. In this way you can automatically keep increasing the amount of life insurance held. Make sure to ask your insurance agent or broker about this type of insurance.

- Not only can life insurance policies fund buyouts after the death of an owner, but some types of life insurance can also help to fund a buyout during an owner's lifetime. In this type of arrangement, the company or the owners take out whole-life insurance policies in the name of each owner, which build up cash surrender values. If an owner retires or becomes disabled before he dies, the company or the continuing owners will cash out the policies they hold on the life of the departing owner and give the cash surrender value of the policies to him in return for a transfer of his ownership interest back to the company or the continuing owners. If the cash surrender value of the policies is less than the buyback price (which it probably will be), then the company or the owners must pay the difference or sign one or more promissory notes to cover what remains of the purchase price plus interest until it is paid off. In other words, the cash value can be used to provide a portion of the purchase price, such as a down payment.

- A variety of alternatives to standard life insurance policies exist that should be discussed with your insurance agent or broker prior to deciding on the best way to fund the buyout of deceased owners. For example, some insurance companies now offer a less-expensive "first to die" life insurance policy that pays when the first of two or more individuals dies. Another alternative is the "adjustable life" policy, whose payoff amount can be increased (with a corresponding increase in premiums) during the life of the policy. As your business becomes more valuable, you can increase the death benefit payable under this type of policy.

 Be sure to ask your insurance agent or broker about all of the life insurance alternatives we have discussed. This short section above should serve as an introduction to insurance funding for buy-sell agreements, and not as advice for choosing and buying insurance policies.

Having the Insurance Policy Set the Buyback Price

We discuss in the text the practical and tax reasons why it can make sense to fund the buyback of a deceased owner's ownership interest with life insurance proceeds. Some buy-sell agreements go further and actually use the payoff value of the life insurance policy as the price to be paid by the company for a deceased owner's ownership interest.

While funding the buyback of an ownership interest from a deceased owner's estate with insurance proceeds obviously makes sense, we don't think it's normally smart to tie the price to be paid for an ownership interest under the agreement to the amount of insurance taken out. A big reason for this is that the insurance policies may not be updated to reflect increased earnings of the company. In such cases, the buyback price paid by the insurance policy will probably be unfairly low. Also, agreements that have an insurance policy fix the buyback price will not fix the value of an ownership interest for estate tax purposes (see Chapter 9, Section B).

Our approach is to have the buy-sell agreement set a buyback price independent of the means used to fund the buyout. Of course, your company can still fund all of the buyback of a deceased owner with life insurance proceeds (by taking out life insurance policies on each owner, and updating these policies regularly to reflect any increase in the value of the ownership interest). But this way, if the policies are not updated fast enough, the family of a deceased owner doesn't bear the full brunt of the oversight.

c. Taxes for Life Insurance Funding

Life insurance funding brings up significant tax issues. We will touch on some of the issues here, but understand that this is a very complex area. When using insurance to fund your buy-sell agreement, you'll undoubtedly be working with an insurance planner and a tax expert. Their advice will be needed.

Here are the normal income tax consequences of buyback arrangements funded by life insurance:

- The purchasers of the insurance (the company or the owners) get no income tax deduction for the amount of the premiums paid.
- Premiums paid by the company or co-owners for a policy on the life of an owner will not be taxable to the insured owner.
- Life insurance proceeds paid to the policy owners (the company or the continuing owners) are generally not subject to income tax—the owners or the company do not have to report the funds as income; the funds are simply used to buy the ownership interest back, usually from the deceased owner's estate.
- Life insurance proceeds will not be included in the estate of a deceased owner for estate tax purposes as long as the proceeds are not payable directly to the estate, and the deceased owner did not own the policy (see the sidebar, "Check the Estate Tax Treatment of Life Insurance Payouts," below). Policy proceeds should be payable to the company or the continuing owners, whoever held the policy.

Check the Estate Tax Treatment of Life Insurance Payouts

To ensure that in an insurance-funded buyout, the proceeds of life insurance are not included in a deceased owner's estate for estate tax purposes, make sure that each insured owner has no "incidents of ownership" in the policy on his life owned by the company or his co-owners, and that the policy proceeds will not be directly available to the owner's estate or inheritors to pay taxes or estate debts. (Although the company or continuing owners can buy the interest from the deceased owner's estate or inheritors with the life insurance proceeds, and the estate or inheritors could then use the proceeds to pay taxes or estate debts.)

If the policy provisions or your buy-sell agreement gives the insured owner an option to purchase a policy on his life prior to death (for example, on the sale of the ownership interest, termination of the buy-sell agreement or cancellation of the policies by the corporation), the IRS may decide that the owners have been given "incidents of ownership" in the policies. If so, the insurance proceeds will be included in a deceased owner's taxable estate (even if the deceased owner never exercised her option to take title to the policy prior to her death). (Our agreement does not provide an owner with the option to purchase the insurance policies that the company or owners hold on his life.)

There's also a special estate tax trap for cross-purchase life insurance arrangements (where the owners individually take out policies on the lives of each other). Namely, when an owner dies, if your arrangement requires his estate to transfer the insurance policies he owned on the lives of the surviving owners back to the surviving owners, the IRS may consider this arrangement a "transfer for value" feature of these policies. In this case, life insurance proceeds paid upon an owner's death would be taxable as part of her estate. (Our agreement does not require an owner's estate to transfer the policies back to the surviving owners.)

Without going further into the ins and outs of these special rules, one bit of advice: You will want your insurance or tax advisor to scrutinize any life insurance arrangement you adopt to fund the buyout of a deceased owner to make sure that insurance proceeds will not be included in the taxable estate of a deceased owner.

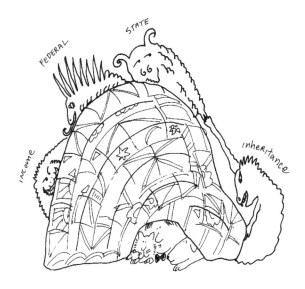

2. Disability Insurance

One way to cope with the problem of funding the buyout of a disabled owner is to call for a long-term installment plan, so that the company or continuing owners can make partial payments to a disabled owner over a number of years. But for larger companies, a better way to cope with this issue is to have your buy-sell agreement require the purchase of disability insurance on all co-owners. This way, if a disability occurs, the insurance policy proceeds can provide a source of funds to allow the company or the co-owners to buy back the interest of a disabled owner without diminishing company or personal cash reserves.

 Life insurance can partially fund the buyout of a disabled owner. Some types of life insurance (for example, whole-life) can help to fund a buyout of a disabled owner by providing cash-surrender values. If an owner becomes disabled, the company or the continuing owners can cash out the policies they hold on the life of the disabled owner and give the cash-surrender value of the policies to her (plus some cash, no doubt—up to the Agreement Price) in return for a transfer of her ownership interest back to the company or the continuing owners. Ask your insurance agent or broker about this possibility.

Disability insurance operates in much the same way that life insurance does to provide funds to buy out a deceased owner's ownership interest. Much of the information we covered in the life insurance discussion above applies here also. In addition, there are several issues specific to disability insurance that you should discuss with your insurance agent or broker to ensure that your policies fund a buyout properly:

- You may want to use your insurance company's definition of "total disability" and provide that the insurance company is the arbiter of whether the co-owner really is totally disabled—that is, the insurance company decides whether an owner's disability will trigger a buyout under your buy-sell agreement. (Our buy-sell agreement says that the insurance company's determination of disability is controlling if disability insurance is used to fund the buyout of a disabled owner. See Section III, Scenario 2, When an Owner Becomes Disabled).

- Your agreement should establish a period of time—a waiting period—that an owner's inability to work for the company must persist before a buyout can occur. You may also want to provide that time spent off work by an owner with a series of illnesses with the same or related causes can be added up to fulfill the waiting period requirement. (Our agreement provides a disability waiting period in Section III, Scenario 2.)

- Your agreement should also specify when the buyout price will be determined. Most agreements use the date the owner stopped working as the date to value the business—since that is the date the owner stopped contributing to the company. This way, any changes in the worth of the company can be attributed to the remaining owners. (Section III, Scenario 2 of our agreement contains an option to allow the buyout price to be determined on the date the owner stopped working or on the date of the buyout.)

Special buy-sell disability insurance policies. Some disability policies are designed just to fund buyouts under buy-sell agreements. These policies usually pay a lump-sum cash benefit of up to $1 million (or up to $1.5 million, if installment benefits are chosen) to fund the buyout of a disabled owner. (If desired, additional financial benefits can also be funded by policy proceeds, such as a wage continuation plan to the disabled owner prior to a buyout of ownership interest.) Be sure to ask your insurance agent or broker about these special policies.

The disability funding clauses we use in our agreement (Section V, (2)) are shown in Excerpt 3.

Check Option 1 for company-purchased disability insurance, Option 2 for owner-purchased disability insurance or neither if you are not interested in funding your agreement with disability insurance. (Section V, (2).)

---

(2) Disability Insurance

☐ **Option 1: Company-purchased disability insurance**

The company will apply for, own and be the beneficiary of disability insurance policies for each owner. The company will take any actions necessary to maintain in force all of the insurance policies it is required to maintain under this section, including paying all premiums, and will not cancel them or allow them to lapse. The policy benefits shall be applied to the purchase price in a buyout of a disabled owner.

☐ **Option 2: Owner-purchased disability insurance**

Each owner will apply for, own and be the beneficiary of disability insurance policies for each other owner. Each owner will take any actions necessary to maintain in force all of the insurance policies it is required to maintain under this section, including paying all premiums, and will not cancel them or allow them to lapse. The policy benefits shall be applied to the purchase price in a buyout of a disabled owner.

Excerpt 3

6

How to Set the Buyback
Price in Your Agreement

By now you should have your eye on the buy-sell clauses that will best handle prospective ownership changes for your company (for example, after reading Chapter 3, you've decided to provide the company and the remaining owners with an Option to Purchase an owner's interest in case he dies or retires). Also, after reading Chapters 4 and 5, you should understand how buyout procedures work and how you'll fund a future buyout. Now, as explained in this chapter, your next big job is to decide how to establish a fair price (the "Agreement Price") for any future buybacks or buyouts that occur. Unfortunately, choosing a price that will be perceived years from now by all owners and the IRS as representing the true value of your company is no easy task. After all, as you read this you can't know if in the years ahead your business will prosper mightily, struggle to make a profit or fail.

A. Why Choose a Price in Advance?

Even with a pile of up-to-date facts, coming up with an accurate price for a small, privately owned business interest is not easy. Unlike publicly traded corporations, there is no public market for small business interests, so it's hard to establish comparative prices for similar businesses. And even if you are able to find out how much similar businesses are selling for, there's no guarantee yours would fetch a similar price. Depending on the economy and competitive pressures in your industry, as well as the health (or lack thereof) of your business, plus many other more subtle factors, the true value of your company could be way more or less.

Although it is hard to value an interest in a small business any time, and even harder to do it years in advance of a sale, it's a job that must be done in order to prepare an adequate buy-sell agreement. If owners neglect to do this, they will have to haggle over price each time an owner's interest is bought by the company or the continuing owners under their buy-sell agreement. And

to make things worse, if the divorce or death of an owner is the reason for a buyout, negotiations are almost sure to be burdened by the emotions of the owner's spouse, inheritors or estate representative, making agreement difficult or impossible. Especially when a divorce is involved, such emotion-laden conflict can even result in a lawsuit. And should a co-owner die, her inheritors can find themselves at a truly unfair disadvantage in the absence of an agreement. For instance, a recently widowed spouse who needs cash to pay a child's college tuition may be easily pressured into selling her ownership interest back to the company or the remaining owners at a too-low price (or a spouse may simply not be familiar with the business and, as a result, not know what a fair price for his interest is).

Hopefully you are now convinced that it's best to include in your buy-sell agreement a price, or a formula—called a valuation method—that can determine a fair price at the time of a buyout. While no price or formula will be perfect, choosing one in advance does have the great advantage of allowing you and your co-owners a chance to think about, discuss and vote on how a reasonable price for the company should be calculated, at a time when none of you are planning to sell out. Just the fact that a particular method was agreed to by all owners is likely to go a long way towards reducing conflict when you or a co-owner leaves. Even if, at the time of an owner's departure, you all agree to modify the Agreement Price to better reflect current realities, the fact that you start with an agreement—not a vacuum—should make the negotiating process easier. Fortunately, there are some techniques that can help you come up with a fair price. Let's look at how to accomplish this.

 In some ways it's easier to establish a price in advance than at any other time. Think of it this way. When you're creating your buy-sell agreement, no owner knows whether she'll be the one to leave and sell her interest (in which case she might want a high agreement price) or whether she'll be one of the owners who will remain and buy out a departing owner (in which case she might want a low agreement price). So even though it's hard to agree on a future price for a new or growing business, making this decision before any owner leaves has huge advantages.

To Avoid Buyback Disputes, Explain Provisions to All Concerned

It's fairly common for an owner's spouse or children or other relatives to object when a company eventually asserts its right (exercises an option) to buy back the shares of a deceased, disabled or divorced owner. Often, these family members have an unrealistically high expectation of the value of the company and are upset if the amount they will receive in a buyout is based on a fairly conservative valuation formula, such as book value. Or put another way, the owner's spouse or inheritors are likely to be highly disappointed not to receive what they consider to be top dollar for their newly acquired share of the business.

Trouble of this sort is particularly likely when key family members have been kept in the dark about the terms of the buy-sell agreement. It follows that you can defuse most potential future problems by making sure that spouses, adult children and any other family members likely to be affected by a future buyout clearly understand the valuation method described in your buy-sell agreement. At a minimum, make sure that the spouses of all owners read and sign your buy-sell agreement (we provide a specific spousal consent provision at the end of our agreement to be signed by spouses). And in case a dispute does arise, it's important to have a mediation and arbitration clause in your agreement, since valuation conflicts are more easily solved outside of the courtroom (see Chapter 8).

Your Buy-Sell Agreement and Estate Taxes

An important reason to set a price or formula in advance concerns "estate taxes"—taxes collected after your death by the government. Carefully setting a price for estate tax purposes can potentially save your estate a lot of dough—which is important if your heirs want to hang on to the business interest they inherit. A good valuation provision can fix the value of your ownership interest at an amount considerably lower than its market value at the time of your death. (And the lower the value your agreement provides, the lower your estate taxes.) Of course, to really save a bundle on estate taxes, the IRS must accept the value set in your buy-sell agreement. The key to getting the IRS to accept it is choosing the right valuation method. We discuss the ins and outs of estate taxes in Chapter 9, Section B.

B. What Valuation Methods Are Based On: Investment vs. Value of the Company

Sometimes new owners imagine that, if they were to leave their company after a few months or years, they'd be entitled to get back all the money they've invested (often called their capital contribution—see sidebar, "Capital Accounts"). This is usually wrong. Rarely is it appropriate for a departing investor or owner to simply get his capital contribution back. Instead, he should get more than he invested if the business does well, or less (possibly even nothing) if it does badly. After all, the point of investing is to make a gain, which, of course, always means you risk taking a loss.

In truth, since the value of a new business is often closely tied to the net value of its assets (that is, company assets minus company liabilities), it often drops at the beginning as the owners' initial cash investments are turned into equipment, inventory, salaries and other start-up costs. Whether the business's worth will then recover and eventually go up, of course, depends on a number of factors, most prominently whether the business quickly finds sufficient customers, meets their needs and turns a profit.

EXAMPLE: Carol and Dick go into business together to clean and repair houses so that their owners will be able to sell them for top dollar. Carol plans on doing industrial-strength cleaning, interior painting and yard work, while Dick will take care of any needed exterior painting, critical repairs and, if called for, minor structural improvements. Each puts up $15,000 as a capital contribution, but Dick and Carol don't get around to writing a partnership agreement, let alone buy-sell provisions. Their first decision is to purchase a van. Rather than looking into the used van market, however, they buy a new vehicle from a dealer for almost $25,000 and have their company name, "Property Moppers," painted on the side. Dick also buys a high-powered washer, a power painter and a set of tools for a total of $4,500. Carol buys what seems like a year's worth of cleaning supplies and paintbrushes for $500.

Two months into it, Property Moppers has only had one job, and because of their inexperience, Dick and Carol spent more to fix the house up than they were paid. Carol, knowing that it takes time to build a business reputation and get a system down, vows to hang in there. Dick, however, is out of patience and tells Carol he wants out. He demands that Carol pay him the $15,000 he put into the company. Carol can't afford to buy Dick out without taking out a home equity loan, something she is loathe to do—at least before she finds someone to do Dick's work. Fearing she may just have to give up the business and sell the equipment, she tries to make a deal with Dick. Eventually they agree to have an appraiser value the current worth of their business assets, with Dick accepting half of that amount for his share.

The appraisal is straightforward. Since Dick and Carol didn't buy anything on credit, the business has no liabilities. Since they don't have any customers, the business has no "goodwill." In short, it's worth the current value of its assets. Although they bought the van for $24,980, the appraiser concludes it has already depreciated by $7,000 ($2,000 of this amount is because they had their name painted on the side, meaning a new owner would have to spring for a whole new paint job). Similarly, although they paid $4,500 for the tools new, the appraiser decides that their current market value is less than half that— $2,000. Finally, the appraiser sets the market value of Carol's cleaning supplies at $20. Adding all the assets up, the appraiser values Property Moppers at $20,000, or $10,000 less than the sum of the owners' capital contributions! Under their agreement, Dick must accept half of that—$10,000—rather than his original $15,000 contribution.

In short, because the value of a company goes up and down depending on the successes or failures of the business, most valuation formulas do not use capital contributions as the basis for a buyback price, but instead use information on sales, profits or assets to come up with the current worth of the company.

Capital Accounts

The term capital account refers to the dollar value of a partner's or LLC member's interest in the business (not counting depreciation or goodwill). An owner's capital account starts off with the value of her initial investment in the business (her capital contribution). Accounting additions and subtractions occur over time as the profits and losses of the company are recorded and as additional capital contributions or distributions are made.

Sometimes the value of these capital accounts is used as the basis for setting the amount each owner gets if the company dissolves—ceases to do business and liquidates its assets. Thus, if a business dissolves in a situation where all creditors of the business have been fully paid off and there's still money left in the business, each owner may be able to be paid back his capital investment. If there is insufficient cash left from a liquidated business to pay each owner the amount in his capital account, the relative percentage of each owner's capital account will be used to split whatever cash is left from the liquidated business (for example, a 50% owner should get 50% of the net cash of a liquidated business).

Since the value of capital accounts usually bears little relationship to the real worth of a business, our buy-sell agreement does not use capital accounts to put a price on ownership interests for buyouts and buybacks.

C. How Our Valuation Provisions Work

1. When the Agreement Buyout Price Applies

Throughout this book and in our buy-sell agreement itself, we refer to the fixed price you choose to govern any buyout—or more likely, the price that will result from the valuation formula you choose—as the "Agreement Price." This Agreement Price will usually control whenever the company or the continuing owners buy an ownership interest, no matter why the buyback was triggered—death, retirement, divorce, disability or any other listed reason.

Specifically, our buy-sell agreement provides that the Agreement Price will be used for all buyouts "unless otherwise provided in the agreement." This qualifying language is necessary because one part of your agreement may include a buy-sell provision that uses a different price. For instance, a Right-of-First-Refusal provision may require the company and the continuing owners to pay the price an outsider has offered for an owner's interest, rather than the Agreement Price (as discussed in Chapter 2). If so, the outsider's price will take precedence over the general Agreement Price.

 Our agreement offers two price options for the Right of First Refusal. As explained in Chapter 2, Section II of our buy-sell agreement gives the company and the continuing owners two price options if an owner is proposing to sell an ownership interest under the Right-of-First-Refusal provision:

- the price the proposed buyer is willing to pay, or
- the Agreement Price (the standard price for buying an interest under your buy-sell agreement—the price or formula you set in your agreement as explained in this chapter).

You may provide that the full Agreement Price is not to be used, or is to be discounted, in other buyout situations as well. For example, as discussed in Chapter 3, your agreement may state that a co-owner who wants out in the first year or two may only be eligible to receive a fraction of the Agreement Price.

2. Figuring the Price for an Individual Owner's Interest

For purposes of convenience, the price provisions in our buy-sell agreement set an Agreement Price that reflects the worth of the whole company. To come up with a price for any individual owner's interest, simply multiply the entire Agreement Price by that owner's ownership percentage. For example, if an owner owns 25% of his company, you'd multiply the Agreement Price by 25% to come up with the price of that owner's share.

3. Choosing a Valuation Provision

Our buy-sell agreement sets forth five alternative valuation provisions. We discuss each below. Once you decide on the one you want, simply check the appropriate box. Having all the valuation provisions in your buy-sell agreement allows you to easily update your method of valuation should the need arise, without having to create a whole new agreement. To change your valuation method at a later date, you can simply line-out your check mark for the valuation method you originally chose and place a new check mark for a different valuation alternative. Naturally, you will want to date and have each owner initial each line-out and addition to your agreement. Or, you can just change your choice in the agreement you saved on disk, and print out a clean copy for signature by the owners.

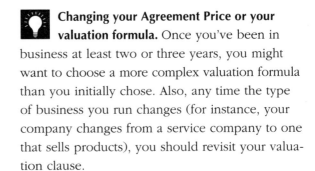 **Changing your Agreement Price or your valuation formula.** Once you've been in business at least two or three years, you might want to choose a more complex valuation formula than you initially chose. Also, any time the type of business you run changes (for instance, your company changes from a service company to one that sells products), you should revisit your valuation clause.

D. Agreeing on a Fixed Price in Advance (Valuation Method 1)

Using a fixed price may not be the best method. For a number of reasons we discuss below, adopting one of several widely used valuation formulas is often, but not always, a better approach than actually inserting a fixed price in your buy-sell agreement. In short, before getting enthusiastic about the first—or any other—valuation alternative, please read the entire chapter.

The most straightforward approach to nailing down a buyback or buyout price for your agreement is to agree upon an actual fixed-dollar price in your buy-sell agreement. This "agreed-value," or "fixed-price," method combines simplicity with certainty. By setting a fixed-dollar value yourself, there is no need to bother with appraisals, accountants or earnings multiples when an owner's interest is being purchased. You simply have to take your buy-sell agreement out of its file, blow off the dust and locate the fixed price in Section VI, Agreement Price.

The fixed-price method also makes it easy for business owners to do estate planning, since they know exactly what the agreed value of their ownership interests will be when they die, and how much their estate may owe in estate taxes, if any. A fixed price can also be useful when considering how to fund the buy-sell agreement in the cases of death or disability, since the owners will know how much life or disability insurance they need to buy. (Do not, however, set the Agreement Price at the amount of an insurance policy. If the company does well, the insurance policies may not be updated to reflect the increased earnings of the company. Simply estimate the amount of insurance you'll need to make a purchase of an interest at the fixed price you decide on.)

Pinpointing a fixed price, however, as the true value of your company can be a difficult task. Using the fixed-price method requires that the owners have business acumen, or at least informed common sense, when it comes to valuing their company. For example, in some companies this means being savvy enough to realize that when a co-owner leaves, he may take most of his share of the business with him. If a company's major business asset consists of a customer or client list, and an owner who departs (but doesn't die or retire) will likely take most of her own customers with her, there may be little value left in the business that the departing owner should fairly be paid for, besides any company assets and equipment. This is true for most service businesses where clientele and reputation are key, like those of tax preparers, interior decorators or hair stylists.

> EXAMPLE: Abe, Emily and Tanya start an interior design business. But when Abe tries to do every color scheme in deep purple, the two women say enough and decide to go their separate ways. Because each of the three decorator/owners has his or her own client list, the only property that needs to be divided consists of furniture and office equipment and, of course, liabilities (debts).

Be conservative when setting a value for your business. We all hope to be hugely successful. But few of us will really become millionaires because of small business ownership. Recognizing this, when you prepare your buy-sell agreement, it's wise to resist galloping optimism.

And also consider that although you will want to be paid a high price for your business interest if *you* will be the first to leave, the tables are turned if you and your co-owners must buy out someone else. If your business is highly overvalued, it may even have to be liquidated to pay off a departing owner.

The major problem with establishing a fixed price in advance is that any value you pick for your business will almost surely be quickly outdated. Depending on your initial outlook and your actual successes or failures, your fixed price should be adjusted up or down to keep pace with business profitability and owner expectations. And after several years of profitable operations, it may make sense to place a value on the ability of the company to draw customers or attract business (called "goodwill"). For example, a small architecture company that specializes in public safety buildings (police, fire and emergency response) may, over the years, build up a very valuable reputation that will help bring in a steady stream of profitable new jobs, thereby increasing the value of the company. It follows that if you use the fixed-price method, you should periodically revise your agreement (we recommend annual updates to change the agreed value shown in your agreement).

Make sure a required re-evaluation actually happens. Even if you plan to annually update your company's agreed value, there is always the danger that this task will be overlooked. Although it's not an adequate substitute for meeting and agreeing on a new price, some co-owners include a back-up clause in their agreement that will automatically adjust the Agreement Price up or down based on the consumer price index or another inflation-tracking mechanism in any year when the co-owners fail to update it.

As you can see, there are can be problems with using a fixed-price, or agreed-value, provision. Because it's usually subjective—and often out of date—a fixed price can create arguments between the buyer of an owner's interest (the company or the continuing owners) and the seller (a departing owner or his spouse, his inheritors or an estate representative). Its subjectivity and unreliability may even subject an agreed-upon price to a court challenge by a departing owner or inheritor, and a judge may refuse to uphold it without real data to back it up. Because of these drawbacks, the fixed-price method is less popular than several of the other methods discussed below, although it is sometimes used to set a low value on a new or small service business, at least until the business has been in operation long enough to make it sensible for the owners to switch to one of the other methods (see sidebar, "Businesses Where an Agreed-Upon Price Often Works").

The language of the agreed-value provision in our buy-sell agreement is shown in Excerpt 1.

Check Valuation Method 1 if you wish to set an agreed value for your company. (Section VI, Valuation Method 1.) Also, insert the agreed value for the entire company in the blank.

Updating your agreement price. Note that the owners can (and should) regularly update the agreed value by preparing and signing a new agreement with a new agreed value or by signing a separate statement. If you use separate statements to update your agreed value, make sure to attach copies to your buy-sell agreement for future reference. (See Chapter 8, Section E, for more on updating your agreement.)

Fixed-price method has a hidden danger. Using this method alone—especially if you agree on a fairly optimistic price—can provide a windfall to an owner who departs early (before the company has become profitable enough to be really worth the agreed-on price). One way to anticipate and cope with this problem is to include a disincentive for leaving early (for example, an owner who leaves in the first year or two receives a discounted agreement price). In short, if you are considering adopting the fixed-price method, consider also adopting a disincentive for early departure (see Section III, Scenario 1 in the agreement and on the worksheet).

Section VI: Agreement Price
Unless otherwise provided in this agreement, the undersigned agree that the method checked below for valuing the company shall be used to determine a price for ownership interests under this agreement.

☐ **Valuation Method 1: Agreed Value**
The agreed value of the company shall be $ *[insert agreed-upon price for entire company, such as "100,000"]* , or such other amount as fixed by all owners of the company after the date of adoption of this agreement as specified in a written statement signed by each owner of the company. If more than one such statement is signed by the owners after the date of adoption of this agreement, the statement with the latest date shall control for purposes of fixing a price for the purchase of ownership interests under this agreement. The value of an individual owner's interest shall be the entire value for the company as determined under this paragraph, multiplied by his or her ownership percentage.

Excerpt 1

Businesses Where an Agreed-Upon Price Often Works

In some companies, an agreed-on price may be a simple and efficient way to provide for how much a business is worth.

- **Service Businesses:** From computer repairs to cutting hair, new service businesses typically have few valuable assets beyond the energies and hopes of their owners. In this context, rather than bothering with trying to determine the worth of the business by more conventional means (for instance, book value, capitalization of earnings, appraisal), the owners may simply agree on what they think the business is worth and revise this figure periodically. Later, if the business grows and succeeds, they may wish to switch to one of the other valuation methods.

- **Closely Held Companies With Just a Few Owners:** Another occasion where it may be appropriate to use the agreed-value method is for small closely held companies where the owners want to maintain close, harmonious relationships. Since the price is set in advance, an individual being bought out is less likely to become paranoid and conclude that the company is manipulating a last-minute valuation process in order to establish an artificially low buyout value. And by establishing the buyout price in the agreement at a reasonably conservative figure—something that owners in smaller companies are likely to do—the company should be able to afford the buyout when the time comes to implement one.

E. Formulas That Calculate a Price at the Time of the Buyout

Why bother with a buyout formula? Because it is almost impossible to value what a growing company will be worth in the future by simply picking a dollar figure. Almost surely, the business's worth at the time of a buyout will turn out to be more or less valuable than you and your co-owners collectively guess.

Because valuing a business interest that will be sold in a future transaction is so difficult, using a valuation formula based on numbers, such as the value of current assets, the level of sales or the amount of profit, can make a lot of sense. Because formulas use regularly updated, factual information, they tend to give a more accurate picture of your company's worth than using a fixed price. The trick is choosing the one of a half dozen or so common valuation methods that best represents the value of your company.

Start by understanding that some valuation methods are more appropriate for certain businesses than others. For instance, for a company that exists only to own real estate, it would make a lot more sense to establish what it's worth by appraising the fair market value of its assets (the buildings and land it owns) and then subtracting its liabilities (the mortgages it owes on), rather than trying to value it based on a multiple of yearly earnings. On the other hand, an assets-based method would work poorly for a small, organic honey company that has been successfully and profitably producing and marketing high-grade honey for the last fifteen years. While the company's only assets might be a few boxes of bees and some mesh jumpsuits and smoke guns, valuing it based on its earnings history would surely be more appropriate.

Here are the most common valuation alternatives used by privately owned small businesses:

- Book value
- Multiple of book value
- Capitalization of earnings method
- Appraisal value.

1. Book Value (Valuation Method 2)

At least at the start, the value of a company's assets minus its liabilities is all many businesses are worth. Recognizing this, the first valuation formula we present uses assets minus liabilities as shown on the most recent year-end balance sheet of the company. Commonly, this is called a company's "book value," but it also goes under the names "net asset value" and "depreciated asset value" (assets are listed on a company's balance sheet at their "depreciated" value—the cost of the asset minus depreciation taken on the asset for tax purposes). Note that a balance sheet usually lists the net amount of assets minus liabilities as the "owners' equity" amount. Theoretically, this figure can be positive (if assets exceed liabilities) or negative (if liabilities exceed assets).

As you no doubt know, your balance sheet is basically a snapshot of your company's assets minus liabilities on a particular date. Assets listed on the balance sheet usually will include cash in the bank, real estate, business equipment and machinery, accounts receivable (money customers owe to the business) and other types of tangible assets. Liabilities usually consist of accounts payable (amounts owed to employees and suppliers), plus the remaining balances on any loans taken out by the company. Balance sheets are typically prepared as of the end of each fiscal (tax) year of a company, and are needed to prepare annual tax returns for the business.

> EXAMPLE: The previous fiscal year balance sheet of Mega-Mania Computer Supplies, Inc. shows assets totaling $320,000 (after depreciation) and liabilities of $200,000. Thus, shareholders' (owners') equity is $120,000. It follows that if the company has issued 1,000 shares, and Joe owns 100 of them (Joe owns 10% of the company), the book value of his shares is 1/10 of total owners' equity, or $12,000.

A big advantage to choosing this method is that it uses figures that are already readily available from the company's financial statements. Because it is so easy to understand and implement, microbusinesses and start-ups often use the book value method. A big drawback to the "snapshot" aspect of the book value method, however, is that it does not give you information on the profitability of the business. Book value usually doesn't measure the value of certain intangible assets such as a strong reputation or customer goodwill, which reflect the ability of the company to continue to earn a good profit—these assets are not reflected on the company's balance sheet. As a result, of all the valuation formulas, the book value method usually results in the most conservative (lowest) valuation figure for a business. (Also, book value can result in a low figure because the depreciated value of assets—their original cost minus any depreciation written off by the company for tax purposes—may be much less than the value of the assets to an outsider.)

For these reasons, book value is most often used by owners of new businesses that have yet to earn a profit or build up goodwill. It is also the best method to use when owners wish to put the company's ongoing survival interests ahead of any individual owner's interest in selling out for top value. Again, this can make excellent sense if a business is just getting off the ground, and the owners are worried that the company (and its remaining owners) will be hard pressed to come up with money necessary to buy back a departing owner's interest under the buy-sell agreement.

> EXAMPLE: Louise, Danny and George form their own company, Digi-Fix, which provides computer-repair services. Each owns one-third of the company. After four years, Danny quits, deciding to turn his white-water rafting hobby into a career as a full-time river guide. On its last fiscal year balance sheet, the company's assets included cash in the bank, depreciated fixed assets (mostly, computers, tools and equipment) and accounts receivable, totaling $95,000. Liabilities consisted of accounts payable plus the current remaining balance on

a small business bank loan taken out by the company two years after its formation, totaling $60,000. The book value of the company—its owners' equity—is the difference between assets and liabilities—$35,000. Using the book value method, each owner's third of the company is worth $11,666 ($35,000 ÷ 3). Assuming that Digi-Fix's buy-sell agreement uses the book value method to value the owner's interests, the company's cash reserves, though modest, are adequate to pay Danny $11,666 for his interest, so the company purchases Danny's interest and continues business operations with the two remaining owners.

The language that we use in our buy-sell agreement to establish the book value method is shown in Excerpt 2.

Check Valuation Method 2 if you wish to use your company's book value (as of the end of the last fiscal year prior to a buyout) to value your ownership interests. (Section VI, Valuation Method 2.)

The book value method often does not make sense for long-term owners. People who work in a business for many years expect to be fairly compensated at retirement or death. Using book value to come up with a buyback price usually won't provide an adequate buyout price. It's far better in this situation to choose one of the other valuation methods below that provide a higher buyout price.

EXAMPLE: Let's return to our Digi-Fix example, but assume now that it has been in operation several more years. Thanks to several very profitable service contracts that extend for several years, the three owners have been able to pay themselves salaries of $80,000 per year for the past few years, while hiring repair people to do much of the work, allowing each owner to put in a three-day work-week.

This time, it's Louise who wants to leave, to spend more time with her two young children. The book value of Digi-Fix's assets on its last fiscal year balance sheet was $125,000, consisting of: $50,000 in equipment tools and office furniture (after depreciation), $35,000 in repair fees owed to the company by customers (accounts receivable) and $40,000 cash. Liabilities totaled $50,000, consisting of $40,000 owed to the local bank, plus various accounts payable totaling $10,000. This means the total owners' equity is $75,000 ($125,000 – $50,000). Louise's interest is worth $25,000—one-third of the total book value of $75,000. Obviously this is a pretty low buyout amount for someone who has been receiving $80,000 every year! True, when Louise leaves, she will no longer have to work those three days per week, and the remaining owners may have to replace her. But surely they can do this for less than $80,000 per year. At any rate, Louise's interest in Digi-Fix seems worth more than $25,000. Using the book value method would be a poor choice in this situation.

☐ **Valuation Method 2: Book Value**
   The value of the company shall be its book value (its assets minus its liabilities as shown on the balance sheet of the company) as of the end of the most recent fiscal year prior to the purchase of an ownership interest under this agreement. The value of an individual owner's interest shall be the entire value for the company as determined under this paragraph, multiplied by his or her ownership percentage.

Excerpt 2

If the book value method will result in too low a buyback figure—as it will for most successful businesses in the long term—consider adopting or switching to one of the other methods set out below.

Businesses Where the Book Value Method Often Works

Valuing an owner's interest at book value is most appropriate for companies whose assets, rather than earnings potential, are the base, or strong point, of the business. As mentioned in the text, this applies to companies just starting out, who probably don't have an established earnings record, and companies with low earnings. Let's look at a few examples of which types of businesses this simple book value approach often works best for.

- **Start-up companies:** When a business is young and has not yet developed a reputation or turned a profit, the true value of the company may well be the amount of the depreciated value of assets, less its liabilities. And because the book value method is based on the business's financial statement, it will not lead to any extra costs for accounting, legal or appraisal fees.
- **Marginally profitable companies:** Especially in a highly competitive field, many companies just aren't able to make much of a profit above their ongoing expenses, such as salaries, rent, utilities and advertising, meaning that an earnings-based valuation method may not reflect their true worth. Nevertheless, the company may have a bright future if it can find a way to break away from the pack. In the meantime, the book value method may do a fairly accurate job of valuing the business.

Adjustments for Owning Real Property

If your business owns considerable real estate (but does not use it mainly for rental income purposes), you may sensibly decide that valuing your company based on its assets (real estate) is more appropriate for your company than valuing it based on its earnings (rental income, for example). Just the same, you may not want to use a straight book value method to value the assets, because this method may not adequately represent the value of your property. Book value can be inappropriate for companies with real estate in particular because (in most geographical areas, anyway) real estate is usually worth more than its depreciated value as shown on the company balance sheet.

To come up with a formula that does a better job of valuing your real property, you'll probably want to provide that real property be valued at its current market value.

EXAMPLE: Let's revisit Digi-Fix. This time assume that the computer-repair company many years ago bought the real property where it does business—in Silicon Valley. Since real estate has skyrocketed in the Valley in the last few years, companies who bought real estate years ago are usually worth quite a bit. The book value method would surely not give any of the owners a fair buyout price, since that method doesn't reflect the appreciated market value of real estate.

If your company owns real estate, you can prevent an unfairly low agreement price from being used in a buyout by selecting the appraisal method in your buy-sell agreement to value your company (discussed in Section 4, below), where a professional will appraise your real estate at its fair market value at the time of a buyout.

💡 **Use several years if your balance sheet numbers fluctuate from year to year.** If your company has been in business several years, but its balance sheet numbers tend to fluctuate widely year to year (for instance, because of large losses at the end of a year or the beginning of the next year), you may want to provide that the book value of your company be derived from several years' balance sheets, not just the balance sheet of the last fiscal year.

2. Multiple of Book Value (Valuation Method 3)

As we mentioned above, if a small business has been up and running successfully for several years, its real value is probably greater than its book value (the balance sheet value of its assets minus the balance sheet value of its liabilities). For an outside buyer, there can be considerable value in the fact that the owners of an ongoing business have done everything necessary to operate profitably (for instance, bought or leased equipment, installed a phone system, rented or bought a building, purchased inventory, developed a clientele, implemented a marketing program, trained employees and established an accounting system). Of course, most of the time, an outside buyer won't be involved in your buy-sell situation —the selling will be between the owners, or between an owner and the company. Nevertheless, knowing what an outsider would pay can give you a good indication of the fair market value of your business interest. That's why it can be sensible to use a valuation formula that treats your entire company as a candidate for sale—a formula that is likely to arrive at a dollar figure that better reflects what an outside buyer would pay for a profitable business.

Enter the "multiple of book value" method. While based on book value, this formula goes beyond measuring the book value of your company's tangible assets to take into account "intangible assets." Intangible assets typically include things whose worth is hard to calculate, such as a desirable lease and the "goodwill" or positive reputation of the business. Other intangible assets include intellectual property (such as patents, copyrights and brand or trade names), mailing lists and the anticipated effect of long-term advertising campaigns.

The Value of Goodwill

Some profitable ongoing businesses are worth significantly more than the balance sheet value of assets minus liabilities because they've earned a good business reputation. That reputation brings in a steady stream of regular business. This intangible asset, which business brokers call "the well-founded expectation of continued public patronage," is more colloquially labeled "goodwill." Taking goodwill into account when setting a buy-sell agreement price rewards the owners for putting their skill and hard work into building up the company.

The concept of business goodwill is especially applicable for successful retail businesses—for example, a restaurant with an excellent location and a big following—but it is often less of a factor for businesses that depend primarily on personalized service. For instance, a carpenter, podiatrist or dentist may have worked hard to acquire personal goodwill, but it's tricky—and sometimes impossible—to transfer the goodwill to another person when the business is sold. Or put another way, when a person who provides individual service retires or dies, much of the value of the business disappears. And, of course, this is especially likely to be true if the owner leaves to open or join a competing business.

Although undoubtedly a real asset, the value of business goodwill is easily overestimated following a change in business ownership. Even loyal customers soon go elsewhere if the quality of a service or product diminishes. For example, the reputation of even the most established restaurant can quickly take a dive if new management takes over and the menu and service don't match previously met expectations. As a rule, the more competition there is in a particular market, the less goodwill is worth—after all, in this age of the pampered consumer, people will quickly go elsewhere if offered even a slightly better service or price.

The multiple of book value method calculates the worth of the company by taking the net asset value (owners' equity) figure from your balance sheet and multiplying it by a predetermined number, called a multiplier. This multiplier—which you and your co-owners will establish in your buy-sell agreement—should be greater than 1 (or greater than 100%, if you use a percentage). That's because the purpose of the multiplier is to increase the Agreement Price of your company beyond its book value to bring it closer to fair market value. Again, because it is so difficult to precisely value goodwill and other intangibles, picking the correct multiplier is at best an imprecise science.

EXAMPLE: Fit-Tite Jeans, Inc., a discount retailer of distressed, stretched-to-fit denim jeans with a desirable location near a big university, has had ten years' worth of steadily increasing business. Most years, both sales volume and profits have jumped by 10% or more. Because customer satisfaction appears to be high, the owners of Fit-Tite expect business to remain good. An outside buyer would probably agree (though maybe not out loud) that customer goodwill should be taken into account when offering a fair price for the business.

Wanting to account for their company's goodwill, the Fit-Tite owners all agree to change the book value formula they adopted as part of their original buy-sell agreement. They reason that it is only fair that any departing owner be bought out at an amount that reflects the hard work she's put in over the years and that better represents what an outside buyer would pay for the business. To accomplish this, the owners adopt a new agreement, selecting the multiple of book value method, and inserting a multiplier of 2 (200%) to double the book value figure taken from the company's last balance sheet.

☐ **Valuation Method 3: Multiple of Book Value**

The value of the company shall be ___*[insert multiplier, one or higher, such as "two"]*___ times its book value (its assets minus its liabilities as shown on the balance sheet of the company) as of the end of the most recent fiscal year prior to the purchase of an ownership interest under this agreement. The value of an individual owner's interest shall be the entire value for the company as determined under this paragraph, multiplied by his or her ownership percentage.

Excerpt 3

The language for the multiple of book value method used in our buy-sell agreement is shown in Excerpt 3, above.

Check Valuation Method 3 if you wish to use a multiple of your company's book value (as of the end of the last fiscal year prior to a buyout) to value your company. (Section VI, Valuation Method 3.) Make sure to insert a multiplier (after consulting an expert if necessary) in the blank.

Use additional years if your balance sheet fluctuates. As with the regular book value method, if your company has been in business several years but assets and liabilities tend to fluctuate fairly widely from one year to the next (for instance, because large expenses accrue at the end of a year or the beginning of the next year), you may want to provide that the book value figures from balance sheets of several years should be used to arrive at an average adjusted book value amount.

3. Capitalization of Earnings (Valuation Method 4)

For established companies only. This method measures a business's value by its profits. If your company is just starting out, or hasn't been in existence very long, it's premature to value your ownership interests by using the capitalization of earnings method since your business has no earnings history. Better to adopt another valuation provision for your first year or two, then switch over to this valuation method later. While we recommend reading this section anyway so you get an idea of what may be in your future, if you're pressed for time, you may want to skip ahead to the appraisal method, below.

Once a company produces a good profit for at least several years in a row and appears to have a promising future, it often makes sense to value it based on a multiple of its annual *earnings*. That's because earnings usually better reflect a small but established company's value than its assets and liabilities do—a solid earnings history is often a pretty good predictor of how the company will perform in the future.

EXAMPLE: Two restaurants are each worth $175,000 according to the book value method (balance sheet assets minus liabilities). But their values diverge if you look at each restaurant's profit picture. After paying each of its three owners a salary of $50,000 per year, Peas and Carrots, Inc. has earned an annual profit averaging $10,000 over the last three years. But Mucho Mocha Corp., which also has three owners and pays the same salaries, produces yearly profits averaging $80,000 per year. Clearly, pushing caffeine beats flogging legumes. Based on the likelihood that (in the immediate future, at least) both businesses' profits will stay near their three-year average, Mucho Mocha is probably worth more than Peas and Carrots. Thus, a book value valuation method, which results in a similar value for both companies, won't produce accurate results for Mucho Mocha Corp. The capitalization of earnings method, which takes into account Mucho Mocha's higher earning capacity, will produce a much fairer result.

Under the capitalization of earnings method, you first determine the company's annual earnings, or profit, by subtracting the cost of doing business from gross revenues. Next you simply multiply the annual earnings by a number, called a multiplier. The selection of a multiplier should depend, at least to some degree, on your company's industry (as well as prevailing interest rates at the time of a buyout—see sidebar, "Rates of Return and Earnings Multipliers," below). That's because once some types of businesses become solidly profitable, they are likely to stay that way, while other types of endeavors are much more likely to produce up and down profits. For example, in the current economic climate, a small educational publishing company with an established and defensible market niche may be valued at about ten times average annual profits. However, a small publisher of fiction—a much chancier venture—is likely to be valued at a much lower multiple of annual profits, perhaps two.

To use the capitalization of earnings method, apply your multiplier to the average annual earnings from several consecutive years—called the "base earnings period." It's almost always a mistake to choose a base earnings period shorter than three years (and the IRS prefers to see figures that represent a five-year average), since doing so would risk a very good or bad year's skewing the results.

EXAMPLE: The four owners of Bean Bag Furniture, Inc. guessed right: They obtained a long-term, low-rent lease on a store in a run-down area that is rapidly becoming one of the trendiest shopping districts in town. After an initial period of marginal returns, their business is just plain booming. For the past three years, net profits, after paying each working owner a decent salary, have averaged $250,000. Now one owner has decided to retire. The owners' buy-sell agreement calls for arriving at the value of the business by multiplying its average net profits for the past three years by two. Thus, Bean Bag's value is $250,000 x 2, or

$500,000. It follows that, since the retiring owner holds one-fourth of the total shares, her interest is worth $125,000 under the capitalization of earnings method.

Capitalization rate is the same as a multiplier. In reading or talking with an expert about the capitalization of earnings method, you may come across the jargon "capitalization rate," or "cap rate." Don't be daunted—the term capitalization rate means exactly the same thing as multiplier—thus, using a cap rate of 10 simply means multiplying your earnings by 10.

The "capitalization of earnings" method requires you to do a fair bit of research, or educated guessing, before you agree on the multiplier to insert in your buy-sell agreement. Many factors should go into choosing a multiplier or capitalization rate, including:

- general economic conditions—for example, if yours is a tourist-based business and the economy is heading towards a recession, your multiplier should be lower than if the economy is growing fast and consumers have plenty of disposable income.
- the nature of your business, including the type of products and services you sell and whether customers are loyal to you or another co-owner. For example, if the service your business sells is highly personal, such as is often true for interior decorators, the company may not do well if a key co-owner leaves, meaning you'll probably want to choose a low multiplier.
- the age of your business. The longer your business has been profitable (especially if profits are stable or growing), the higher the multiplier you'll normally want to choose.
- the risk—or lack thereof—inherent in operating your business. For example, if your business is under assault by new competitors and profits are falling, it's probably worth a lot less than if the reverse is true.

- recent sales of interests in similar, small businesses. But make sure the comparable sales figures you look at are both current and truly comparable.

Choose a realistic multiplier. One experienced small business advisor we know recommends against using a multiplier higher than three times profits averaged over the last three years. Anything more could cripple the business with too high a buyout price. However, some experts say that, for a somewhat larger business with a superb earnings history, a highly desirable market niche and a solidly positive cash flow, it can sometimes make sense to pay as much as ten times earnings.

Because there are so many factors that can affect the choice of a multiplier, using this method is often most sensible in an industry where the multiplier has been generally defined and accepted in the trade. Construction companies, retail stores and restaurants are examples of businesses where it can be reasonably easy to obtain information on standard industry multipliers.

People who regularly buy and sell businesses are a good source of information. Business appraisers and brokers, especially those who specialize in a particular industry, often can tell you what sorts of multipliers are in general use in your type of business. Trade publications that report prices paid for businesses that change hands are another good source of information.

The capitalization of earnings clause in our buy-sell agreement is shown in Excerpt 4.

Check Valuation Method 4 if you wish to use the capitalization of earnings method to value your ownership interests. (Section VI, Valuation Method 4.) Also, insert the multiplier and the number of years to be used as the base earnings period into the blanks.

Rates of Return and Earnings Multipliers

To really understand how the capitalization of earnings method works, it helps to understand what the term "rate of return" means. This is the percentage of an investment that a buyer expects to get back each year. For instance, if you put $100,000 in a certificate of deposit (CD) with an interest rate of 5%, your rate of return on that investment would be about 5%, meaning you'd make about $5,000 in interest each year. In terms of buying a small business, to get a 5% rate of return on a purchase price of $100,000, the company would have to earn profits of $5,000 per year. If you, as an investor, had the option of putting your $100,000 into a guaranteed CD or into a small business, to get the same annual profits of $5,000 per year, you'd probably take the CD. Why put your money in an inherently risky small business when you are guaranteed the same return from an insured bank? Obviously, a 5% rate of return on a business investment is an unacceptably low rate given the risk inherent in any small business.

In valuing a business based on its earnings, the multiplier, or capitalization rate, varies inversely with the expected rate of return. If a company uses a multiplier of 20 (20 times annual earnings), a buyer would expect a rate of return of 5% (100% ÷ 20). Of course, if the company uses the much lower multiplier of 5, a buyer would get a far more desirable 20% rate of return (100% ÷ 5).

Rate of Return	Multiplier/Cap Rate
5%	20
8%	12.5
10%	10
15%	6.67
20%	5
25%	4
30%	3.33
50%	2

The multiplier you choose will vary depending on a number of factors, including the rate of return paid by other investments. That's because, as mentioned above, the rate of return a buyer will want to achieve when investing in an inherently risky small business will be substantially *above* what he could get if he placed his money in a U.S. government bond or other comparably safe investment. And it's also likely to be at least somewhat above the return a buyer would antici-pate receiving by investing in the stock market. For example, if the stock market has averaged a 16% rate of return over the last few years, a 10% rate of return from a small business (and thus a multiplier of 10) won't look nearly as good as it would if the stock market's recent average rate of return was 5%. In this case, an investor in a small business would probably be looking for at least a 20% rate of return (and thus a multiplier of no higher than 5).

☐ **Valuation Method 4: Capitalization of Earnings (Adjusted for Income Taxes)**
The value of the company shall be determined on the basis of _[insert multiplier, one or higher, such as "two"]_ times the average net earnings (annual gross revenues of the company minus annual expenses and minus any annual federal, state and local income taxes payable by the company) for the _[insert number of years, typically "three" or more]_ fiscal years of the company (or the number of fiscal years the company has been in existence, if fewer) that have occurred prior to the purchase of an ownership interest under this agreement. The value of an individual owner's interest shall be the entire value for the company as determined under this paragraph, multiplied by his or her ownership percentage.

Excerpt 4

Earnings Figure May Not Accurately Represent True Profit

Keep in mind that a savvy business owner (with the help of a creative accountant) can often take perfectly legal steps to make a business appear more or less profitable than would otherwise be true. For example, the owners can agree to pay themselves and their relatives salaries and bonuses that are way more or way less than the industry averages. Or a business can temporarily show chunky profits by skimping on new product development or postponing major expenses.

If you think your balance sheet may need adjusting before it fairly states your profit, you may want to have a professional appraiser or business valuation expert make appropriate adjustments so that the numbers reflect the earning value of your company more realistically and accurately.

Fine-tuning your formula. You can make your valuation method as complicated or as uncomplicated as you wish, but whichever method you choose, your price or formula should be reasonable, fair and affordable. Depending on your company's circumstances, you may wish to provide for the earnings formula to:

- weigh your earnings average to reflect a recent upward earnings trend (counting the most recent year's earnings the most)
- provide for a partial allocation of annual earnings in case an owner leaves in the middle of a fiscal year.

These adjustments are beyond the scope of this book—if you're interested in including them in your buy-sell agreement, we recommend you get an expert's help.

4. Appraisal Value (Valuation Method 5)

By now it may seem that you have to be a financial wizard to come up with a fair buyback price or an appropriate valuation formula for a small business. Don't worry—there is an easy, if more expensive, way out: You can adopt a provision that simply provides for your business's value to be established by a professional business appraisal at the time of a buyout.

The appraisal method involves agreeing to hire one or more professional appraisers who will decide the value of your business for you at the time of a buyout. Here is the way the appraisal method often works: As part of the buyout process, the buyer (usually the company or the remaining owners) and the seller (the departing owner, the representative of a deceased owner's estate or the ex-spouse of a divorced owner) each choose an appraiser to value the company. If the appraisers come up with the same price, or more likely a similar price, often the parties can negotiate a mutually agreeable price. But if the appraisers arrive at very different values, a typical buy-sell agreement requires the two appraisers to choose a third appraiser to make yet another appraisal, which is used as the agreement price. The appraised value is binding on all parties.

Choose an appraiser in advance. One way to reduce the possibility of future disputes and to hold down expenses is to agree in advance on one appraiser that all owners have confidence in. For example, if you and your co-owners set up a small software company and select an appraisal provision as the valuation method in your buy-sell agreement, you should think about finding and designating an appraiser who intimately knows the software industry, and preferably your segment of it. If you can't find a particular person, you may want to at least specify in your agreement a specific firm where the appraiser will come from, or at least require specific credentials for the appraiser (such as a CPA or an accredited appraiser).

Although using an appraisal approach to value your company may seem like a safe, conventional approach, there are a few potential drawbacks. Here are several:

- Having an appraiser can reduce guesswork and, hopefully, conflict, but it can also be expensive and time-consuming. Business valuations usually cost a minimum of $1,000 —and up to $2,500 for $100,000 companies, up to $5,000 for $500,000 businesses and $10,000 and above for larger companies. Using two or three appraisers will double or triple these amounts. In short, for a small business, appraisal costs can eat up a chunk of cash.

- Unlike most other valuation methods, establishing your business's value based on a time-of-sale appraisal does not provide a valuation figure you can look to in advance of a buyout. This can mean an owner who is contemplating leaving the company or adopting an estate plan won't have essential information she needs. This also means the company or co-owners will not know how much life or disability insurance to take out or how much liquidity will be needed to fund a potential buyout. (See sidebar, "Ongoing Appraisal Packages," for a way around these problems).

- It may be difficult, even for a professional appraiser, to subjectively but fairly value a small private company whose shares are not traded on any exchange, especially if one of the principals has died or is leaving the business. While naming an appraiser in your buy-sell agreement takes a big step toward avoiding conflict, if tension between owners is already present, the appraisal process can still be rancorous and political. You always take the risk that one party or another will contest the appraisal based on a claim that the appraiser unfairly favored the other side.

- It can take some time to get an appraiser's report, unless you have the good fortune of finding an appraiser who is both experienced in your line of business and prompt. To avoid delays, your agreement should set a certain period for the selection of an appraiser (this also prevents one of the owners from using the appraiser selection process as a delay tactic) and for the appraisal itself.

Business Valuation: How to Identify the Players

Anyone can value a business—there is no license requirement. We suggest, however, hiring a appraiser with professional credentials, who has been tested for proficiency and understanding of the fundamentals of appraisal concepts and ethics. As in many other fields, the business valuation industry has created its own professional designations. While many appraisers are also certified public accountants, the American Society of Appraisers (a widely respected, private accreditation group) uses these designations:

- AM (Accredited Member): requires two years of full-time appraisal experience
- ASA (Accredited Senior Appraiser): requires five years of full-time appraisal experience
- FASA (Fellow Appraiser): an Accredited Senior Appraiser who has been recognized by ASA's International Board of Governors for outstanding services to the appraisal profession and/or the Society of Appraisers.

Ongoing Appraisal Packages

Some business appraisal firms offer an ongoing "buy-sell agreement service." For a set price, they will perform annual valuation "checkups" on your company, giving you and your co-owners a dependable annual valuation that will normally withstand IRS scrutiny. It's also helpful for insurance, estate planning and business planning reasons to have handy a reasonably recent estimation of your company's value. As an added bonus, before any buybacks actually occur, you'll get to know and trust your appraiser and he'll get to know the strengths and weaknesses of your business.

The appraisal valuation language in our agreement, shown in Excerpt 5, provides for the mutual selection of one appraiser, or if that doesn't work out, it provides a mechanism for choosing two or three appraisers.

☐ **Valuation Method 5: Appraised Value**

The value of the company shall be its fair market value as determined by an independent appraiser mutually selected by Buyer(s) and Seller of the ownership interest subject to purchase under this agreement. If Buyer(s) and Seller are unable to agree upon an independent appraiser within 30 days, Buyer(s) and Seller, within the next 10 days, shall each select an independent appraiser. If the two selected appraisers are unable, within 60 days, to agree on the fair market value of the company, then the two appraisers shall select a third independent appraiser within the next 10 days, who shall, within 30 days, determine the fair market value of the company. All costs of an appraiser mutually selected by Buyer(s) and Seller or of a third appraiser selected by two appraisers shall be shared equally by Buyer(s) and Seller. All costs of an individually selected appraiser shall be paid by the party selecting the appraiser. The value of an individual owner's interest shall be the entire value for the company as determined under this paragraph, multiplied by his or her ownership percentage.

Excerpt 5

Check Valuation Method 5 if you wish to use an appraisal (at the time of purchase of an ownership interest by your company or continuing owners) to set the agreement price for a buyout. (Section VI, Valuation Method 5.)

There are many other ways to value your business. Although we include the most common types of valuation methods in our buy-sell agreement, we do not have the space to include the many different versions of each. And we obviously don't have the facts necessary to tailor our agreement to exactly match the needs of your business. Whether yours is a manufacturing, wholesale, retail or service business, it's important to recognize that a more custom-tailored valuation method may lead to a more accurate estimation of the worth of ownership interests in your company. Talk to your legal and accounting advisers about their experiences and recommendations, and to other business owners in your field about how they would go about valuing their business. If you're still interested in learning about more elaborate, detailed formulas, you'll need to do more reading (we list several resources in Chapter 10) or see an expert. ■

CHAPTER

7

Choosing Payment Terms for Buyouts

The payment terms in your buy-sell agreement control how and when the buyer must make payments to the seller under any buyout that arises under the buy-sell agreement. (For our purposes, the buyer will probably be the company or the continuing owners; the seller a selling owner, his family members or his estate representative.)

Lest you think these are just annoying financial details that can be handled quickly at the time of a buyout, consider that payment terms often affect the most important aspect of a buyout—the price that the buyer is willing to pay and the seller is willing to accept. For instance, terms that are more favorable to the buyer, such as a low-interest installment plan that extends over 5 years, can allow the seller to receive a higher price. In contrast, payment terms that favor the seller, such as an immediate, one-time, lump-sum cash payment, might lower the price the buyer is willing to pay.

Because payment terms can have a great effect on the success of any buyout that arises under your buy-sell agreement, you want to pick a payment plan that is perceived as fair to both buyer and seller. A departing owner who is selling his interest, of course, usually will want to receive payment for her interest fairly quickly, while the buyer—the continuing co-owners or the company itself—often will want to make payments over time. But it's important to realize that both sides have an interest in establishing terms that make it possible for your company or the continuing owners to exercise a buyout (if payment terms are too severe, your company or co-owners may not be able to afford them). For example, payment terms that require a 100% lump-sum cash payout right away can prevent even the most successful companies from buying back an owner's interest. Or if the company does make the purchase, such harsh payment terms may unfairly hamper or even destroy the business.

But in case you are tempted to provide extremely lenient buyout terms to benefit the buyer (for example, low payments over many years),

remember to balance your concern for the continued well-being of the company with the need to minimize inconvenience to a departing owner—or her family, if the owner has died. (After all, this could be you or your family.) Depending on the circumstances, a departing owner or her family normally has a legitimate interest in getting the buyback money reasonably fast. Aside from the obvious reasons of needing money for expenses, waiting a period of years to be paid off carries big risks. For example, if the remaining owners make bad business choices, they could render the business insolvent, with the result that the departing owner or her family may never receive all—or a substantial portion of—the buyout price. And, of course, how and when the buyback will occur can be of intense concern if the departing owner is pulling out precisely because she doesn't trust the others.

Your choice of payment terms may depend on where the funds to purchase an owner's interest will come from. If you opt to fund a buyout with life and/or disability insurance (discussed in Chapter 5), some buyout scenarios will be funded. But what about a situation where insurance can't pay for the buyout, such as after an owner's divorce? If the company or all of the co-owners are affluent, you may choose to payoff a buyout rather quickly, say within one year. But especially if you can't afford insurance and the business is cash-short, you'll probably want to opt for less stringent payment terms.

Of course, you can't know ahead of time what payment terms will work for both parties in a particular buyout situation. But choosing a fair payment plan now will at least give you a starting point to negotiate from when an actual buyout looms.

Payment-term provisions are not written in stone. Any payment-term provision you adopt can be changed if all owners agree. For instance, suppose your payment-term provision calls for a five-year payment plan, with interest at 10% per year on the unpaid balance. Now, suppose seven years after you sign your agreement, when your business is prosperous, a departing owner says, "You know, I'd like to get as much cash as I can now to invest in a new business. I propose that you pay me, right now, 60% of what I would have received over a five-year payment plan." If this seems fair to the remaining owners, all can agree to substitute the lump-sum payment for the five-year payment plan (you will want to get unanimous written consent of all owners to this arrangement, and place a copy of the signed consent in your company records book).

Following are several common ways to set up payment terms.

A. Lump-Sum Cash Payments

This method requires the buyer to pay the full amount of the buyback price in cash within a specified number of days from the date the buyer provides a Notice of Intent to Purchase to the seller.

The lump-sum payment provision in our buy-sell agreement is shown in Excerpt 1.

If you wish to choose the full cash payment alternative, check this provision on your worksheet. (Section VII, Payment Terms Alternative

1.) Insert in the blank the numbers of days (from the date of the company's Notice of Intent to Purchase) by which payment must be made.

Again, we believe requiring a lump-sum payment can be highly problematical, since the company or the continuing owners are unlikely to have sufficient cash on hand and, unless the business is extremely solvent, may be unable to obtain a loan from a bank to fund the cash buyout of the ownership interest. The unhappy result may be that the company or the continuing owners may not be able to exercise their buyout rights to avoid having a new owner come on board. This means an owner's inheritor or ex-spouse may be allowed to hold on to his ownership interests—just the result the buy-sell agreement is designed to avoid.

Don't tie the payment to insurance proceeds. Your buy-sell agreement should not call for a lump-sum payment that is tied specifically to the amount of life or disability insurance proceeds (see sidebar, "Having the Insurance Policy Set the Buyback Price," in Chapter 5, Section C1b for reasons why). Our approach is to have the buy-sell agreement set a buyback price independent of the means used to fund the buyout. But, you can provide that life insurance proceeds will be used as a down payment—see Section C, below.

Section VII: Payment Terms
Unless otherwise provided in this agreement, the undersigned agree that the payment terms checked below shall be used for the purchase of ownership interests under this agreement.

☐ **Payment Terms Alternative 1: Full Cash Payment**
Cash payment for the Seller's ownership interest shall be made by Buyer(s) to Seller within _[insert number of days, typically "30 or "60"]_ days of the date the company provides a Notice of Intent to Purchase to the Seller under this agreement.

Excerpt 1

B. Equal Payments Under an Installment Plan

With this approach, the company or the buying owners pay the purchase price in installments. (Also see Section C, below, for a combined cash and installment buyback.) You can adopt any installment payment schedule that you and your co-owners conclude is most likely to meet your needs—perhaps providing for equal payments over a number of months or years. It's also possible to provide for payments to increase or decrease over a number of years (perhaps tied to future levels of profits) or for periodic payments with interest added. Of course, without a down payment, the seller has an interest in receiving payments for his interest fairly quickly, probably over no more than one to three years.

The provision in our agreement that calls for equal payments over a specified term, with interest added is shown in Excerpt 2.

 If you wish to provide in your buy-sell agreement for monthly payments of principal and interest, check this alternative on your worksheet. (Section VII, Payment Terms Alternative

2.) Insert in the blanks the number of months over which payments will be made, the interest rate, the due date of the first installment and the monthly installment due date.

C. Combined Cash and Installment Payments

This method specifies an initial cash payment on the buyout date followed by periodic payments of the purchase price plus interest until the full amount is paid. A down payment of one-quarter to one-third of the buyout price is usually reasonable, followed by installment payments for three to five years. Of course, with a higher down payment, a longer installment period may be acceptable.

 Insurance proceeds can fund the down payment used to buy a deceased or disabled owner's interest. Obviously, you can use any life or disability insurance proceeds taken out on an owner to fund the down payment required to purchase a disabled or deceased owner's interest (for a discussion of insurance funding, see

---

☐ **Payment Terms Alternative 2: Monthly Installments of Principal and Interest**
Buyer(s) shall pay Seller the purchase price for an ownership interest in equal installments over a term of _[insert term for repayment in months, such as "24"]_ months, with interest added to the amount of each installment computed at an annual rate of _[insert interest rate]_ and compounded annually on the unpaid continuing balance of the purchase price of the ownership interest. The first installment payment shall be made to Seller by Buyer(s) on _[insert date of first installment payment]_, and the continuing payments shall be made to Seller by Buyer(s) on the _[insert payment due day, typically "1st"]_ of every month, until the full purchase price, together with any interest owed, is paid in full.

Excerpt 2

Chapter 5). We don't specifically tie the down payment to insurance proceeds in our provision below since this really isn't necessary—if insurance proceeds are available, you can use them at the time of the buyout to fund the down payment if you decide to do so.

The provision from our buy-sell agreement that calls for a cash down payment followed by the installment purchase of an ownership interest is shown in Excerpt 3.

If you decide to use the combined cash and installment payment alternative, check this provision in your worksheet. (Section VII, Terms Alternative 3.) Insert in the blank the amount of the down payment, the number of days in which the down payment must be made, the number of months over which payments will be made, the interest rate, the due date of the first installment and the monthly installment due date.

D. Interest-Only Installment Payments

Using this payment method, payment of the purchase price is postponed until a future date. Until this future date, the company makes installment payments of interest only. We rarely recommend this approach, except possibly in the first year or two of a new business or in a family business situation where affluent members of an older generation are looking for a generous way to transfer ownership to their children without making an outright gift.

☐ **Payment Terms Alternative 3: Partial Cash Payment, Followed by Monthly Installments of Principal and Interest**

The purchase of an ownership interest shall be accomplished as follows: An initial cash payment of _[insert the cash amount of the purchase price to be paid up-front, such as "$40,000"]_ shall be paid by Buyer(s) to Seller within _[insert number of days for down payment, such as "30"]_ days of the date the company provides a Notice of Intent to Purchase to Seller. The remainder of the purchase price shall be paid by Buyer(s) to Seller in equal installments over a term of _[insert term for repayment in months, such as "24"]_ months, with interest added to the amount of each installment computed at an annual rate of _[insert interest rate]_ % and compounded annually on the unpaid continuing balance of the purchase price of the ownership interest. The first installment payment shall be made by Buyer(s) on _[insert date of first installment payment]_ , and the continuing payments shall be made by Buyer(s) on the _[insert payment due day, typically "1st"]_ of every month, until the full balance of the purchase price, together with any interest owed, is paid in full.

Excerpt 3

If you wish to choose the interest-only installment alternative, check this provision in your worksheet. (Section VII, Terms Alternative 4.) Insert in the blanks the date for full payment of the purchase price, the interest rate, the date of the first installment payment and the monthly installment due date.

The provision in our buy-sell agreement that allows interest-only installment payments is shown in Excerpt 4.

A CHECK AT LAST

At the time of a buyout, this method may need to be used as a temporary payment method. Occasionally, when a co-owner leaves, neither the company nor the co-owners can afford to fund the buyout method provided by their buy-sell agreement. If so, all may agree to substitute an interest-only agreement such as this one on an interim basis.

☐ **Payment Terms Alternative 4: Monthly Installments of Interest Only, With a Final Payment for the Full Purchase Price**

Buyer(s) shall pay Seller the purchase price for an ownership interest on *[insert future date for full payment of purchase price]* . Until such date, Buyer(s) shall pay Seller monthly payments of interest, computed at an annual rate of *[insert interest rate]* % on the purchase price for the ownership interest. The first installment payment of interest shall be made by Buyer(s) on *[insert date of first installment payment]* , and the continuing installment payments of interest shall be made by Buyer(s) on the *[insert payment due day, typically "1st"]* of every month, until payment of the full amount of the purchase price by Buyer(s) as specified above. On the date for full payment of the purchase price by Buyer(s), interest owed on the purchase price from the date of the last payment of interest by Buyer(s) to the date of payment of the purchase price shall be added to and included with the payment of the purchase price by Buyer(s).

Excerpt 4

E. Customized Schedules of Payments

With this method, set amounts are paid at set times (for example, one-quarter of the purchase price, with interest, anytime during the following four calendar quarters). Obviously, the total of all payments should equal the full amount of the buyback price to be paid for the ownership interest, plus any interest charged on the financed amount. This might make sense for seasonal businesses, or for businesses that make most of their annual income once a year.

If you are interested in customizing your own payment terms, make a notation on your worksheet now. Write down whatever terms you're thinking of, including dates for payment, any applicable interest rates and the number of months over which payments will be made. (Section VII, Terms Alternative 5.)

☐ **Payment Terms Alternative 5: Customized Schedule for Payment for Ownership Interest**
Buyer(s) shall pay Seller the purchase price for the ownership interest according to the schedule and other terms included below:
[specify the amount and dates of a customized payment schedule]

Excerpt 5

Completing Your Buy-Sell Agreement

I n this chapter we cover the last few sections of our buy-sell agreement. Some of these final provisions contain accepted legal "boilerplate" language that will protect current and future owners, which has proven to be legally sound, if not readily readable. You should not change any of this language (nor will you have to check any options on your worksheet or on the buy-sell agreement itself for this chapter). Simply read the provisions in this chapter and you'll be ready to sign your agreement!

A. Resolving Buyout Disputes

Even the best buy-sell agreement—one that clearly and fairly covers every possible eventuality —can't guarantee a future free of disputes. Human nature being what it is, if business owners are not on good terms during a buy-sell situation, one owner (or his inheritors or his ex-spouse) may pick a fight with the others. And even if the owners are getting along personally, it's possible to disagree as to the value of a business interest. For example, a departing owner may assert the purchase price the company has offered to pay him is unfairly low because the valuation method in the agreement wasn't properly followed.

For these and other reasons, it makes sense to provide a structured procedure right in your buy-sell agreement for resolving conflicts in case a serious dispute arises. Then, if the owners can't negotiate a solution or compromise and a spat does ensue, all owners will have the security of knowing there is a method in place to resolve the dispute fairly, quickly and without having legal fees bankrupt all involved. To help meet these goals, our buy-sell agreement provides a way to resolve disputes using "alternative dispute resolution"—ADR for short.

ADR is a catchall term that describes a number of methods used to resolve disputes out of court, including negotiation, mediation and arbitration. The common denominator of all ADR methods is

that they are faster, less formal, cheaper and often less adversarial than a court trial. Our agreement utilizes the two most effective out-of-court mechanisms for resolving disputes: mediation and arbitration.

1. Litigation

First let's take a look at how regular court litigation works (or doesn't work), if only to demonstrate why it's almost always a rotten choice for resolving small business disputes. First, if lawyers must be hired to represent each side in a small business conflict, the resources of the company and the involved owners will quickly be drained. Simply put, legal fees can be astronomical. To understand why, realize that business lawyers usually charge $150 to $350 per hour—and a single case can take hundreds of hours of an attorney's time in depositions and other trial preparation before the case even goes to trial. In short, when you add up the legal expenses of both sides, going to court can, and often does, cost more than the dispute is worth.

Add to this the fact that litigation can drag on for months or even years, during which time your business may be in limbo, and you have a true recipe for disaster. In fact, many small businesses simply fall apart before the court fight is over.

Third, keeping conflicts out of a public courtroom can be very important to small business owners. Understandably, they don't want to expose trade secrets or private financial information, or have to air their dirty laundry in public. For example, if you go to court over the expulsion of a co-owner who has a drug or alcohol abuse problem, some very personal matters could be brought up, such as a laundry list of all the embarrassing things the owner had done under the influence. Revealing such information to the public could affect your company's reputation, not to mention ruin your business partner's life. Likewise, if you rely on consumers to buy products or services from you, you'll want to keep up your public image. For instance, if one of your co-owners becomes disabled in a tragic accident, and you and the other co-owners attempt to stop his salary and force him to sell out, you could engender a wave of bad local publicity that could damage your business for many years.

Fourth, filing a lawsuit is a hostile and aggressive act. So as not to jeopardize your case, your lawyers may even forbid you to speak with opposing co-owners (even if you need and wish to cooperate to keep the business functioning). Also, many attorneys will all but insist on using every means possible to win, even if it means showing your co-owner in the worst possible light, or dragging his family through the mud. And, of course, behavior like this is highly likely to cause your adversary to retaliate in kind. Continuing your business relationship in circumstances like these is all but impossible.

Fifth, many times small business disputes do not raise legal claims that can be effectively pursued in court. For example, if two partners are in a major disagreement about who should control different aspects of the business, but there has been no violation of the owners' agreement and

no legal damages, chances are the co-owners won't be able to resolve their problem in court.

Lastly, small businesses are particularly vulnerable to losing a court case. They usually carry less comprehensive insurance and have less capital than larger companies. As a result, they are at an increased risk of being wiped out by even one oversized court award.

2. Mediation

Compared to litigation, mediation is inexpensive, quick, confidential, less risky and almost always available for small business disputes. In a nutshell, mediation is a process where the parties to a dispute try to come to a voluntary agreement with the help of an outside, neutral third party: the mediator. A mediation session is an informal process that takes place without rules of evidence and other court-like protocols (though it does follow a defined structure—see sidebar, "The Stages of Mediation"). With the help of their mediator, the parties decide what issues need to be resolved and what procedure should be followed to solve their dispute.

The Stages of Mediation

Many people think that mediation is a totally unstructured process in which a friendly mediator chats with the disputants until they suddenly drop their hostilities and work together for the common good. In fact, mediation is a carefully designed process designed to help the disputing parties craft a detailed written solution to their problem. True, compared to the 19th century formalism of an American trial court, mediation is informal, but that's not a bad thing.

Stage 1: Mediator's Opening Statement. After the disputants are seated at a table, the mediator introduces everyone, explains the goals and rules of the mediation and encourages each side to work cooperatively toward a settlement.

Stage 2: Disputants' Opening Statements. Each party is invited to tell, in his or her own words, what the dispute is about and how he or she has been affected by it, and to present some general ideas about resolving it. While one person is speaking, the other is not allowed to interrupt.

Stage 3: Joint Discussion. The mediator will try to get the parties to talk directly about what was said in the opening statements. This is the time to determine what issues need to be addressed.

Stage 4: Private Meetings With the Mediator (called "caucuses"). Often considered the guts of mediation, the private caucus is a chance for each party to meet privately with the mediator (usually in a nearby room) to discuss the strengths and weaknesses of his or her position, and new ideas for settlement. The mediator may caucus with each side just once, or several times, as needed. Often the mediator helps each party to focus on their real needs (and to put aside less essential issues). Although it may take hours or even days, this eventually causes the parties to abandon emotionally laden side issues and come to terms with the best way to resolve the major issues.

Stage 5: Joint Negotiation. After the private caucuses, the mediator may bring the parties back together to negotiate directly.

Stage 6: Closure. This is the end of the mediation. If an agreement has been reached and the parties are ready, they can write up and sign a legally binding contract. Otherwise the mediator may draw up a written summary of their agreement and suggest they take it to lawyers for review. If no agreement was reached, the mediator will review whatever progress has been made and advise everyone of their options, such as meeting again later or going to arbitration.

All parties to a dispute must agree to mediation and be able to mediate. If one party refuses or perhaps isn't competent to participate, the dispute cannot be mediated. If one party may be mentally disabled, you'd be better off going to court, where a judge or lawyer can protect his interests.

Precisely because a mediator has no power to impose a decision, but encourages would-be antagonists to arrive at their own compromised solution, participants are usually less paranoid and more open to creative proposals to resolve a dispute. In fact, partly because of this, business ownership transition problems are quickly becoming a well-developed specialty in the private dispute resolution world. Here are just a few of the many other reasons why mediation is particularly well suited for business disputes:

- Mediation costs a lot less than litigation. Fees start at $1, 200 or so per party for a full-day session, but can go higher, depending on how long mediation lasts, how specialized your dispute is and which firm or mediator you choose. You should count on at least a couple of days for small business mediation, maybe as much as a week or two if your dispute is complicated. Still, the cost will be a pittance compared to taking the same dispute to court.

- Mediation spares the disputants the fear of the courtroom, where a judge or jury can stun one party with a big loss. Because the mediator has no authority to impose a decision, nothing can be decided unless both parties agree to it. Knowing this greatly reduces the tension felt by all parties— people who choose mediation tend to be more relaxed and open to compromise. And if for any reason you don't feel the mediation session is productive, you can call it off. For instance, if one party isn't cooperating—he insists that he's right and is not willing to hear the other side, he doesn't agree with the advantages of mediation or he's just a loud-mouthed jerk—you may not want to waste any more time in mediation, and instead go straight to arbitration (see Section 3, below).

- People who arrive at a joint decision are much more likely to abide by it than are people who have a decision imposed on them by a judge. This is key when an ongoing business is involved, since mediation greatly increases the likelihood that the solution will actually work.

- When you have to keep working with your co-owner (or a member of her family) and you want to remain on good terms, mediation is usually the best choice. Unlike a judge, a mediator will not place blame. Just the opposite: His job is to help each party evaluate their goals and options in order to find a solution that works for everyone. For instance, during litigation, it's common to call a witness just to show the judge or jury the bad character of the person you're up against; in mediation this would be completely irrelevant, and therefore is almost never done. And since neither side needs to personally attack the other, each is able to save face and, hopefully, continue some sort of business and personal relationship with the other after the dispute is over.

- Unlike court, mediation is not limited to solving the dispute at hand. Often, issues are discussed in mediation that would not be legally relevant in court, but which are highly important to the parties. This allows the parties to address the issues that may have created the dispute in the first place, including problems that stem from different communication styles and clashing personalities. In short, if undiscovered or ongoing problems surface during mediation, the parties, with the help of the mediator, can work them out.

- Mediation can be particularly helpful if you're having trouble communicating and negotiating with the other party; the mediator will help you make your points and not allow the other side to intimidate you. In fact, even the experience of talking civilly to each other and working cooperatively toward a solution can help business owners restore their relationship; some consider it a kind of business therapy.

• Mediation is also a good choice when you don't want to air your company's and co-owners' dirty laundry. Mediators take a vow of confidentiality, so you can be assured that you won't read about what your co-owner told your mediator about you in the local paper. Especially for family businesses —where a contested court case can tear a family apart—mediation is almost surely the better choice. Because of the privacy, the civility and the encouragement it provides to co-owners to come to a compromise, it offers many distressed families a positive way to begin a healing process that will go beyond the particular dispute.

When and if the parties do come up with a solution, the mediator should help them put the agreement in writing, usually as a legally binding contract. The negotiated solution can include whatever you've agreed to, including issues not thought to be important when the mediation began.

For example, it can set up a plan for you and the departing owner to work together in the future (perhaps a retiring owner agrees to sell out as part of the settlement, but the company agrees that it will hire him to do consulting work for two years).

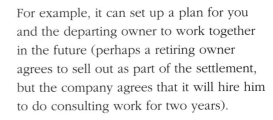

Choosing a Mediator

To find a mediator, ask for recommendations from colleagues or small business lawyers or associations, or look in your local yellow pages under mediation services for a private dispute resolution company.

It's important to choose a mediator with experience in small business disputes, in particular in disputes arising out of buy-sell agreements. And in some situations you may want to seek out a mediator with more specialized knowledge. For example, if your conflict is over the value of an owner's interest, then experience in business valuation techniques or at least general financial know-how will be necessary. Likewise, if you're trying to structure a complicated installment payment plan with an eye toward minimizing taxes, the mediator should have some tax savvy. Or, if you and your co-owners are arguing over the worth of a patent, she should have a technical background.

Use experts as consultants. Small business lawyers or tax experts can also be used in a consultative role as part of mediation. Often they make no appearances at the mediation session itself, but stand by to review settlement proposals. But be sure to have any experts you need lined up before you begin mediating. When proposals start flying, you obviously need to have your advisor at the ready to check them out, to recommend any necessary changes and to consider the tax consequences.

3. Arbitration

Arbitration, another form of alternative dispute resolution, is actually more like court than like mediation. Like mediation, arbitration is a non-court procedure for resolving disputes and uses a neutral third party—called an arbitrator (or sometimes, there are several neutral parties that make up an arbitration panel). However, in binding arbitration, the parties themselves are not expected to arrive at a voluntary agreement (although, of course, they are always free to do so). Instead, each side presents its version of the dispute to the arbitrator, who then issues a written decision that is binding on the parties. Although arbitration is more structured and trial-

---

Section VIII: Resolution of Disputes

Mediation Followed by Arbitration

Except as may otherwise be provided in this agreement or a later one dated and signed by all owners, any dispute concerning the contents of this agreement, if it cannot be settled through direct negotiation, shall first be submitted to mediation according to the terms specified below. All parties agree to try in good faith to settle the dispute by mediation before resorting to arbitration or litigation.

(a) An owner, an owner's legal representative, the spouse or ex-spouse of an owner, the executor or administrator of a deceased owner's estate or any other party with an interest in this company who wishes to have a dispute mediated shall submit a written request for mediation to each of the other owners of the company. Mediation shall commence within 15 days after the date of the written request for mediation.

(b) Any decision reached by mediation shall be reduced to writing, signed by all parties, and shall be binding on each party. The costs of mediation shall be shared equally by all parties to the dispute.

(c) Each party to the mediation process shall cooperate fully and fairly with the mediator in any attempt to reach a mutually satisfactory compromise to a dispute. If the dispute is not resolved within 30 days after it is referred to the mediator, the dispute shall be submitted for arbitration according to the terms specified below or on terms agreeable to all parties at the time the dispute is submitted to arbitration.

(d) Within 15 days of the delivery of the notice of intention to proceed to arbitration to all parties, each party shall reply in writing to the arbitrator, stating his or her views of the nature and appropriate outcome of the dispute.

(e) The arbitrator shall hold a hearing on the dispute within 15 days after replies have been received from all parties, or, if all replies have not been received, no later than 30 days after the giving of notice of intention to proceed to arbitration.

(f) At the arbitration hearing, each party shall be entitled to present any oral or written statements he or she wishes and may present witnesses. The arbitrator shall make his or her decision in writing, and his or her decision shall be conclusive and binding on all parties to the dispute.

(g) The cost of arbitration, including any lawyer's fees, shall be borne by the parties to the dispute equally unless the arbitrator directs otherwise.

Excerpt 1

like than mediation, the fact that it uses relatively informal rules of evidence and procedure means that it's almost always faster than going to court. Also, arbitrators have a bit more leeway than judges to impose commonsensical solutions, rather than being bound to follow the letter of the law.

If an unhappy losing party decides to sue in court in an attempt to overturn the arbitrator's decision (in fact, such lawsuits occur infrequently), she is almost sure to lose. That's because the court will not overturn the arbitrator's decision unless the arbitrator was blatantly biased or unfair (for example, had an undisclosed conflict of interest). In other words, once the arbitrator makes a decision, the fight is over.

In short, while more formal than mediation, arbitration is almost always quicker and less expensive than going to court, and definitely more private.

4. Our Solution

Arbitration is required by our buy-sell agreement only if negotiation and mediation prove unsuccessful. In other words, disputants are encouraged to mediate first, arbitrate second (if necessary) and litigate not at all. In fact, few disputes ever get past the mediation stage, since in mediation disputants are highly motivated to arrive at a compromise they can live with, rather than risking an arbitrator's imposing a less palatable one. The language of the dispute resolution clause we use in our buy-sell agreement is shown in Excerpt 1, above.

Our dispute resolution clause is not optional. We assume all readers will agree in their buy-sell agreement to attempt to mediate their disputes and, if mediation fails, to arbitrate instead of going directly to court. Of course, you can change this provision, for example, by not requiring arbitration if mediation fails, but we don't think this is the best course—for the reasons given earlier, a court case should be avoided if at all possible.

B. Placing a Legend on Your Ownership Certificates

For companies that issue certificates. Usually corporations are the only companies that issue ownership certificates to their owners (in the form of stock certificates). Although LLCs can issue membership certificates to owners, most do not. If your company does not issue certificates or other documents representing ownership interests, skip ahead to Section C.

Most states require the placement of a notice, or "legend," on stock certificates whenever the interests they represent are subject to transfer restrictions—to let owners and outsiders know that interests in the company are subject to these transfer restrictions and can be bought back by the company and its owners pursuant to the buy-sell provisions that your company has adopted.

We believe the placement of a legend on certificates also is essential to remind owners, and give notice to others who may get their hands on ownership interests, that interests cannot be disposed of at will, but only under the terms of your buy-sell agreement. If you don't do this, you invite confusion and controversy later by successors to ownership interests who claim ignorance of the existence of your buy-sell restrictions.

Excerpt 2 shows the language of our buy-sell agreement's Section IX, which requires the placement of a legend on certificates. Our legend also says that your secretary or other equivalent officer of the company will provide a copy of the text of your buy-sell provisions to any requesting person, whether an owner or not. Make sure to honor any such requests.

Here's how to comply with this section of the agreement:

- **Existing Certificates.** The secretary of the company should gather up all the outstanding certificates issued to the company's existing owners, and type the legend required by Section IX of the buy-sell agreement in capital letters on the front of all certificates.

- **New Certificates.** Make sure to also type this legend on any new certificates issued to future owners. One way to ensure this is to type the legend on all blank certificates that remain in your corporate or LLC records binder. When these certificates are issued to new owners, the legend will already be on them and you will not have to remember to perform this task.

Order new certificates if the legend won't fit. If there is insufficient room on your current certificates to type the legend, or if you wish to have this legend printed on new certificates by a legal stationer, order new certificates. (Some states allow the use of the back of certificates, but we don't like this idea—an owner may not flip the certificate over to read the language on the back.) Simply exchange the new certificates bearing the printed legend with the old certificates held by your current owners. Make sure to note the cancellation of the old certificates and the issuance of the new certificates in your company's transfer ledger or records binder.

C. Binding All Future Owners Under Your Buy-Sell Agreement

The next section of our buy-sell agreement, Section X, ensures that new owners in the company will be legally bound to the terms of the buy-sell agreement. *All* future holders of ownership interests, whether they have received an interest by sale, gift, will or trust or otherwise, are subject to the terms of the buy-sell agreement. Excerpt 3 shows the first part of the provision we use in our agreement.

Section IX: Placement of Notice of Transfer Restrictions on Certificates

(a) The following statement must appear conspicuously on each ownership certificate issued by the company:

THE INTERESTS REPRESENTED BY THIS CERTIFICATE ARE SUBJECT TO RESTRICTIONS UPON TRANSFER AND ARE REDEEMABLE PURSUANT TO PROVISIONS CONTAINED IN AN AGREEMENT AMONG THE OWNERS OF THE COMPANY. FOR A COPY OF THIS AGREEMENT, CONTACT THE SECRETARY OR EQUIVALENT OFFICER OF THE COMPANY AT THE PRINCIPAL OFFICE OF THE COMPANY AT __*[insert company's address]*__

_____ .

(b) The secretary or other equivalent officer of the company shall provide to any owner or third person upon written request and without charge a copy of this agreement.

Excerpt 2

Section X: Continuation of Restrictions

All heirs, successors and assigns to an ownership interest in the company will be bound by the terms of this agreement.

Excerpt 3

Although this formality is recommended, without signing it, new owners may not actually be legally bound to follow the buy-sell agreement, even if the restrictions are printed on the certificate or other evidence of ownership.

EXAMPLE: George and Harry have owned and managed a mortuary for 40 years as a corporation. Having bought the building that houses the mortuary and owning a large share of a local cemetery, the business has come to be worth a lot of money. Getting on in years, George starts to gift shares to his children, hoping to avoid eventual estate taxes. George does not require his children to sign the company's shareholder (buy-sell) agreement before receiving shares. Soon after receiving shares in the corporation, George's son Michael decides he doesn't want to follow in his father's footsteps and become an undertaker, so he sells his shares to one of George and Harry's competitors. Since Michael never signed the agreement, it would be very hard, if not impossible, to get a judge to void the transfer of shares.

Problems can also arise if a recipient of an ownership interest wants to hold on to her interest in the company but never signs the agreement. If, for instance, Michael from the above example gets divorced, and his spouse receives his ownership interest in a divorce settlement, the company cannot require the spouse to sell her ownership interest back to the company. For this reason, any time family members receive interests in the company by gift, they, as well as their spouses, should be required to adopt the buy-sell agreement.

Our agreement requires all new owners, and their spouses, to sign the buy-sell agreement before taking an ownership interest in the company. The second part of Section X from our buy-sell agreement is shown in Excerpt 4.

In the future, whenever a new owner joins your company, add this owner's name (and her spouse's name, if applicable) to your buy-sell agreement and have the new owner sign it. You can simply add a new date and signature line at the bottom of your original agreement for the new owner to date and sign, or you can prepare a new one, having all old and new owners sign it. This latter approach gives you a chance to review your agreement to make sure it still works for all owners. For example, when a new owner buys into the company, you may want to change the valuation and payment alternatives in Sections VI and VII of the agreement, if the economic circumstances of your corporation or the personal preferences of your owners have changed since the adoption of, or last update to, your agreement. (See Section E, below, for updating your agreement.)

D. Signing Your Agreement

Assuming you have read this entire book up to this point, filling out the worksheet as you go along, you should now transfer the choices you marked on your worksheet to the buy-sell agreement provided with this book, on the tear-out form in Appendix C or on the forms disk that accompanies this book. Next, we recommend you bring your draft buy-sell agreement for review by a lawyer, tax expert or other professional with

---

Before receiving a purchased, donated or otherwise transferred interest from an owner or an owner's legal representative, the owner or the owner's legal representative will require any purchaser, donee or transferee, and his or her spouse, to sign this buy-sell agreement, agreeing to be bound by its terms.

Excerpt 4

experience in buy-sell agreements. (See Chapter 10 for how to find an expert.)

Finally, you've come to the last step in completing your agreement—signing it! On the last page of the buy-sell agreement, you'll find Section XI, which contains blank lines for the signatures of the owners and their spouses. Have each owner and spouse print his or her name and the date in the spaces provided, and then sign the agreement.

CONGRATULATIONS! You and your co-owners are now protected by a buy-sell agreement!

 To add provisions to an existing document. If you have decided to add your buy-sell provisions to an existing organizational document (such as your partnership or LLC operating agreement), simply cut and paste the buy-sell provisions into the existing document, without the signature page. We recommend that you add the provisions to the end of the existing document, but you can insert them anywhere you wish. Of course, when adding these provisions to the document, you will want to change the paragraph numbering or lettering of the buy-sell provisions to conform to the numbering or lettering scheme of your existing organizational document. Make sure all owners (and their spouses) sign and date the new agreement.

E. Updating Your Buy-Sell Agreement in the Future

As we have discussed elsewhere, it's important to review your buy-sell agreement periodically to make sure it reflects the current economic realities of your company and the present expectations of your owners. It is particularly important to review Sections VI and VII of the agreement, where you check the methods to be used to value ownership interests, and the payment terms to pay for them, for purposes of a buyout under your agreement. Some experts recommend doing this each year, at the owners' annual meeting.

If all owners agree to make changes to the buy-sell agreement, you can date and have all owners initial changes on the original agreement itself, or you can prepare a new one and have it dated and signed by all owners.

There's another way to update your valuation provision if you have selected the agreed-price valuation method (Valuation Method 1) in Section VI. This provision lets you change the buyout price to be paid for interests by having all owners sign a written statement that specifies a new agreed-upon price. Below is a sample statement you can copy and use for this purpose:

Owner Consent to New Agreement Price for Interests in the Company

The undersigned owners of ___*[name of company]*___, representing all the voting owners on the books of this company on the date shown below, agree that in any purchase or sale of ownership interests under the owner agreement, dated ___*[date of signing of your owner buy-sell agreement]*___, unless otherwise stated in a provision of such agreement other than Section VI, for the purposes of determining the purchase price for individual ownership interests, the entire value of the company shall be $ ___*[insert agreed-upon price for entire company, such as "100,000"]*___. The value of an individual owner's interest shall be the entire value for the company as determined under this paragraph, multiplied by his or her ownership percentage.

The price stated in this statement shall supersede any price specified in Section VI of the above-mentioned buy-sell agreement, and shall supersede any price specified in any statement dated and signed by owners prior to the date of this statement, shown below.

Dated: _____

Signed: ___*[signatures of all current owners]*___

If you use a written statement like this, be sure to attach it to your buy-sell agreement.

Update your price whenever your financial outlook changes. Even if you and your co-owners do not sign a new statement annually, make sure to do so whenever financials in your business take a significant upturn or downturn (for instance, your payroll costs increase significantly, with a resulting reduction in owners' equity as shown on your last fiscal year-end balance sheet, or your annual profits go up significantly three quarters in a row, and you expect this trend to continue).

Don't forget to add new owners to your buy-sell agreement, as discussed in Section C, above. You can simply add a new date and signature line at the bottom of your original agreement for the new owner to date and sign, or you can prepare a new one, having all old and new owners sign it. ■

Income and Estate Tax Issues

Tax consequences are obviously important whenever business interests are transferred. The adoption of particular provisions in your buy-sell agreement as well as the actual buyout of an owner's interest according to those provisions can have important income and estate tax consequences. For this reason, it is crucial to have your buy-sell agreement reviewed by a skilled tax advisor to make sure that a buyout will have the appropriate tax consequences for the seller, buyers, inheritors and other people intended to be benefited by a buyout under your agreement.

In this chapter we flag some of the basic federal income and estate tax issues involved with buyouts of ownership interests in partnerships, LLCs and corporations. The tax implications of buy-sell provisions and the tax consequences of using a particular buyout method are complicated, and we don't cover all the rules and exceptions—just enough to give you a good start when seeking more specific, individually tailored advice from your tax advisor.

A. Buy-Sell Income Tax Issues

Let's start by looking at some of the fundamental income tax issues surrounding a buyout of an owner's interest. Right at the beginning of this discussion, we encounter a technical tax term—the concept of "income tax basis" in an ownership interest.

1. Tax Basis and Capital Gains Tax Treatment

As you probably know, the term "income tax basis," or simply "basis," refers to the value assigned to property for the purposes of determining the taxable gain or loss from it after it is sold. Calculating your exact basis in an ownership interest (with the help of a tax advisor) is crucial, because this is the number that the IRS uses to determine if you've made a profit when you sell your business interest.

Generally, your income tax basis in an ownership interest is the cash amount you pay, along with your current basis in any property you transfer, to buy the interest. If you transfer property that's subject to a debt that the business assumes—for example, you transfer real estate subject to a mortgage—your basis in your interest is decreased by the amount of the assumed debt (in effect, the business refunds to you the amount of the debt attached to your capital contribution). In a partnership, where owners are personally liable for the debts of the business, your share of accounts payable and other liabilities of the business at the time of your capital contribution increases your basis in your partnership interest.

Over time, this original basis in your ownership interest is adjusted up or down. For example, in a partnership or LLC (or a corporation that elects S corporation tax treatment), your basis in your ownership interest is increased when profits are allocated to you, and decreased when losses are allocated. These allocations occur automatically at the end of the tax year of the partnership or LLC whether or not profits are actually paid out, and are known as each owner's "distributive share." Your basis in a partnership interest also increases when the business incurs additional liabilities (takes out a loan). In addition, your basis in an LLC or partnership interest is decreased whenever you receive a cash distribution from the business —for example, when profits are actually paid to you—although you do not pay tax on these profits (since taxes were paid when the profits were allocated to you) unless they exceed your basis in your interest. Obviously, figuring your basis in an ownership interest at the time of its formation, during the course of its operations or at the time of a buyout of your ownership interest is anything but obvious to most of us, and this is just one of the important tasks that should be referred to a tax advisor.

There are different types of basis in partnership and LLC ownership interests. In a partnership or an LLC, there are two types of basis: the owner's individual basis in her business interest —called her "outside basis"—and the partnership or LLC's separate basis in its assets—called its "inside basis." In our discussion of basis in this section, unless we say otherwise, when we refer to a partner's or LLC owner's basis in her ownership interest, we mean the partner's or LLC owner's "outside basis" in her interest.

Your profit (gain) when you sell your ownership interest is calculated by subtracting your tax basis in your ownership interest (your original basis plus or minus adjustments) from your sale proceeds.

EXAMPLE: Barbara is a shareholder and vice president of Biz Wiz, a small C corporation (this means a regular corporation that has not elected S corporation tax treatment) with four other owners. As part of its initial stock issuance, Barbara's company issues her 3,000 shares in exchange for her cash payment of $70,000, plus the patent she owns for "Biz Wiz" software. Her current basis in her patent of $30,000 plus her cash payment of $70,000 are added to make up her starting basis of $100,000 in her newly acquired corporate shares. When Barbara leaves the company four years later, no adjustments have been made to her original basis in her shares. Under the terms of the buy-sell provisions in the shareholder agreement signed by Barbara and her co-owners, her ownership interests are appraised and purchased by the company for $125,000. Barbara recognizes a gain (profit) of $25,000—the $125,000 sales price minus her basis of $100,000 in her shares.

You can expect to pay a tax on any gain you make when you sell your ownership interest. In most cases, your profit should be eligible to be taxed at capital gains tax rates. The capital gains rates vary according to how long you owned your ownership interest—either as a long-term investment, a mid-term investment or a short-term investment. Without listing the various capital gains rates and holding periods, which change regularly, the main point is this: Capital gains rates are lower than ordinary individual income rates paid by the owners, so it's an advantage to have the profit from a sale of an ownership interest taxed at capital gains rates.

EXAMPLE: Let's revisit Barbara. After owning her shares in Biz Wiz (in which her tax basis is $100,000) for several years, she sells them back to Biz Wiz for $125,000. Her $25,000 profit is eligible for long-term capital gains treatment (we'll assume a 20% capital gains tax rate), rather than ordinary income tax treatment. Had Barbara's sale not qualified for capital gains tax rates, she would have been taxed on the sale proceeds at a 31% rate—her personal income tax bracket.

 Shareholders can exclude some gains. Shareholders in active C corporations may be able to exclude from their gross income 50% of the capital gain realized from selling originally issued shares held for more than five years. If you are a shareholder of a C corporation, ask your tax advisor about this possibility.

Okay, we've established that capital gains tax treatment is normally the way to go when selling an ownership interest. And we've also seen that having a higher basis in your ownership interest results in the recognition of less capital gain, and, therefore, the payment of less tax when the interest is sold. Below, we discuss special IRS rules that affect the basis of an ownership interest and your eligibility for capital gains tax treatment when your ownership interest is bought out under a buy-sell agreement.

What the Term "Capital Account" Means

It is easy to confuse "capital account" balances with other accounting and tax terms, such as an owner's basis in his interest or his distributive share of profits and losses. To avoid this, just think of a capital account balance as the amount that an owner can expect to be paid if the business is liquidated and split up among the owners (assuming there is sufficient cash left after all creditors have been paid).

When a partner or LLC member contributes cash or property to a company, her capital account is credited with the cash amount or fair market value of the contribution. When profits are allocated to the owner at the end of the tax year of a partnership or LLC, her capital account balance goes up (the business owes her this money); as distributions are made, such as payments of draws or profits, her capital account balance goes down (the business no longer owes this money to her).

In fact, an owner's capital account balance may be used in a partnership or LLC operating agreement as the price an owner receives for a buyout of the owner's interest. As long as the assets of the partnership or LLC are appraised and adjusted on the balance sheet of the company just prior to the buyout (an increase in assets results in proportionate increases to the balances in the owners' capital accounts), payment of the capital account balance to a departing owner can represent a fair value for her interest. If you're interested in using this method to value ownership interests in an LLC or partnership, choose the appraisal method in Chapter 6—a professional appraiser can handle these calculations for you.

a. Stepped-Up Basis at Death of Owner

When you leave a business interest to someone at death, either by will or by a probate-avoiding living trust, your inheritor's tax basis in the property is normally equal to its fair market value as of the date of your death. Because fair market value is likely to be higher than your original tax basis in the interest (assuming appreciation over the years), it is often said that at death the tax basis of a business interest is "stepped up" to its fair market value. (Actually, this is a simplification of the rule, since the basis of inherited property is adjusted up *or down* to its fair market value as of the date of death.) Assuming your interest has appreciated, this adjusted-value rule can save the inheritor a lot in taxes, and can make leaving your business interest at death a better choice than selling or giving it away shortly before death.

EXAMPLE: Bill paid $25,000 for an ownership interest in BJB, a company he owns along with his wife Judy and her brother Bob. His company's buy-sell agreement allows an owner to leave his ownership interest to whomever he wishes in his will, and that inheritor has the right to force BJB to buy back the ownership interest at its current fair market value (to be established by a professional appraiser). Bill dies, leaving his ownership interests to his daughter, Amy. Within 60 days, Amy demands that BJB buy back the interest she recently inherited. BJB gets an appraisal for Bill's interest for $200,000 and buys it from Amy for this amount. Amy does not owe any capital gains or income taxes, since at Bill's death her income tax basis in the ownership interest was automatically "stepped up" to the fair market value of $200,000, and her sale proceeds were also $200,000. (If her basis in the ownership interest had not been stepped up, but had stayed at Bill's original basis of $25,000, Amy would have had to report and pay taxes on capital gains of $175,000 when she sold her ownership interest back to BJB.)

Other issues may be important in the sale or transfer of your business interest. Here we just demonstrated the general rule that property receives a stepped-up basis at death. But in some cases, if a business is very valuable today but faces much uncertainty in the years ahead, waiting to transfer an ownership interest at death in order to save on taxes may be a poor choice. In short, you'll need to assess your business prospects, family needs and tax situations to decide the optimum time and manner to sell or transfer your small business interest.

b. No Change of Basis for Gifts of Interests

Unfortunately, this "stepped-up" basis rule does not apply to gifts. If you give away all or part of your business interest during your lifetime, the person who receives the interest will take it at the same tax basis as yours was when you made the gift. Or put another way, when you give away ownership interest, you give it away at *your* tax basis, *not* at the interest's fair market value when you make the gift.

> EXAMPLE: Let's go back to Bill and Amy. Imagine that instead of waiting to leave his ownership interest in BJB to Amy upon his death, Bill gives it to her while he's living. Amy takes the interest at Bill's basis of $25,000. Several years later, after Bill dies, Amy sells her interest for $200,000. Unfortunately, instead of owing no capital gains tax, as would be true if Bill had waited and left his share of BJB to Amy at his death (her tax basis in BJB would have been stepped up to its current market value of $200,000), Amy owes a whopping capital gains tax. In the eyes of the IRS she has realized a taxable gain of $175,000 ($200,000 − $25,000).

It follows that, if you're an elderly owner, it may not make sense to give away interests in your business to family members during your lifetime, unless if these family members will take

over their share of the company on a long-term basis (assuming the buy-sell agreement allows this, of course), in which case no capital gains tax will be due for many years. Instead, it may make better sense to wait until your death to leave your ownership interest to your heirs, who will then inherit it with a basis equal to its stepped-up fair market value. If your heirs sell it relatively soon after, they should pay little or no capital gains tax.

2. Tax Basis of the Continuing Owners

In Chapter 4, we discussed why the buy-sell agreement included in this book allows the company and then the continuing owners the opportunity to purchase a departing owner's interest. A big advantage of this approach is that the decision as to whether the company or the continuing owners will make the purchase doesn't have to be made until a particular buyout situation presents itself. This allows the owners of the company to evaluate the tax advantages and disadvantages of several different buyout scenarios. But when the time comes for a buyout, the decision as to whether to have the company or the continuing owners purchase an ownership interest can have significant tax consequences. We look briefly at some of these tax consequences below.

a. When the Continuing Owners Buy an Owner's Interest

Let's start by focusing on a simple truth. When the continuing owners buy a co-owner's interest out of their own pockets they have spent additional personal funds to increase their ownership interest in their company.

> EXAMPLE: Amanda, Beth, Chris and their father each own 150 shares in Shortcuts, Inc. (They each own 25% of the company.) When their father decides to retire, Amanda, Beth and Chris buy his 150 shares (the corporation does

not buy any shares itself). According to their buy-sell agreement, they split the purchase of the shares equally, buying 50 shares apiece. Amanda, Beth and Chris now each own 200 shares. (Also, now they each own 33% of the company, instead of 25%.)

It follows that each buying owner's tax basis in her ownership interest will increase by the amount of cash each owner paid to buy the departing owner's shares.

EXAMPLE: Let's fill in the details of the Short-cuts example above. Amanda, Beth and Chris each had a basis of $15,000 in their original shares—that is, each paid $15,000 to buy their original 150 shares. When their father decided to retire, Amanda, Beth and Chris each paid $5,000 for 50 of his shares. Amanda, Beth and Chris now own 200 shares each (33% of the company), and each has a basis of $20,000 in their increased ownership interests.

This type of direct purchase by the continuing owners may be just what the continuing owners want. It lets them increase their bases in their interest so that in the future, when one of them wants to sell the shares, there will be less of a taxable gain (less difference between tax basis and the sales price) and therefore less capital gains taxes to pay.

Continuing owners must come up with the funds for a buyout. Of course, unless life and disability insurance will fund a buyout, the continuing owners will have to use personal funds or borrow money to purchase a departing owner's interest. And, if a shareholder has to take dividends from his corporation, to fund the buyout, the funds will be subject to double taxation— once as income to the corporation, and again when received by the shareholder. Similarly, partners or LLC members will be taxed when taking draws from their businesses to fund buyouts (a draw is simply an advance distribution of profits by a

partnership or LLC to owners, and is taxed to owners at their individual income tax rates). In short, these considerations simply demonstrate that the decision as to who buys a departing owner-ship interest—the company or the continuing owners—is a complex one where input from a tax expert is necessary.

Watch out for tax terminations. If the con-tinuing owners of a partnership or LLC buy out a majority owner, the business may terminate for tax purposes. See Section A4, below, for further details.

b. When the Company Itself Buys an Owner's Interest

When the company itself buys a co-owner's inter-est, however, it's a slightly different story.

EXAMPLE: Amanda, Beth, Chris and their father each own 150 shares in Shortcuts, Inc., or 25% of the company. When their father decides to retire, the corporation buys back (redeems) his 150 shares and cancels them. Although Amanda, Beth and Chris still only own 150 shares apiece, they now each own 33% of the company.

Obviously, when a company buys back a departing owner's interest, whether it's a corpora-tion, LLC or partnership, each continuing owner ends up owning a larger fraction of the company, since there are fewer owners. And assuming the business stays on a steady course, each owner's larger share can be sold for more than would have been true before the company bought back an owner's interest. However, from a tax point of view, when the company itself buys a departing owner's interest, the continuing owners' tax basis does not go up (since they did not actually purchase any interest or invest more dollars). The result is that each owner may owe higher capital gains taxes when he eventually sell his interest than if each owner had personally bought a share of the departing owner's interest in the business.

For this reason, if a co-owner is selling his interest, you and your co-owners may want to buy it yourselves, rather than having the company pay for it. But this decision isn't usually this simple. Also key to the decision of whether the company or the continuing owners should purchase a departing or deceased owner's interest is whether the sale proceeds will be taxed as a capital gain or as ordinary income to the seller. We look at this issue in the next section.

3. Tax Treatment of a Sale of an Ownership Interest

First, the good news. Generally, when an owner sells an ownership interest, whether it be shares in a corporation or an ownership interest in a partnership or LLC, the sale is normally eligible for capital gains tax treatment (which saves tax dollars as discussed above). But, of course, there are technical tax requirements and exceptions that you will want to discuss with a tax advisor to make sure your sale or purchase of an interest under your buy-sell agreement actually qualifies for this treatment. Let's look at some of the general rules for corporations, partnerships and LLCs.

a. Buyouts of Partnerships and LLC Interests

When the continuing owners buy out a departing owner in a partnership or an LLC, any gain on the sale—more specifically—the excess of the sales price over the transferor's basis—is normally taxed to the transferring owner at capital gains tax rates. Also included in the sale and taxed to the selling owner is her share of any partnership or LLC liabilities. Also realize that the basis of a partner or LLC member is adjusted up or down at the time of sale for the amount of profit or loss allocable to the owner for the portion of the tax year prior to the sale.

> EXAMPLE: Mary sells her partnership interest to her partner for $25,000. Her basis in her interest is $15,000 and her share of partnership liabilities is $5,000. At the time of the sale, Mary's share of partnership profits for the current tax year is $1,000. Her adjusted basis is $16,000—her $15,000 basis adjusted up by $1,000 for her share of current-year profits. Her taxable gain is thus $14,000 ($25,000 selling price plus her $5,000 share of partnership liabilities, minus her $16,000 adjusted basis). Mary will owe capital gains taxes on $14,000.

⚠ **Exception.** If a portion of the purchase price is allocated to unrealized receivables (rights to payments by the business for past or future goods or services) or substantially appreciated inventory (their market value exceeds 120% of their basis) of the partnership or LLC, it is taxed at ordinary income rates to the selling owner, rather than given capital gains treatment.

When the business itself—the partnership or the LLC, not the continuing owners—purchases the interest of a departing owner (called a "liquidation" of the owner's interest), capital gains treatment for the seller's gain is not a sure thing. The selling owner *may* be eligible for capital gains tax treatment on her gain from the sale, *or* she may have to pay ordinary income taxes on the sale proceeds. Tax analysts see this as a tax flexibility afforded partnerships and LLCs—they can structure the liquidation of an owner's interest by the partnership or LLC any way they agree (but if you are the seller who must pay a 31% tax or higher on the sale proceeds, you may be less thrilled at that prospect).

Here's a quick summary of the three ways a partnership or LLC can handle buyouts for tax purposes:

1) If a buyout of the interest of a retiring or deceased owner qualifies under IRC Section 736(b) as an "exchange for an interest," the payment should receive capital gains treatment. Capital gains taxes are due on the amount by which the sales price exceeds the owner's basis in the interest (although technically, the payment of cash reduces the owner's basis in his interest, and if the basis is reduced to zero, the owner pays capital gains taxes on the excess).

Exceptions. If a portion of the payment is for unrealized receivables and the company is a service business, that portion will be taxed to the selling owner at ordinary income tax rates rather than be given capital gains treatment. Also, if any portion of the price is a payment to the selling owner for goodwill of the business, it will be taxed to that owner at ordinary income tax rates, unless the partnership or LLC operating agreement specifically provides for payment for goodwill.

2) If the payments for an ownership interest are determined with reference to the income of the business, they will be considered a payment to a partner of her distributive share —that is, her share of profits in the partnership or LLC. In this case, the selling owner (or his estate) will owe ordinary income taxes on the entire sales price. The distributive shares allocable to the remaining partners are reduced (this is similar to the partnership getting a deduction for the payment).

3) If the sale is considered by the IRS as a "guaranteed payment," the selling owner pays ordinary income taxes on all of the sale proceeds. The partnership is entitled to a deduction for the amount paid.

We won't cover the technical requirements and exceptions to the above rules. Just make sure to have your tax advisor analyze potential and future buyouts under your buy-sell provisions to make sure you will obtain the desired tax result when and if the time comes for the buyout of an owner's interest by your partnership or LLC.

Ask your tax advisor about goodwill payments. If you plan to include goodwill in your buyout price, you may wish to amend your partnership or LLC operating agreement to specifically provide for a reasonable payment to a selling owner for his share of goodwill in the business (so that a selling owner doesn't have to pay ordinary income tax rates on the portion of the buyout price allocated to goodwill). Your tax advisor can help you decide if you should do this and can add the necessary language to your agreement to meet the tax rules. (Even though courts have allowed retroactive amendments to partnership agreements to include this language after a buyout, we recommend you make any necessary changes prior to effecting a buyout under your buy-sell provisions.)

b. Buyouts of Corporate Shares

The good news is that most buyouts of a corporate shareholder's entire ownership interest should qualify for capital gains tax treatment by the owner or his estate. But, again, there are technical exceptions you should go over with a tax advisor if they appear problematic to you.

When the continuing shareholders buy out a departing owner, the transaction normally should qualify for capital gains tax treatment—the selling owner pays capital gains taxes on the excess of the sales price over the owner's basis in the interest. But there are more than a few tax wrinkles that arise if the corporation is the buyer (when the corporation itself buys a departing or deceased owner's shares, it is called a "redemption").

Here's the basic rule: If a redemption by the corporation of an owner's shares qualifies under IRC Section 302 as an "exchange," then capital gains tax rules apply: The selling owner (or his estate) pays capital gains taxes on the amount by which the sales proceeds exceed his basis in the transferred shares. But if the buyout does not qualify as an exchange, ordinary income taxes are due on the entire sales price (not just the amount of the sales price that exceeds the seller's basis)! Obviously, a seller or his estate will want the buyout to qualify as an exchange under the tax rules.

Fortunately, most buyout scenarios qualify as exchanges, and are therefore eligible for capital gains tax treatment. That's because the buyout of the *entire* interest of an owner qualifies as an exchange. But watch out for any of the following circumstances when your corporation redeems stock under your buy-sell agreement:

- The corporation buys less than all of an owner's interest. For example, your corporation may be exercising its Right of First Refusal under your agreement to purchase shares offered by a shareholder to an outsider, but the outsider is planning to buy less than all of the shareholder's stock. In this case, the corporation has a right to buy less than all the shares of the selling shareholder, and the purchase won't automatically qualify as an exchange.
- Both the corporation and the continuing shareholders are buying an owner's shares (our agreement allows both the company and the continuing owners to participate in buyouts). Again, if the continuing shareholders buy some of a departing owner's shares, the corporation is buying less than all the shares of an owner and the transaction won't automatically qualify as an exchange.

- The corporation is a family business. Even though the corporation purchases all the shares of a departing owner, it might not be purchasing her entire interest under the technical definition of an exchange. That's because the rules say that shares owned by an owner's relatives (spouse, children, grandchildren and parents) will be attributed to the owner. Unless the corporation buys out all of the owner's shares plus all shares owned by the owner's relatives, the redemption does not automatically qualify as an exchange.

If you are concerned about a corporate buyout of shares not automatically qualifying as an exchange eligible for capital gains tax treatment—because the corporation is buying less than all the owner's shares or because relatives of the owner will own shares in the corporation after the buyout—there are some special rules that still allow the purchase to qualify as an exchange (for example, a partial buyout of a deceased shareholder's shares to pay his estate taxes may qualify for capitals gains treatment—we discuss this exception further in Section B4e, below). We won't go into the details of these other special rules. Just be aware of the basic requirement for capital gains treatment stated above and, if you anticipate problems, ask your tax advisor for more information about these special tax rules.

4. Income Tax Termination of Partnerships and LLCs

Another tax trap related to buyouts is that they can trigger a "tax termination" of a partnership or LLC. (Corporations continue legally and for tax purposes despite changes in share ownership.)

First, let's distinguish a "legal termination" of a partnership or LLC from a "tax termination." Under state statutes—specifically, in states that have adopted the Uniform Partnership Act (UPA)—a partnership may legally terminate when a partner dies, leaves or otherwise transfers an ownership interest, or when a new partner is admitted into a partnership. A legal termination, if it does occur, is mostly just a nuisance, and means the remaining or newly constituted partners should adopt a new partnership agreement specifying capital, profits, loss and management rights and responsibilities—in other words, they need a new contract to continue doing business. Of course, this is something any partnership or LLC should consider doing whenever an ownership interest if transferred or additional owners are brought in. The main point, though, is that the business of the partnership, and its financial and tax operations, stay on a steady course even if the partnership is legally terminated.

You can prevent legal termination. Partnerships in states that have adopted the Revised Uniform Partnership Act, as well as LLCs in most states, can avoid the imposition of this legal termination rule by saying in their partnership or LLC operating agreement that the partnership or LLC legally continues despite changes in ownership. Our agreement says this in the introduction.

There are situations, however, where a buyout of an owner can trigger a tax termination, and this is a more serious problem. Specifically, Section 708 of the Internal Revenue Code says that a partnership or LLC is terminated for tax purposes if, within a 12-month period, there is a sale or exchange of 50% or more of the total interests in partnership or LLC capital and profits. Fortunately, large transfers of interests by gift, will, inheritance and buyouts by the partnership or LLC itself do not count, but large buyouts of a departing owner by the continuing partners or LLC members do.

Here's the problem: If, under the terms of your buy-sell agreement, the continuing owners buy out the interest of a majority owner, the partnership or LLC is terminated for tax purposes. This means the books of the company are closed and all assets are considered to have been distributed to the continuing partners or LLC members, who then are assumed to have put these distributed assets into a new partnership or LLC. Obviously,

the tax effect of this type of forced tax termination can be enormous and costly, so you will want to make sure you do not run afoul of this tax provision when you effect a buyout under your buy-sell agreement. Ask your accountant for additional information to avoid triggering this tax provision well in advance of any buyout.

Don't ignore state tax issues. Some states tax transfers of ownership interests in at least some contexts. In a few states, a sales tax may even apply to sales of business assets. And, of course, many states and localities impose transfer taxes on real estate or other assets. Be sure to ask your tax advisor about your state's taxes.

B. Buy-Sell Estate Tax Issues

You are, or will soon become, a small business owner. If your enterprise is even moderately profitable, your estate—all the real estate and personal property you own when you die, including your ownership interest—will most likely be subject to estate tax. This in turn makes you a candidate to engage in at least basic estate planning, which simply means planning how to pass along your property at death in the most efficient and cost-effective way.

Often, the primary estate planning concern for owners of a small business is planning to pass their ownership interest (or, more likely, the proceeds from selling it to the surviving owners) to the next generation with the least amount of red tape and taxes. In the first two subsections of this section we offer a thumbnail sketch of the primary estate planning devices used to accomplish this goal, and then we describe how it's possible to use your buy-sell agreement to lower your eventual estate tax liability. (Essentially, the key to using your buy-sell agreement to help lower estate taxes is to use the right valuation formula—the formula that sets the buy-sell Agreement Price for ownership interests. We show you how to do this in Section 3, below.)

Keep in mind that if you and your co-owners are young, you may buy and sell many businesses in your lifetime, so the business you own now may not affect your estate taxes at all. In addition, the tax laws may change many times in the next few decades. In short, younger readers will probably be wise not to sweat estate taxes *too* much, but, of course, it's always wise to look ahead. On the other hand, if you're in your 40s—and especially if you are older—you will want to pay close attention to this chapter.

Estate planning—and especially estate taxes—are complicated and often-changing areas. In this chapter we provide some basic information about general estate tax rules. Once you understand the basics, you will be better positioned to further discuss these issues with your tax advisor.

No Income or Capital Gains Taxes When Your Heirs Inherit Property

Some people worry that their heirs will have to pay income taxes on the money they receive after their death. This will not happen. Specifically, any property your inheritors receive from your estate at your death will not be considered income, so they will not owe income taxes. And because they inherit property at its current market value (remember, inherited property gets a stepped-up basis equal to fair market value at death), they probably will not have to pay capital gains taxes if they sell it promptly, since, technically, they will not have experienced a gain.

1. What Are Estate Taxes?

If you're very familiar with estate taxes (including the changes made by the Taxpayer's Relief Act of 1997), as well as all possible exclusions from the estate tax (the personal exemption, the family business deduction and the marital deduction) and the various ways of lowering your eventual taxes (gifts and minority discounts), you may want to skip ahead to Section 3 and read about structuring your buy-sell agreement for optimum savings on estate taxes. But if you are even a little hazy on this subject, we advise you to at least breeze through the first two sections so as not to miss any tax-saving hints.

First, a brief overview of estate taxes.

a. Federal Estate Tax

The federal estate tax is often called a "death tax" (although as we'll see, with the help of its partner the "gift tax," it also works to tax many valuable gifts made during life). In a nutshell, when you die, the federal government may attempt to take a large bite out of your property in the form of estate taxes. These taxes will technically be owed by your estate, but for all intents and purposes, your heirs will be the ones paying them, since all taxes paid out of your estate will reduce their inheritance.

Fortunately, as discussed in Section 2a, below, the government provides a "personal exemption," which allows every person to leave a certain amount of property free from estate taxes ($650,000 in 1999, increasing to $1 million in 2006). For the vast majority of Americans, this personal exemption is high enough so that they'll never have to worry about estate taxes. But you, as a successful small business owner, may not be able to rest as easily. If the value of your estate is higher than the personal exemption amount in the year you die, your estate will owe estate taxes unless you leave your property in one of the few ways that allow it to qualify for a deduction. For instance, any property, including a business interest, you leave to your spouse passes free of estate tax, using what's called the marital deduction.

Put bluntly, unless you take steps to adopt a sensible estate tax-saving plan, chances are the government, rather than your heirs, will receive a big slice of your estate! And if you leave your share of your business to your heirs with the expectation that they'll take over for you, you could even be saddling them with such a hefty federal estate tax bill that they may have to sell the business just to have the cash to pay the estate taxes. For example, assume that Mr. Gadfly owns a business worth $2 million, which he manages with his two children. His goal is to leave the business to the kids, who have expressed a desire to continue the business. But there is a major problem: Without planning to avoid estate taxes, Mr. Gadfly's estate will owe an estate tax of about $435,000 (assuming Mr. Gadfly dies in the year 2006 or later). In order to pay these estate taxes, the junior Gadflys may have no choice but to sell all or part of the business.

Federal Estate Tax Rates Effective in 1999

Estate Over	But Under	Effective Rate of Tax
$ 0	$ 650,000	0%
650,000	750,000	37
750,000	1,000,000	39
1,000,000	1,250,000	41
1,250,000	1,500,000	43
1,500,000	2,000,000	45
2,000,000	2,500,000	49
2,500,000	3,000,000	53
3,000,000	infinity	55

In addition, a 5% tax surcharge applies to estates from $10 million up to $21 million, and, to make things harder on the well-to-do, the personal exemption is phased out for estates in this bracket. What this means is that a straight 60% tax will be taken from estates over $21 million! For people facing these estate taxes, seeing an estate planning expert is a necessity.

b. State Death Taxes

In this chapter we concentrate on how to pass your business interest to your inheritors while paying the least amount of *federal* estate taxes. The majority of states either don't collect death taxes at all, or they dovetail them with federal taxes—through what's called a "pick-up tax" or a "sponge tax"—with the result that you pay no more than the federal government would take on its own. Either way, you don't have to worry about death taxes in any of those states.

A minority of states, however, impose their own death taxes—usually called "inheritance taxes." The following states still collect death taxes over and above federal taxes:

Connecticut	Maryland	New York
Delaware	Michigan	North Carolina
Indiana	Mississippi	Ohio
Iowa	Montana	Oklahoma
Kansas	Nebraska	Pennsylvania
Kentucky	New Hampshire	South Dakota
Louisiana	New Jersey	Tennessee

Fortunately, because state rates are so much lower, state inheritance taxes are a minor annoyance compared to federal estate taxes. (But in some states, property left to nonrelatives can face a fairly hefty tax.) You'll also be glad to know that, for the most part, what works to reduce federal estate taxes will also work to lower state death taxes, without your having to do any other special planning. But there is an exception to this rule. In states that do collect a separate death tax, most do not allow a deduction for family businesses as the feds do. So if your estate will be sizable (say, your business interest is worth more than a few hundred thousand dollars), you may want to look into your state's law while you're planning your estate.

 Death tax rules for all states are summarized in *Plan Your Estate*, by Denis Clifford and Cora Jordan (Nolo Press).

Death taxes on property outside the United States. If you own property or run a business in another country, your estate may owe estate taxes in that country. If this is your case, you should see an estate planning attorney. International estate tax planning is beyond the scope of this book.

2. Is Your Estate Likely to Owe Taxes?

Before you spend time learning how you can structure your buy-sell agreement to reduce or eliminate potential taxes, let's first see if your estate is likely to owe estate taxes. As mentioned above, there are exemptions and deductions a business owner can use to whittle down the part of his estate that will be subject to estate taxes.

a. Personal Exemption

As mentioned above, after an individual dies, the IRS will take estate taxes from her estate *only if it is over a certain amount*—called the personal exemption amount. The personal exemption amount is $650,000 in 1999 and will increase steadily until it tops out at $1 million in 2006. Because of the personal exemption, every individual can leave a sizable amount of property to his heirs without worrying that his estate will owe taxes on it. For example, if you were to die in 1999 and the net value of your business interest plus the rest of your property is $600,000, your estate wouldn't owe any estate taxes. But say you leave $1 million worth of property. Then your estate would owe taxes on $350,000 (the difference between $1 million and $650,000); your estate's tax bill would be approximately $136,500.

Increases to the Personal Exemption

The personal exemption is scheduled to rise steadily over the next decade:

Year	Personal Exemption	Exemption for a Couple
1999	$650,000	$1,250,000
2000	$675,000	$1,300,000
2001	$675,000	$1,350,000
2002, 2003	$700,000	$1,400,000
2004	$850,000	$1,700,000
2005	$950,000	$1,900,000
2006 and after	$1,000,000	$2,000,000

EXAMPLE: If you were to die in the year 2002, leaving $1 million worth of property to your children, your estate would owe estate taxes on $300,000 ($1 million minus the $700,000 exemption). The estate taxes would be approximately $117,000. If you could keep chugging until 2006, your estate wouldn't have to pay any taxes on your $1 million worth of property! (Of course, estate tax laws can change again, so these scheduled increases in the personal exemption amounts may not be current in 2006.)

If you are married, you and your spouse each have a personal exemption. For example, if both you and your wife were to die at the same time in 2002, leaving a shared-ownership business interest worth $2 million, your estate would owe estate taxes on only $600,000 ($2 million minus the two $700,000 exemptions); the tax would be about $234,000. In 2006, spouses who die at the same time will be able to leave their co-owned estate of $2 million without incurring any estate tax.

b. Marital Deduction

The marital deduction is a huge exception to the rule that all property you own when you die (over the personal exemption amount) is taxed before it passes to your inheritors. This deduction allows you to leave as much property to your spouse as you want without incurring federal estate taxes (as long as the spouse receiving the property is a U.S. citizen). As a result, many married couples start their estate planning by assuming that each spouse will leave all his property to the surviving spouse, who will then leave all the remaining property to the children upon her death. Unfortunately, this common way of thinking can lead to a substantial estate tax that could easily have been avoided.

Let's see why this is true. If you leave your entire estate directly to your spouse when you die, your estate won't owe any estate taxes because of the marital deduction. (Thus, when you leave everything to your spouse, it doesn't matter if your estate is over the personal exemption amount discussed just above.) But with the addition of your property, your spouse will have a much larger estate—maybe even double the size of her original estate. This spells trouble if the surviving spouse's estate will be over $1 million in 2006 or beyond. That's because, after your spouse dies, she'll have only one $1 million personal exemption—her own—to use against all that property. (She can't "save" your personal exemption to be used on her estate after she dies, even if your estate didn't use your personal exemption at your death.) So unless your spouse spends or gives away enough money, as might occur if she is likely to outlive you for many years or your family will have high expenses (educating several children, for example), with only one personal exemption, your spouse's estate is likely to owe a big pile of estate taxes. Put bluntly, in many situations (usually with elderly couples, roughly the same age), using the marital deduction to leave valuable business interests to a surviving spouse results in a higher overall estate tax burden when the second spouse dies.

> EXAMPLE: Walt and Helen are partners with another couple in a luxurious resort/spa in Utah. Each person's interest is worth about $1 million. Walt dies in 2006 and leaves his share of the business to his wife. Walt's estate does not owe any federal estate taxes on his owner-ship interest because of the marital deduction. With the addition of Walt's ownership interest, Helen's estate increases from $1 million to $2 million.
>
> Helen dies in 2007. Her $2 million estate exceeds the exemption amount for one person ($1 million in 2007). Stiff federal estate taxes are levied on the excess ($2 million – $1 million = $1 million); Helen's estate will owe about $450,000 in estate taxes.

One way around this tax is to have both spouses leave at least some property directly to their children, up to the personal exemption amount. That way, each spouse gets to use his entire personal exemption. But many couples are loathe to do this, worrying that, should the surviving spouse have high expenses or medical problems during her remaining years, she might burn through her one-half of the total estate and need at least a portion of the property the other spouse left directly to the kids.

Luckily, it's possible to devise a plan that will enable the couple to use their two personal exemptions while allowing the surviving spouse to use the property left by her deceased spouse. Using an "AB trust" (sometimes called an exemption trust, marital bypass trust, credit shelter trust or marital life-estate trust), each spouse puts her one-half of the property in trust. The surviving spouse can receive all the income from the trust holding the deceased spouse's property (and even spend the principal for her "health, education, maintenance or support") during her lifetime. At her death, whatever remains of the principal in the trust passes to the ultimate beneficiary (often children or grandchildren) free of estate tax.

 Make Your Own Living Trust, by Denis Clifford (Nolo Press), enables you to create an AB trust, and the forthcoming 3rd edition of Living Trust Maker software (Nolo Press) can create an AB trust for you.

c. Special Family Business Estate Tax Deduction

Obviously, the marital deduction won't help single people (and even many married folks need to create an AB trust to avoid the tax trap it can create). Luckily, another deduction is available— the family business deduction. While family business interests still have to pass under the estate tax guillotine on their way to the owners' heirs, this deduction can help dull the blade. Let's see if your business might be eligible.

➡️ If you aren't planning on leaving your business to your family after you die—for instance, your business partners will buy out your share upon your death—this deduction won't

apply to you, and you can skip ahead to Section 3. Same goes if you leave the business to your family members, but they don't want to continue the business—your estate won't be eligible for this special tax break.

Here's how the family business deduction works: It excludes from estate taxes a maximum of $675,000 from a qualifying business owner's estate. Plus, you can combine this deduction with the personal exemption (which is always available to every taxpayer). For example, a business owner who dies in 1999 and qualifies for the family business deduction will be able to leave a business interest worth $1.3 million free of estate tax ($675,000 for the family business deduction, and $625,000 for the personal exemption).

⚠️ **Use of the family business deduction will become less valuable in a few years.** Presently the family business deduction is worth an extra $675,000. Unfortunately, Congress has put a cap of $1.3 million on the combined business and personal exemptions. By 2006, when the personal exemption is slated to increase to $1 million, the small business exemption will do you far less good—it will only give you an extra deduction of $300,000, unless Congress raises this $1.3 million ceiling.

Unfortunately, no matter what the year, there's a big chance your business won't be eligible for this deduction at all. Why? Because Congress created this special estate tax break to help family businesses to survive only when they're passed from generation to generation, to protect the inheritors of a family business from having to sell it to pay high estate taxes. In short, if yours isn't a family business that will be passed along to the next generation, who will continue to operate it for the long-term, this deduction will do you no good. And to ensure that only true family businesses receive the benefits of this deduction, the IRS has created a long list of conditions. Try not to get dizzy when you read them:

- At least 50% of the business must have been owned by one family, 70% of the business by two or 90% by three families. If more than one family owns the business, the family seeking the business deduction must own 30% of the business. (Members of "one family" include your spouse, your parents or grandparents and your children or grand-children, and their spouses.)

- The value of the deceased owner's share of the business must be more than 50% of the value of her entire gross estate.

- The deceased owner (or members of her family) must have worked for or actively managed the business for at least five of the eight years preceding her death.

- The inheritors of the business interest must be family members or long-time employees who have been involved in the business for at least 10 years.

- The inheritors must work in the business for 10 years following the death of the owner. (If the inheritors stop working in the business or sell their interest within 10 years, part or all of the estate tax savings must be paid back to the government.)

- The interests in the business must not have been publicly traded in the last three years.

- The deceased owner must have been a citizen or resident of the United States, and the company must be located in the United States.

 If you are interested in using this deduction, talk to a small business or tax expert. Chances are you'll have to structure your business differently than would otherwise be the case.

Because of these strict requirements, many businesses won't be eligible for the family business deduction. If yours is one of them, and it is likely to be worth more than $1 million in 2006, you'll want to read on. And the same is true even if your business interest will be eligible for this deduction, but it's worth over $1.3 million.

d. Gifts of Ownership Interests

Assuming your estate will still owe estate taxes after consideration of the personal exemption, the family business deduction and, for married couples, the marital deduction (including the possibility of creating an AB trust), all is not lost. One obvious solution is to simply give away some of your property before death. If you're thinking, "I don't need a book to tell me how to do that," you're likely wrong. Because the federal government imposes a "gift tax" (as part of its unified estate and gift tax scheme), giving away property free of tax can be a complicated business.

How can giving away your money help you avoid estate taxes? Let's first briefly explain how the federal gift tax works. All gifts, unless they are tax-exempt (discussed immediately below), will be added up and taxed at your death, just like the property that remains in your estate at death. Fortunately, the personal estate tax exemption that we discussed above ($650,000 in 1999, up to $1 million in 2006) may be applied to lifetime gifts. But if a person were to give away more than the exempt amount, the excess property left at death would be subject to estate tax.

Luckily, some gifts are exempt from the estate and gift tax altogether (in other words, are completely nontaxable). Nontaxable gifts will not use up any of the personal exemption available to your estate when you die. Here is the short list:

- gifts to your spouse (because of the marital deduction discussed above)
- gifts to a qualified tax-exempt nonprofit organization (for example, a charity)
- direct payments for school tuition and medical expenses of family members
- gifts of under $10,000 per year per person to anyone.

EXAMPLE: Each year for the rest of your life you can give your son and your daughter $10,000 each, without incurring estate or gift taxes or eating into your personal exemption. Your spouse can also give $10,000 per year to each child tax-free. And both of you can also make tax-exempt gifts to your children's spouses and kids.

The $10,000 annual gift tax exemption is the basis for many long-term estate tax-saving strategies. This makes sense when you realize you and your spouse could give a total of $100,000 to five people each year without being taxed, and you can repeat this act of generosity every year. Following are some of the ways you can use $10,000 taxable gifts to pass on your ownership interest to exactly the same people who would receive it at your death while avoiding estate taxes.

A common method used by many business owners is to give their children small interests (valued at $10,000 or less) in the business each year over many years. Typically, to keep control of the business, an owner gives away less than a majority of her interest (or if the business is incorporated, creates a second class of nonvoting stock and gives these away).

The slow gifting approach is not always best! If the worth of your business is likely to increase very rapidly, you might be better off not giving away your interest to your children in $10,000 increments over the years. Instead, you could come out ahead by giving them a large chunk now. Here's why. If the value of your company skyrockets, your ownership interest will be worth much more in years to come than it is now, making it harder to give away a significant portion of your ownership interest in $10,000 increments. True, if you make a gift now, you may have to pay a gift tax, but you'll do so based on your business's current, comparatively low, value. The big savings result because, by the time the business goes way up in value, it will already be owned by your kids—meaning, of course, that at your death no estate tax will be due on the increase.

Unless your business is quite small, you may wonder if giving away small portions of your

share will work to save a significant amount of estate tax. Because of a tax concept that allows you to discount the value of a minority business interest, the answer is often yes. "Valuation discounts" allow a business owner to give away more of the business in one year while staying under the $10,000 gift tax exemption threshold. Essentially, owners can lower the value of certain types of ownership interests for tax purposes, in order to be able to give more ownership interest away every year.

The value of an ownership interest can be discounted for tax purposes based on certain characteristics that seem to make it less valuable in the marketplace generally. One of these is whether a business interest is big enough to have a controlling vote (51% or more of the voting interests of a company) or is a minority interest (49% or less of a company's voting interests). Based on the fact that minority interests are often worth much less when a business is sold, they are valued by the IRS at a discount.

Buy-sell agreement provisions restricting the transfer of ownership interests can also make an ownership interest less valuable (called a valuation discount for "lack of marketability"). The rationale for this discount is that outside buyers might not want to pay as much for an ownership interest with restrictions on transfers as they would for a freely marketable interest.

What this all adds up to is that when either a restricted or noncontrolling interest in a business is given away, it's valued at about 20%–40% less than if it were a controlling or nonrestricted interest. And when a minority interest can't be freely marketed (when the discounts are combined), it may be worth 30%–60% less.

Why is this important when it comes to gifting a portion of your ownership interest? Simple. The lower the value of one percentage point of a company (or share, in the case of a corporation), the more percentage points (or shares) of the company that will fit under the $10,000 annual gift tax exclusion. For example, if one percentage point of a company is worth $10,000 without discounts, an owner could obviously transfer only one percentage point (1%) of the company per year to a child before exceeding the annual $10,000 gift tax exemption. But if the ownership interest is eligible for a combined valuation discount of, say, 50%, each percentage point of the company can be valued at $5,000 for IRS purposes, meaning that the owner could transfer two percentage points of the company ($20,000 in actual value) per year to his child before exceeding the annual $10,000 gift tax exemption. For example, if a husband and wife each transfer 2% of their company to each of their children for six years, they can transfer $480,000 (or 48% of the company) to their kids, and still remain in control of the business. (Without using discounts, the parents would only be able to transfer $240,000, or 24% of the company, in six years.)

Giving away your interests early avoids appreciation. As an added bonus, the portion of the company that is given away during life will appreciate in the kids' hands, not the parents", meaning the kids won't have to pay taxes on its increase in value, as would be the case if the parents waited to give their interest to their kids until after their death.

Since the IRS tends to examine valuation discounts very closely—due to the opportunity for abuse—we strongly suggest that you seek the advice of a tax expert before using a valuation discount on your gift tax return. When you do, be prepared to provide the IRS with an explanation of the basis for the discounts and the amount of discounts taken.

Family Limited Partnerships and LLCs

A "family limited partnership" (or a "family limited liability company") can be a good estate tax-savings vehicle, although it has come under recent fire from the IRS. These business structures are really no different from regular limited partnerships and LLCs, except that the partners and members are all family members.

Here is how these devices work. The owners of closely held businesses create family limited partnerships and LLCs, keeping the controlling interest (the interest of a general partner or a management interest in an LLC) to themselves and giving the nonvoting ownership interests (limited partner interests in limited partnerships or nonmanaging membership interests in LLCs) to family members. Because these noncontrolling business interests can be subject to valuation discounts, a larger share of the business can be transferred to family members, under the $10,000 annual gift tax exemption. By combining discounts for lack of marketability, minority ownership and lack of control over management and income, the value of a limited partnership or LLC interest can be valued at a much lower amount than would be the case for the same interest in a publicly traded corporation.

The IRS attempts to disallow any family limited partnership whose sole purpose appears to be to reduce taxes. In short, any downward adjustments made to the value of a limited partnership interest must have valid business reasons.

Generation-Skipping Transfer Tax

Years ago, the federal government caught on to the fact that the affluent would sometimes try to escape estate taxes by giving lots of property directly to grandkids or even great-grandkids. The idea was to pay just one gift tax, instead of two or three rounds of estate taxes when each generation died. To clamp down, Congress enacted what's called the "generation-skipping transfer tax." Now the government places an extra tax on nonexempt property left or given to a grandchild—at a gouging flat rate of 55%. You can, however, give up to $1million directly to your grandchildren (in total, not $1 million to each) without triggering the extra tax. Of course, this property is still subject to regular estate taxes when you die (just not when the middle generation dies).

Further reading on estate planning. In this book we focus primarily on how owners of a small business can limit, or at least establish controls on, the transfer of ownership interests to outsiders, including spouses, family members, inheritors and outside purchasers. Please realize that this is a different goal from how a business owner can best plan her estate to minimize probate costs and estate taxes and to assure the orderly and efficient passing of property to heirs upon the owner's death. Fortunately, another Nolo Press book directly addresses estate taxes: *9 Ways to Save on Estate Taxes*, by Denis Clifford (Nolo Press). And if you are interested in developing a comprehensive estate plan, including writing a will, making a trust, getting insurance and avoiding probate, check out *Plan Your Estate*, by Denis Clifford and Cora Jordan (Nolo Press). It presents a good survey of the specialized estate planning devices used by families to pass ownership interests to the next generation with minimum financial pain.

3. How Your Buy-Sell Agreement Can Affect Estate Taxes

If you or one of your co-owners does not plan on being succeeded by a family member when you die or retire (probably the majority of the readers of this book), this section will probably not be helpful to you. Why? While never fun, paying estate taxes is less of a burden for heirs who do not plan on taking over the family business—that is, for those heirs who receive cash, or property that can easily be sold for cash. After all, an heir who receives $1 million in cash and gives the government one-third of it is still getting a good sum of money. If this describes you and your business partners, you may wish to skip ahead to Chapter 10.

We include this section for family business owners who want to pass their interests on to their children or other relatives who want to continue the business without being overburdened by estate taxes. If, after investigating the personal exemption, the marital deduction, the family business deduction and gift tax exemption rules, you've found that your ownership interest may still be subject to the federal estate tax, and you are an owner of an intergenerational family business, you may be able to craft your buy-sell agreement to lower your eventual estate tax liability. By "intergenerational family business" we mean a business where at least one co-owner will leave his interest to heirs who will keep ownership of the business interests they inherit and work in or help manage the business for more than a few years (assuming the buy-sell agreement and your co-owners allow this).

If your business qualifies for the family business deduction, you can leave up to $1.3 million tax-free. If you can use the family business deduction successfully to avoid all estate taxes, it obviously doesn't make sense to gear your buy-sell agreement toward manipulating estate taxes.

➡ **If estate taxes aren't on your horizon.** People who are in their 20s, 30s or even 40s and in good health probably won't need to worry about estate taxes for decades—during which time estate tax rules will likely change many times. If this describes you and your business partners, you may want to just draft a sensible buy-sell agreement and forget about estate taxes for the next 20 years.

For small business owners whose heirs will succeed them, drafting a buy-sell agreement with an eye toward estate tax concerns can be important. Here's why: If the bulk of the property you leave to your heirs consists of a largely nonliquid (not readily changeable into cash) interest in a small business (for example, one-third of a large furniture rental company), your heirs may not have any available resources to pay a hefty estate tax bill. If your estate tax debt is large enough, your heirs might even have to sell the ownership interest and pay the taxes out of the receipts. Or, if they try to hold on to the business and pay estate taxes at the same time, they might have trouble keeping the company afloat.

EXAMPLE: Dick, with the help of his three sons, Dan, Bob and Jonathan, had built up a successful custom glass-manufacturing business by the time he died in 2000. His sons inherit the business, but little other property. Before filing an estate tax return, they hire a CPA to do an appraisal of the business, which comes out to $5 million. As a result, Dick's estate owes $2,198,000 in taxes.

The glass company has few liquid assets— its capital is tied up in equipment and inventory, its profits routinely paid out as salaries and bonuses. And Dick's sons, who are in the process of educating their children, certainly don't have an extra $2,198,000 lying around. Rather than trying to make hefty payments to the IRS for years in an amount that might hobble the company, the sons sell the glass outfit for $4 million to pay off the taxes. After

all was said and done, they took home a measly $900,000 apiece. Because of their Dad's poor planning, they paid more estate taxes than necessary and had to sell the family business and find other work.

This is where buy-sell agreements can help. To avoid an estate tax squeeze, in some circumstances you can structure your agreement to legally minimize taxes. As we discussed in Chapter 6, your buy-sell agreement will normally specify a price, or a formula for setting the price, for your ownership interest. The key for estate planning is choosing a conservative price or valuation formula in your agreement, to set the value of your ownership interest at an amount considerably lower than its market value at the time of your death. The lower your agreement price, the lower your estate taxes. Keep in mind that the same valuation clause will set the price not only for estate tax purposes, but also the Agreement Price for any transaction arising under the buy-sell agreement.

💼 Please realize that using your buy-sell agreement to avoid estate taxes is a relatively sophisticated form of tax planning, and can be a tricky business. If you (possibly with your family members) own 50% or more of your business, the IRS may think that your only reason for adopting a buy-sell agreement is to lower estate taxes, not to set up transfer restrictions and fair buyback procedures for the co-owners to rely on prior to their deaths. And the IRS audits almost all family business transfers from one generation to the next that occur through buy-sell agreements, so it's doubly important to see a tax expert in this case.

The IRS will accept the value your buy-sell agreement places on ownership interests in your business at the time of your death—even if this value is below fair market value when you die— as long as the price or formula you use in your buy-sell agreement represented the fair market value of interests in the business *at the time you created your agreement*. Assuming the valuation provision in your buy-sell agreement comes up with a lowish price—that is, a price that's lower than the fair market value of the business at your death—your estate taxes will be lower.

⚠ Setting a low price can be detrimental.
There's a hidden danger to establishing a low valuation of your business in an effort to save on estate taxes. It could in fact be counterproductive for at least one, and often several, reasons. If you have to retire early, perhaps because you or a family member has health problems, you'll want to be able to sell your interest back to the company for a price that represents its current fair value (not a price tied to the value of the interest at the time of your agreement to save on estate taxes).

The IRS will do what it can to prevent you from unfairly using an artificially low Agreement Price to reduce estate taxes. The IRS will only accept your Agreement Price if your agreement satisfies six rules:

Rule 1: Your buy-sell agreement must give the company or the continuing owners an option to purchase a deceased owner's interest from his estate.
This is a very common buy-sell provision—called an Option to Purchase a Deceased Owner's Interest in our agreement (discussed in Chapter 3)—that many business owners wish to include in their buy-sell agreements for nontax reasons. Even if the company never exercises its right to purchase the interest back from the estate, having an Option to Purchase a Deceased Owner's Interest in the agreement fulfills this requirement.

⚠ A low Agreement Price could be to your heirs' disadvantage. If your heirs decide they do not want to take over the business after all, but want to sell the interest they inherit—most likely back to the company or continuing owners

pursuant to the buy-sell agreement—a low Agreement Price may hurt them. In this case, they would be better off receiving a higher price for the interest and paying proportionately higher estate taxes.

Rule 2: The Agreement Price must be "determinable and reasonable."
Your Agreement Price must be able to be calculated easily and objectively from your agreement. In practice, this means you must use a fixed price or an objective formula (like book value or capitalization of earnings) as a way to determine the price of the ownership interests. (We discuss how to choose a valuation method in Chapter 6.)

Rule 3: Under the agreement, an owner cannot sell her ownership interest at a price higher than the general Agreement Price.
Your buy-sell agreement may not allow an owner to sell her ownership interest at a higher price during her lifetime, at least without offering it to the company or the other owners first at the Agreement Price. This means that the price that is applicable after an owner's death must be used in all ownership transfer situations, such as when an owner wants to be bought out of the business. A right of first refusal will pass this test only if it gives the company or the continuing owners the option to buy a selling owner's interest *at the Agreement Price*, not at the price an outsider has offered (discussed in Chapter 2).

Of course, just because your buy-sell agreement does not specifically say that a sale of ownership interests at a higher price is okay doesn't mean that it can't be done—when all owners agree, any provision in the buy-sell agreement can be rewritten or ignored. But if the buy-sell agreement is ignored and the IRS finds out, you can say goodbye to being able to use the Agreement Price for estate tax purposes. Likewise, if one owner (a majority owner, for instance) has the sole authority to change the agreement at any time, the IRS may decide that the owner wasn't really bound by the agreement during her lifetime.

Rule 4: Your buy-sell agreement must not merely be a "device" to transfer your business interest to your heirs without paying estate taxes.

If the IRS finds that your intent in creating your buy-sell agreement was to lower estate taxes, it will ignore your Agreement Price and appraise the property itself. However, if the buy-sell provisions accomplish a valid nontax purpose—namely, keeping ownership interests within the control of the founders of a small, closely held company—then it's okay if they have the collateral tax result of fixing the value of shares at a price lower than their future market value.

⚠ **Agreements made late in life are risky.** If you or a co-owner is in poor health or advancing years when you make your buy-sell agreement, your estate is likely to be subject to more intense scrutiny than otherwise. The IRS is more likely to think that your agreement is acting like a will or trust, rather than a legitimate business agreement to restrict ownership, and that you created it only for the purpose of passing on your ownership interest free of as much tax as possible.

Rule 5: Your buy-sell agreement must be a "bona fide business arrangement."

This requirement—which is very similar to the last one—says that your buy-sell agreement must have been adopted for a valid business purpose, such as to limit ownership and control of the company to the original group, or to ensure continuity of management. In other words, a clearly nominal value or a set of buy-sell provisions that have no "teeth" (that are discretionary in effect) will not look like the real thing to the IRS. Also, your buy-sell agreement must be enforceable against *all* of the co-owners. For example, a buy-sell agreement that requires the estate of a deceased minority owner to sell her interest back to the company while allowing the heirs of a majority owner to hold onto their interest would be risky.

Rule 6: Your buy-sell agreement must be similar to fair business arrangements entered into by unrelated persons in the same industry.

If you use a standard measure of value—such as book value or a multiple of earnings—that's commonly used in your type of business, you should be okay, even if your interest could fetch more in the open market. But if your buy-sell provisions contain an incredibly low fixed price that bears no relationship to reality, you may have problems with the IRS if it would be hard to prove that the fixed Agreement Price is fair and might be used in an arms-length transaction.

⚠ **Don't completely ignore the value of goodwill.** If your company has been around long enough for it to develop a good reputation and a reliable customer base, and possibly even recognizable brand names and trademarks, it's a poor idea to use a formula that completely ignores these factors. For instance, the book value method, which will undoubtedly give you a low agreement price, is likely to be questioned by the IRS if other successful businesses like yours are typically valued and bought and sold at market values in excess of book value.

⚠ **Penalties for undervaluing your business interest.** The IRS can slap your estate with a sharp penalty if it discovers that your buy-sell agreement grossly undervalued your business interest. If the IRS concludes your business interest was undervalued by 50% or more, the IRS will penalize your estate 20% of the unpaid tax. And the IRS can penalize your estate as high as 40% of

the unpaid tax if your business interest was undervalued by at least 75%. This is in addition to having to pay the readjusted tax itself, not to mention possible interest owed, court costs and lawyers' fees.

4. Lessening the Pain of Paying Estate Taxes

When a deceased owner's heirs hang onto their share of the business, they may not have the cash to pay the estate tax bill if it's a large one. If you or a business owner dies and the estate owes estate taxes, there are some creative ways to pay them.

a. Alternate Valuation Date

The IRS provides that the executor of your estate can elect to value your estate six months after the date of your death (called the alternate valuation date). Thus, if a catastrophe hits your business, or it simply misses a step or two without you, and it's worth less six months after your death than it was on the date of death, your executor can choose to use the alternate valuation date.

b. Life Insurance

One way to protect your heirs from an estate tax squeeze is by purchasing life insurance, which will be paid to your inheritors upon your death and used to pay any debts, taxes and bills your estate may owe. Assuming that you or your future inheritors have adequate cash to buy life insurance for this purpose, you shouldn't be the owner of the policy—if you are, the policy payout will be included in your estate at death, needlessly raising your estate taxes. One obvious solution is for your children to buy the insurance on your life. But you must be extremely careful to avoid having any "incidents of ownership" in the policy, mean-

ing that there can be no record of your making the premium payments for the life insurance.

c. Deferral and Installment Payments for Family Businesses

For family businesses only. This deferral is only available for heirs who are going to hold on to the business interests they inherit. If you aren't planning on leaving your business to your family after you die—for instance, your business partners will buy out your share upon your death—your estate won't be allowed to defer its tax bill.

The inheritors of qualifying small business interests can delay the payment of estate taxes for five years so that they can prudently plan for such a big expense. During those five years, interest accrues on the estate tax bill. (But the tax on the first $1 million of the business's value is eligible for a 4% interest rate.) Once the five years are up, the estate taxes may be paid off in up to ten equal annual installments. If your heirs wish to use this option, they can't sell 50% or more of their interest before the tax is paid off. If they do, the entire amount of estate tax becomes due immediately.

To qualify for deferral and installment payments, the following requirements must be met:

1. the value of the business interest must exceed 35% of the deceased owner's total estate, AND

2. either:
   - the business must have had 15 owners or fewer (when the deceased owner was alive), or
   - the deceased owner must have owned at least 20% of the company.

Watch out for installment plans and estate taxes. The IRS will not allow an estate to use the estate tax installment plan if the business interest has been sold to the company for a 15-

year promissory note whose payments are set to coincide with estate tax payments. The IRS treats this as a sale of 50% or more of the interest. Your estate could be obligated to pay the estate taxes in full immediately, even though you are receiving payments for the sale of your ownership interest over 15 years. You may instead want to schedule a series of smaller buybacks over a period of years.

d. Special Rules for Valuing Business Real Estate

For family businesses only. These special rules are only available for heirs who are going to hold onto the business interests they inherit. If you aren't planning on leaving your business to your family after you die—for instance, your business partners will buy out your share upon your death—your estate won't be allowed to value their property using these rules.

Real estate used in a family business can be valued for estate tax purposes at its value for its present use, rather than at its "highest and best" use. For example, an old warehouse on the edge of town used by your business doesn't have to be valued for its worth as a location for a strip mall or a housing tract development, but can be valued on the basis of its worth as a storage facility. The reduction is limited to $750,000, indexed for inflation, beginning in 1999.

Several requirements must be met for the rule to apply:

- The value of the family business must be at least 50% of the owner's overall estate.
- The value of the real estate of that business must be at least 25% of the owner's overall estate.
- The owner must leave the family business to a family member.
- The deceased owner (or members of her family) must have used the real estate for

the business for at least five of the eight years preceding her death.

- There are restrictions on the sale and use of the real estate for 10 years (and, in some cases, 15 years) after the estate tax break. During this time, the family must agree to notify the IRS if the property is sold or no longer used for the business, and may be required to repay some or all of the estate taxes if the ownership or use of the real estate changes.

e. Partial Buybacks to Pay Estate Taxes

This method is only available for corporations. If your business is not a corporation, skip ahead to Chapter 10.

We touched upon an exception to the requirement that a buyout by a corporation of an owner's interest must be of the entire interest to qualify as a capital gains exchange in Section 3B, above. This exception has to do with the partial purchase by a corporation of a deceased owner's shares to pay for estate taxes. Let's look at this exception a little more closely here from the estate tax side.

The IRS allows the estate of a shareholder to sell back just enough of the deceased shareholder's ownership interest to the corporation to meet estate taxes, funeral expenses, final bills and probate and other fees—using what is called a "Section 303 redemption" under the Internal Revenue Code.

There are two requirements here:

- the value of the ownership interest must make up at least 35% of the estate of the deceased owner (after expenses and deductions), and
- the estate or the heirs (whoever is selling off part of the ownership interest) must be responsible for paying the estate taxes and other final costs, though they don't actually have to use the money for this purpose.

For a deceased owner's estate or inheritors to be able to force a sale of only part of the deceased owner's interest, your buy-sell agreement must specifically state that an owner's estate or inheritors can force a *partial* buyback of a deceased owner's interest. The key here is "partial"—often buy-sell agreements (ours included) are written to only allow the estate or inheritors to be able to force the company or the continuing owners to buy all of the deceased owner's interest.

If you think your inheritors will want to hold on to their interest, and the company and your buy-sell agreement will allow this, you can provide for a partial redemption to pay estate taxes by changing (slightly) our provision called Right of Estate, Trust or Inheritors to Force a Sale. Go to Section III, Scenario 3, Option 2 of the contract. The first sentence in subsection (a) is shown in Excerpt 1. Simply cross out "all, but not less than all," and add "any."

If you are interested in providing for partial redemptions, on your worksheet, make a note to change the above language in Section III, Scenario 3, Option 2.

☐ **Option 2: Right of Estate, Trust or Inheritors to Force a Sale**

   (a) When an owner dies, the executor or administrator of the deceased owner's estate, or the trustee of a trust holding the deceased owner's ownership interest, or the deceased owner's inheritors can require the company and the continuing owners to buy ~~all, but not less than all~~ **any**, of the deceased owner's ownership interest by delivering to the company within 60 days a notice of intention to force a sale ("Notice of Intent to Force a Sale") in writing.

Excerpt 1

Lawyers, Tax Specialists and Resources

Much of the work involved in forming a buy-sell agreement involves considering and discussing your options with your co-owners and then filling in the blanks. Most knowledgeable and motivated business owners can competently do the work themselves. But there are some issues that we've flagged throughout the book, and especially in Chapter 9, *Income and Estate Tax Issues*, that may need the expertise of a tax planner. Other decisions involve a mix of financial and legal savvy and are likely to be best made with the input of an experienced small business lawyer or a tax attorney. In the sections below, we provide a few tips to help you in your search for competent expert information, assistance and advice.

A. How to Find the Right Lawyer

Many small businesses can't afford to hire a lawyer to create a buy-sell agreement from scratch. Often a knowledgeable self-helper can sensibly accomplish the whole task. Other times, it makes sense to briefly consult with a lawyer about your buy-sell agreement at an interim stage, or have the paperwork reviewed upon completion.

You already have taken one positive step in the direction of making your legal life affordable by deciding to use this book to prepare your buy-sell agreement. Depending on the size of your business and the complexity of your agreement, your next step is likely to be to find a cooperative lawyer who will answer whatever questions you may have and perhaps draft a customized clause here or there for your agreement.

You obviously don't want a lawyer who wants to draw up an overly legalistic agreement from scratch, while running up billable hours as fast as possible. Instead, you need what we call a legal coach—someone who is willing to work with you, not just for you. Under this model, the lawyer works to help draft your own agreement.

You don't need a big-time corporate lawyer. There is a big lawyer surplus these days, and many newer lawyers, especially, are open to nontraditional business arrangements. Look for a lawyer with some small business experience, though preferably in your field or area of operations, and some buy-sell agreement experience. For the most part, you don't want a lawyer who works with big corporations. Not only will this person deal with issues that are far from your concerns, but he or she is almost sure to charge too much.

Don't Ask a Lawyer for Tax Advice

When it comes to the tax implications of buy-sell agreements, accountants often have a better grasp of the issues than lawyers (except for tax attorneys, who may have a special tax law degree). And an added bonus is that although tax advice doesn't come cheap, accountants often charge less than lawyers.

1. Look and Ask Around

When you go looking for a lawyer, don't start with phone books, legal directories or advertisements. Lawyer referral services operated by bar associations are equally unhelpful. These services simply supply the names of lawyers who have signed on to the service, often accepting the lawyer's own word for what types of skills he or she has. A better approach is to talk to people in your community who own or operate businesses you respect. Ask them about their lawyer and what they think of that person's work. If you talk to half a dozen business people, chances are you'll come away with several good leads. Other people, such as your banker, accountant, insurance agent or real estate broker, may be able to provide the names of lawyers they trust to help them with business matters. Friends, relatives and business associates within your own company may also have names of possible lawyers.

2. Talk to the Lawyer Ahead of Time

When you call a lawyer, announce your intentions in advance—that you are looking for someone who is willing to answer a few questions or review your buy-sell agreement, whichever your case may be. Ask the lawyer if she has experience in drafting buy-sell agreements—most lawyers (including small business lawyers) are not very familiar with this area of the law. The ideal lawyer should have experience with small businesses, taxes and estate planning.

If the lawyer seems agreeable to this arrangement, ask if you can come in to meet with her for a half-hour or so. Although many lawyers will not charge you for this introductory appointment, it's often a good idea to offer to pay for it. You want to establish that you are looking for someone to help you help yourself, not for a free ride.

At the interview, re-emphasize that you are looking for a nontraditional "legal coach" relationship. Many lawyers will find this unappealing—for example, saying they don't feel comfortable reviewing documents you have drafted using self-help materials. If so, thank the person for being

frank and keep interviewing other lawyers. You'll also want to discuss other important issues in this initial interview, such as the lawyer's customary charges for services, as explained further below.

Pay particular attention to the rapport between you and your lawyer. Remember—you are looking for a legal coach who will work with you. Trust your instincts and seek a lawyer whose personality and business sense are compatible with your own.

3. Set the Extent and Cost of Services in Advance

When you hire a lawyer, get a clear understanding about how fees will be computed. Some lawyers bill a flat amount for document review; others bill to the nearest six-, ten- or twenty-minute interval. Whatever the lawyer's system, you need to understand it.

Especially at the beginning of your relationship, when you bring a big job to a lawyer, ask specifically about what it will cost. If you feel it's too much, don't hesitate to negotiate.

It's a good idea to get all fee arrangements—especially those for good-sized jobs—in writing.

SO MUCH FOR THE SMALL TALK! HOW MUCH DO YOU CHARGE?

In several states, fee agreements between lawyers and clients must be in writing if the expected fee is $1,000 or more. But whether required or not, it's a good idea to get it in writing.

How Lawyers Charge for Legal Services

There are no across-the-board rules on how lawyers' fees are to be charged. Expect to be charged by one of the following methods:

- **By the hour.** In most parts of the United States, you can get competent services for your small business for $150 to $250 an hour. Newer attorneys still in the process of building a practice may be available for paperwork review, legal research and other types of legal work at lower rates.
- **Flat fee for a specific job.** Under this arrangement, you pay the agreed-upon amount for a given project, regardless of how much or how little time the lawyer spends. Particularly when you first begin working with a lawyer and are worried about hourly costs getting out of control, negotiating a flat fee for a specific job can make sense. For example, the lawyer may draw up a real estate purchase agreement for $300, or review and finalize your buy-sell provisions for $500.
- **Retainer.** Some corporations can afford to pay relatively modest amounts, perhaps $1,000 to $2,000 a year, to keep a business lawyer on retainer for ongoing phone or in-person consultations, routine pre-meeting minutes review or resolution preparation and other business matters during the year. Of course, your retainer won't cover a full-blown legal crisis, but it can help you take care of ongoing minutes and other legal paperwork (for example, contract or special real estate paperwork) when you need a hand.

---

4. Confront Any Problems Head-On

If you have any questions about a lawyer's bill or the quality of his or her services, speak up. Buying legal help should be just like purchasing any other consumer service—if you are dissatisfied, seek a reduction in your bill or make it clear that the work needs to be redone properly (a better buy-sell agreement, a more comprehensive lease, etc.). If the lawyer runs a decent business, he or she will promptly and positively deal with your concerns. If you don't get an acceptable response, find another lawyer pronto. If you switch lawyers, you are entitled to get your documents back from the first lawyer.

Even if you fire your lawyer, you may still feel unjustly wronged. If you can't get satisfaction from the lawyer, write to the client grievance office of your state bar association (with a copy to the lawyer, of course). Often, a phone call from this office to lawyer will bring the desired results.

B. Finding the Right Tax Advisor

Buyout scenarios necessarily involve tax issues and questions, such as, "Is it more tax-advantageous to have the company itself or the continuing owners buy a departing owner's interest?" Luckily, many of these issues won't raise their ugly heads until it's time for an actual buyout. But while you're forming your buy-sell agreement, you may have concerns about the tax aspects of the various buy-sell provisions we provide. To get good answers in these areas may require the expert advice of a tax advisor. Depending on the issue before you, this advisor may be a certified public accountant, a financial or investment advisor or a buy-sell agreement specialist.

Whatever your arrangement, consider the same issues for finding, choosing, using and resolving problems with a tax professional as those discussed in Section A, above, for legal services. Shop around for someone recommended by small business people you respect, or who is otherwise known to you as qualified for the task. Again, you may be able to take advantage of the lower rates offered by newer local practitioners or firms. Your tax person should be available over the phone to answer routine questions, or by mail or fax to handle paperwork and correspondence, with a minimum of formality or ritual. It is likely that you will spend much more time dealing with your tax advisor than your legal advisor, so be particularly attentive to the personal side of this relationship.

Tax issues are often cloudy and subject to a range of interpretations and strategies, so it is absolutely essential that you discuss and agree to the level of tax-aggressiveness you expect from your advisor. Some small business owners want to live on the edge, saving every possible tax dollar even at the risk that tax practices will be challenged by the IRS or state tax agents. Others are willing to pay a bit more in taxes to gain an extra measure of peace of mind. Whatever your tax strategy, make sure you find a tax advisor who feels the same way you do, or is willing to defer to your more liberal or conservative tax tendencies.

As with legal issues that affect your business, it pays to learn as much as you can about corporate and employment taxation. Not only will you have to buy less help from professionals, but you'll be in a good position to make good financial and tax planning decisions. IRS forms, business and law library publications, trade groups and countless other sources provide accessible information on corporate tax issues. Your accountant or other tax advisor should be able to help you put your hands on other good materials.

C. Resources

Law is information, not magic. If you can look up necessary information yourself, you need not purchase it from a lawyer—although if it involves important issues, you may wish to check your

conclusions with a lawyer, or use one as a sounding board for your intended course of action.

Much of the research necessary to understand your state's business law can be done without a lawyer by spending a few minutes in a local law or business library. Even if you need to go to a lawyer to sort out a particular legal question, you can give yourself a leg up on understanding the legal issues surrounding your question by reading practice manuals prepared for lawyers and law students at law and business libraries.

How do you find a law library open to the public? In many states, you need to look only as far as your county courthouse or, failing that, your state capitol. In addition, publicly funded law schools generally permit the public to use their libraries, and some private law schools grant limited access to their libraries—sometimes for a modest user's fee. If you're lucky enough to have access to several law libraries, select one that has a reference librarian to assist you. Also look through the business or reference department of a major city or county public library. These often carry business statutes as well as books on business law and taxation useful to the small business owner.

In doing legal research for a corporation or other type of business, there are a number of sources for legal rules, procedures and issues that you may wish to examine. Here are a few:

- **Federal laws.** These include the tax laws and procedures found in the Internal Revenue Code and Treasury Regulations implementing these code sections.
- **Administrative rules and regulations.** Issued by federal and state administrative agencies charged with implementing statutes, state and federal statutes are often supplemented with regulations that clarify the statute and contain rules for an agency to follow in implementing and enforcing the statute.
- **Case law.** Case law refers to all federal and state court decisions, which interpret statutes and sometimes make new law, known as "common law."

- **Secondary sources.** Also important in researching corporate and business law are sources that provide background information on particular areas of law. One example is this book. Others are commonly found in the business, legal or reference section of your local bookstore.

Unfortunately, tax law is not as easy to learn as some other areas of business law. The present tax code contains over 3,000 pages of very fine print and changes from year to year. So in many cases, going straight to a tax expert will save you a lot of time and frustration. If you do have a specific question you'd like to find the answer to and you're very brave, here are a few tips to follow:

- You can find the tax code itself (Title 26 of the United States Code) on Cornell Law School's Website at http://www4.law. cornell.edu/uscode/26/. This is a very useful site that lets you search for a specific code section by number or key words.
- The IRS interprets the tax code through a series of regulations, and federal court decisions further interpret the law. You can find regulations at http://www4.law.cornell. edu/cfr/26cfrI.htm or in the law library. For court decisions, try www.findlaw.com, or ask your law librarian for *US Tax Court Reports.*
- Your law library should have a good selection of secondary sources, among them *The Arthur Andersen Tax Guide* (Perigle Books), *Consumer Reports Tax Guide* (Consumer Reports Books), *Federal Taxation of Income, Estates and Gifts* (Bittker) and *The Arthur Young Tax Guide* (Ballantine Books).
- A Website maintained by private tax professionals, www.unclefed.com, contains helpful tax articles and a directory of tax professionals.

Resources for Valuation Methods

If you decide you want to explore valuation methods beyond the basics we presented in Chapter 6, you can research any one of a number of alternative routes. But keep in mind that other valuation methods will probably be more complicated, and the more complicated your method gets, the more sense it makes to use a time-of-sale appraisal. There are a number of good books that concentrate on business valuation techniques for small businesses, including *Valuing the Privately Held Business,* by Blackman (Probus Publishing) and *The Handbook of Business Valuation,* by West and Jones (Wiley & Sons).

Resources From Nolo Press

Below are a few titles published by Nolo Press that we believe offer valuable information to the small business person:

- *Legal Guide to Starting and Running a Small Business,* by Fred S. Steingold. This book is an essential resource for every small business owner, whether you are just starting out or are already established. Find out how to form a sole proprietorship, partnership or corporation; negotiate a favorable lease; hire and fire employees; write contracts; and resolve business disputes.

- *The Employer's Legal Handbook,* by Fred S. Steingold. Employers need legal advice daily. Here's a comprehensive resource they can refer to over and over again for questions about hiring, firing and everything in between. The only book that compiles all the basics of employment law in one place, it covers safe hiring practices, wages, hours, tips and commissions, employee benefits, taxes and liability, insurance, discrimination, sexual harassment and termination.

- *Tax Savvy for Small Business,* by Frederick W. Daily. Gives business owners information they need about federal taxes and shows them how to make the best tax decisions for their business, maximize their profits and stay out of trouble with the IRS.

- *How to Write a Business Plan,* by Mike McKeever. If you're thinking of starting a business or raising money to expand an existing one, this book will show you how to write the business plan and loan package necessary to finance your business and make it work. Includes up-to-date sources of financing.

How to Use the Forms Disk

The forms in Appendixes B and C are included on a 3½" floppy disk in the back of the book.

This forms disk is formatted for the PC (MS-DOS), and can be used by any PC running Windows or DOS. If you use a Mac, you must have a Super Disk drive and PC Exchange, or a similar utility, to use this disk. These files can be opened, filled in and printed out with your word processing program or text editor.

 The disk does not contain software, and you do not need to install any files. The forms disk contains only files that can be opened and edited using a word processor. This is not a software program. See below and the README.TXT file included on the disk for additional instructions on how to use these files.

How to View the README File

If you do not know how to view the file README.TXT, insert the forms disk into your computer's floppy disk drive and follow these instructions:

- Windows 95: (1) On your PC's desktop, double-click the My Computer icon; (2) double-click the icon for the floppy disk drive into which the forms disk was inserted; (3) double-click the file README.TXT.
- Windows 3.1: (1) Open File Manager; (2) double-click the icon for the floppy disk drive into which the forms disk was inserted; (3) double-click the file README.TXT.
- Macintosh: (1) On your Mac desktop, double-click the icon for the floppy disk that you inserted; (2) double-click on the file README.TXT.
- DOS: At the DOS prompt, type EDIT A:README.TXT and press the Enter key.

While the README file is open, print it out by using the Print command in the File menu.

A. Copying the Disk Files Onto Your Computer

Before you do anything else, copy the files from the forms disk onto your hard disk. Then work on these copies only. This way the original files and instructions will be untouched and can be used again. Instructions on how to copy files are provided below. In accordance with U.S. copyright laws, remember that copies of the disk and its files are for your personal use only.

Insert the forms disk and do the following:

1. Windows 95 and 98 Users

(These instructions assume that the A: drive is the source you want to copy from and that the C: drive is the location you want to copy the files to.)

Step 1. Double-click the My Computer icon to open the My Computer window.

Step 2. Double-click the A: drive icon in the My Computer window to open the drive window.

Step 3. First, choose Select All from the Edit menu (Ctrl+A). Then choose Copy from the Edit menu (Ctrl+C). Then close the drive window.

Step 4. Double-click the My Computer icon to open the My Computer window.

Step 5. Double-click the C: drive icon in the My Computer window to open the drive window.

Step 6. Choose New... from the File menu, then choose Folder to create a new, untitled folder on the C drive.

Step 7. Type "Buy-Sell Forms" to rename the untitled folder.

Step 8. Double-click on the "Buy-Sell Forms" folder icon to open that folder.

Step 9. Choose Paste from the Edit menu (Ctrl+V).

2. Windows 3.1 Users

(These instructions assume that the A: drive is the source you want to copy from and that the C: drive is the location you want to copy the files to.)

Step 1. Open File Manager.

Step 2. Double-click the A: drive icon at the top of the File Manager window.

Step 3. Choose Select Files... from the File menu to open the Select Files dialog box.

Step 4. First, click the Select button to select all the files on the floppy disk. Then click the Close button to close the Select Files dialog box.

Step 5. Choose Copy... from the File menu to open the Copy dialog box.

Step 6. In the TO box, type C:\BUYSELL and click OK. Click OK again when you're asked if you want to copy the selected files to the C:\BUYSELL directory.

3. Macintosh Users

Step 1. If the BUYSELL folder is open, close it.

Step 2. Click on the BUYSELL disk icon and drag it onto the icon of your hard disk.

Step 3. Read the message to make sure you want to go ahead, then click OK.

4. DOS Users

(These instructions assume that the A: drive is the source you want to copy from and that the C: drive is the location you want to copy the files to.)

Step 1. To create a directory named "BUYSELL" on your C: hard disk drive, type the following at the DOS prompt:

     C: <ENTER>
     CD\ <ENTER>
     MD BUYSELL <ENTER>

Step 2. To change to the BUYSELL directory you just created, type:

     CD BUYSELL <ENTER>

Step 3. To copy all the files from the floppy disk (in your A: drive) to the current directory, at the C:\BUYSELL> prompt, type:

     XCOPY A:*.* /s <ENTER>

All of the files in all directories on the floppy disk will be copied to the BUYSELL directory on your C: drive.

B. Creating Your Documents With the Forms Disk Files

The forms on this disk are in two file types (or formats):

- the standard ASCII text format (TXT)
- rich text format (RTF).

ASCII text files can be read by every word processor or text editor including DOS Edit; all flavors of MS Word and WordPerfect (including Macintosh); Windows Notepad, Write and WordPad; and Macintosh SimpleText and TeachText.

RTF files have the same text as the ASCII files, but have additional formatting. They can be read by most recent word processing programs including all versions of MS Word for Windows and Macintosh, WordPad for Windows 95 and recent versions of WordPerfect for Windows and Macintosh.

To use a form on the disk to create your documents you must (1) open the file in your word processor or text editor; (2) edit the form by filling in the required information; (3) print it out; (4) save your revised file.

The following are general instructions on how to do this. However, each word processor uses different commands to open, format, save and print documents. Please read your word processor's manual for specific instructions on performing these tasks.

DO NOT CALL NOLO'S TECHNICAL SUPPORT IF YOU HAVE QUESTIONS ON HOW TO USE YOUR WORD PROCESSOR.

Step 1: Opening a File

To open a file in your word processor, you need to start your word processing program and open the file from within the program. This process usually entails going to the File menu and choosing the Open command. This opens a dialog box where you will tell the program (1) the type of file you want to open (either *.TXT or *.RTF) and (2) the location and name of the file (you will need to navigate through the directory tree to get to the folder/directory on your hard disk that you created and copied the disk's files to). If these directions are unclear you will need to look through the manual for your word processing program—Nolo's technical support department will NOT be able to help you with the use of your word processing program.

Which File Format Should You Use?

If you are not sure which file format to use with your word processor, try opening the RTF file first. Rich text files (RTF) contain most of the formatting included in the sample forms found in this book and in Appendixes B and C. Most current Windows and Macintosh word processing programs, such as Microsoft Word or WordPerfect, can read RTF files.

If you are unable to open the RTF file in your word processor, or a bunch of "garbage" characters appear on the screen when you do, then use the TXT files instead. All word processors and text editors can read TXT files, which contain only text, tabs and carriage returns; all other formatting and special characters have been stripped.

Windows and Mac users can also open a file more directly by double-clicking on it. Use File Manager (Windows 3.1), My Computer or Windows Explorer (Windows 95 and 98) or the Finder (Macintosh) to go to the folder/directory you created and copied the disk's files to. Then, double-click on the specific file you want to open. If you click on an RTF file and you have a program installed that "understands" RTF, your word processor should launch and load the file that you double-clicked on. If the file isn't loaded, or if it contains a bunch of garbage characters, use your word processor's Open command, as described above, to open the TXT file instead. If you directly double-click on a TXT file, it will load into a basic text editor like Notepad or SimpleText rather than your word processor.

Step 2: Editing Your Document

Fill in the appropriate information according to the instructions in the file and in the book. Underlines are used to indicate where you need to enter your information, frequently followed by instructions in brackets. Be sure to delete the underlines and instructions from your edited document. If you do not know how to use your word processor to edit a document, you will need to look through the manual for your word processing program—Nolo's technical support department will NOT be able to help you with the use of your word processing program.

Editing Forms That Have Check Boxes

Some of the forms have check boxes before text. The check boxes indicate:

- optional text, which you choose whether to include or exclude
- alternative text, where you select one alternative to include and exclude the other alternatives.

If you are using the tear-out form in Appendix C, you simply mark the appropriate box to make your choice.

If you are using the forms disk, however, instead of marking the check boxes, you do the following:

Optional text

If you **don't want** to include optional text, just delete it from your document.

If you **do want** to include optional text, just leave it in your document.

In either case, delete the check box itself, as well as any instructions.

Alternative text

First delete all the alternatives that you do not want to include.

Then delete the remaining check box, as well as any instructions.

Step 3: Printing Out the Document

Use your word processor's or text editor's Print command to print out your document. If you do not know how to use your word processor to print a document, you will need to look through the manual for your word processing program—Nolo's technical support department will NOT be able to help you with the use of your word processing program.

Step 4: Saving Your Document

After filling in the form, do a "save as" and give the file a new name. THESE FILES ARE "READ-ONLY," SO YOU WILL NOT BE ABLE TO USE THE SAVE COMMAND. THIS IS TO MAKE SURE THAT YOU DO NOT DELETE THE UNDERLINES AND INSTRUCTIONS, SO YOU CAN CREATE ADDITIONAL DOCUMENTS WITHOUT RECOPYING THE ORIGINAL FILE FROM THE FLOPPY DISK. MAKE SURE NEVER TO EDIT THE ORIGINAL FILE ON YOUR FLOPPY.

If you do not know how to use your word processor to save a document, you will need to look through the manual for your word processing program—Nolo's technical support department will NOT be able to help you with the use of your word processing program. ■

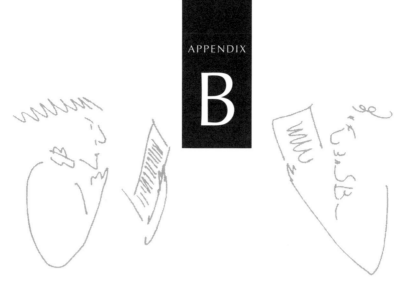

APPENDIX

B

Buy-Sell Worksheet

Buy-Sell Worksheet

Section I: Introduction

When you're ready to draft your agreement, insert into the blanks in Section I of the agreement this information in the following order:

- Date you'll sign your agreement
- City and state in which you'll sign your agreement
- Name of the 1st owner
- Name of the 2nd owner
- Name of the 3rd owner
- Name of the 4th owner
- Your company's name

Section II: Limiting the Transfer of Ownership Interests

Refer to Chapter 2.

☐ **Option 1: Right of First Refusal**

    ☐ **Option 1a: Price and terms in offer**

    ☐ **Option 1b: Price and terms in agreement**

    ☐ **Option 1c: Right of First Refusal applies to sales to current owners**

    ☐ **Option 1d: Right of First Refusal does not apply to sales to current owners**

☐ **Option 2: Transfers to relatives can be made without restriction or approval notwithstanding any other provision in this agreement.**

Notes: _____

_____

_____

_____

_____

_____

_____

_____

_____

_____

Section III: Providing the Right to Force Buyouts
Refer to Chapter 3.

Scenario 1. When an Active Owner Retires or Quits the Company's Employ

☐ **Option 1:** Option of Company and Continuing Owners to Purchase a Retiring Owner's Interest

☐ **Option 2: Right of Retiring Owner to Force a Sale**

   ☐ **Option 2a: Disincentive period, with illness/injury exception**

   Number of years _____

   Disincentive percentage _____

   ☐ **Option 2b: Disincentive period, without illness/injury exception**

   Number of years _____

   Disincentive percentage _____

Scenario 2. When an Owner Becomes Disabled

☐ **Option 1:** Option of Company and Continuing Owners to Purchase a Disabled Owner's Interest

Number of months _____

   ☐ **Option 1a: Date disabled owner stops working**

   ☐ **Option 1b: Date of buyout**

☐ **Option 2: Right of Disabled Owner to Force a Sale**

Number of months _____

   ☐ **Option 2a: Date disabled owner stops working**

   ☐ **Option 2b: Date of buyout**

Notes: _____

_____

_____

_____

_____

_____

_____

_____

_____

Scenario 3. When an Owner Dies

☐ **Option 1:** Option of Company and Continuing Owners to Purchase a Deceased Owner's Interest

☐ **Option 2: Right of Estate, Trust or Inheritors to Force a Sale**

Scenario 4. When an Owner's Interest Is Transferred to His or Her Former Spouse

☐ **Option 1:** Option of Company and Continuing Owners to Purchase Former Spouse's Interest

Scenario 5. When an Owner Loses His or Her Professional License

☐ **Option 1: Option of Company and Continuing Owners to Purchase Interest of an Owner Who Has Lost His or Her Professional License**

    ☐ **Option 1a: The full Agreement Price according to Section VI of this agreement**

    ☐ **Option 1b: Decided by an independent appraisal, according to the Appraised Value Method in Section VI of this agreement**

    ☐ **Option 1c: The Agreement Price as established in Section VI of this agreement, decreased by _____%**

Percentage agreement price will be decreased by _____

Notes: _____

_____

_____

_____

_____

_____

_____

_____

_____

_____

_____

Scenario 6. When an Owner Files for Personal Bankruptcy

☐ **Option 1: Option of Company and Continuing Owners to Purchase Interest of an Owner Who Has Filed for Bankruptcy**

Number of days notice required before bankruptcy _____

Scenario 7. Encumbrance of Interest

☐ **Option 1: Encumbrances Allowed Subject to Option of Company and Continuing Owners to Purchase Encumbered Interest**

☐ **Option 2: No Encumbrance Allowed**

Scenario 8. Expulsion of Owner

☐ **Option 1: Option of Company and Continuing Owners to Purchase an Expelled Owner's Interest**

    ☐ **Option 1a: Any criminal conduct against the company (such as embezzlement)**

    ☐ **Option 1b: A serious breach of the owner's duties or of any written policy of the company, or**

    ☐ **Option 1c** _____.

    Additional reason for expulsion _____

    ☐ **Option 1d: The full Agreement Price according to Section VI of this agreement**

    ☐ **Option 1e: Decided by an independent appraisal, according to the Appraised Value Method in Section VI of this agreement**

    ☐ **Option 1f: The Agreement Price as established in Section VI of this agreement, decreased by _____%**

    Percentage agreement price will be decreased by _____

Notes: _____

_____

_____

_____

_____

_____

_____

_____

_____

Section IV: Buyout Procedure

Refer to Chapter 4.

(1) Option of Company and Continuing Owners to Purchase an Interest

    (b) Number of days that your company will have to make its buyback decision _____

    (c) Number of days that the continuing owners will have to make their individual buyback decisions _____

(2) Right to Force a Sale

    (b) Number of days that your company will have to make its buyback decision _____

    (c) Number of days that the continuing owners will have to make their individual buyback decisions _____

Section V: Funding

Refer to Chapter 5.

(1) Life Insurance

    ☐ **Option 1: Company-purchased life insurance**

    ☐ **Option 2: Owner-purchased life insurance**

(2) Disability Insurance

    ☐ **Option 1: Company-purchased disability insurance**

    ☐ **Option 2: Owner-purchased disability insurance**

Notes: _____

_____

_____

_____

_____

_____

_____

_____

_____

_____

_____

_____

_____

_____

Section VI: Agreement Price
Refer to Chapter 6.

☐ **Valuation Method 1: Agreed Value**

Price for the entire company _____

☐ **Valuation Method 2: Book Value**

☐ **Valuation Method 3: Multiple of Book Value**

Multiplier _____

☐ **Valuation Method 4: Capitalization of Earnings (Adjusted for Income Taxes)**

Multiplier _____

Number of years that earnings will be based on _____

☐ **Valuation Method 5: Appraised Value**

Notes: _____

_____

_____

_____

_____

_____

_____

_____

_____

_____

_____

_____

_____

_____

_____

_____

Section VII: Payment Terms
Refer to Chapter 7.

☐ **Payment Terms Alternative 1: Full Cash Payment**

Number of days when full payment will be due _____

☐ **Payment Terms Alternative 2: Monthly Installments of Principal and Interest**

Term for repayment (in months) _____

Annual interest rate _____

Date first installment payment will be due _____

Payment due day (day of the month) _____

☐ **Payment Terms Alternative 3: Partial Cash Payment, Followed by Monthly Installments of Principal and Interest**

Down payment _____

Number of days until down payment will be due _____

Term for repayment (in months) _____

Annual interest rate _____

Date first installment payment will be due _____

Payment due day (day of the month) _____

☐ **Payment Terms Alternative 4: Monthly Installments of Interest Only, With a Final Payment for the Full Purchase Price**

Future date for full payment of purchase price _____

Interest rate _____

Date first interest payment will be due _____

Interest payment day (day of the month) _____

☐ **Payment Terms Alternative 5: Customized Schedule for Payment for Ownership Interest**

Dates and amounts to be paid under a customized payment schedule _____

_____

_____

_____

Section VIII: Resolution of Disputes
Refer to Chapter 8.

Be sure to read this provision before signing the agreement.

Section IX: Placement of Notice of Transfer Restrictions on Certificates
Refer to Chapter 8.

Be sure to read this provision before signing the agreement.

Section X: Continuation of Restrictions
Refer to Chapter 8.

Be sure to read this provision before signing the agreement.

Section XI: Signatures
Refer to Chapter 8.

Be sure to review your buy-sell agreement with your tax advisor or small business lawyer before you date and sign the agreement. Make sure that all married owners have their spouses sign the agreement.

Notes:

APPENDIX

C

Buy-Sell Agreement

Buy-Sell Agreement

Section I: Introduction

This agreement ("Agreement") is made on _____ , at

_____ ,

among _____ ,

_____ ,

_____ and

_____ ("Owners"),

and _____ ("Company").

Owners wish to restrict the ownership of the company to the present owners and to persons with whom they may comfortably and easily deal, and to provide for the purchase of the ownership interest of any owner who dies or otherwise withdraws under the terms of this agreement.

The legal existence of the company shall not terminate upon the addition of a new owner or the transfer of an owner's interest under this agreement, or the death, withdrawal, bankruptcy or expulsion of an owner.

"Seller" refers to an owner who is selling an ownership interest, or the estate representative, trustee or family member of a deceased owner or the ex-spouse of a divorced owner or other seller under this agreement.

"Buyer" refers to the company and/or the continuing owners who are purchasing an ownership interest.

"Agreement Price" refers to the dollar amount that results from the use of the option checked in Section VI of this agreement at the time of the proposed sale.

"Available interest" refers to the owner's interest that has become available for purchase by the company or continuing owners of the company as a result of a provision in this agreement.

It is hereby agreed:

Section II: Limiting the Transfer of Ownership Interests

Check Option 1 below if you want the company and continuing owners to have a Right of First Refusal when an owner considers transferring his or her ownership interest.

☐ Option 1: Right of First Refusal

(a) No owner ("transferring owner") shall have the right to sell, transfer or dispose of in any way any or all of his or her ownership interest, for consideration or otherwise, unless he or she delivers to the company written Notice of Intent to Transfer the interest stating the name and the address of the proposed transferee and the terms and conditions of the proposed transfer. Delivery of this notice shall be deemed an offer by the transferring owner to sell to the company and the continuing owners the interest proposed to be transferred.

If the proposed transfer is a sale of the owner's interest, these terms shall include the price to be paid for the interest by the proposed transferee, and a copy of the offer to purchase the interest on these terms, dated and signed by the proposed transferee, shall be attached to the notice.

(b) The company and the nontransferring owners then have an option, but not an obligation (unless otherwise stated in this agreement), to purchase the interest proposed for transfer, and may do so within the time and according to the procedure in Section IV, Provision 1 of this agreement.

If the company and the nontransferring owners do not elect to purchase all of the interest stated in the notice, the transferring owner may then transfer his or her interest to the proposed transferee stated in the notice within 60 days after the end of the nontransferring owners' purchase option, according to the procedure in Section IV, Provision 1 of this agreement.

(c) Price and terms

You must check either Option 1a or Option 1b below if you checked Option 1, "Right of First Refusal," above.

☐ Option 1a: Price and terms in offer

If the proposed transfer is a sale of the owner's interest, the company and the nontransferring owners shall have the right to purchase the interest of the transferring owner only at the purchase price and payment terms stated in the Notice of Intent to Transfer submitted to the company by the transferring owner. The price and terms in this notice override the general Agreement Price selected in Section VI of this agreement and the agreement terms selected in Section VII.

If the proposed transfer is a gift of the owner's interest, the company and the nontransferring owners shall have the right to purchase the interest of the transferring owner at the Agreement Price selected in Section VI and according to the manner of payments and other terms of the purchase as established in Section VII of this agreement.

☐ Option 1b: Price and terms in agreement

The company and the nontransferring owners shall have the right to purchase the interest of the transferring owner at the Agreement Price selected in Section VI and according to the manner of payments and other terms of the purchase as established in Section VII of this agreement.

(d) Potential transferees

You must check either Option 1c or Option 1d below if you checked Option 1, "Right to First Refusal," above.

☐ Option 1c: Right of first refusal applies to sales to current owners

The Right-of-First-Refusal clause in this agreement shall apply to all potential transferees, whether they are current owners of any interests in the company or not.

☐ Option 1d: Right of first refusal does not apply to sales to current owners

The Right-of-First-Refusal clause in this agreement shall only apply to those potential transferees who are not current owners of any interests in the company.

(e) This Right-of-First-Refusal clause shall not apply to an owner's transfer of an ownership interest to a trust as long as the following conditions are met:
i) the power to revoke the trust remains with the grantor (the owner of the interest), and
ii) the grantor (the owner of the interest) is a trustee of the trust.

If either of the above conditions ceases to be true, this change will subject the ownership interest to this Right-of-First-Refusal.

Check Option 2 below if you want an owner to be able to give away an ownership interest freely without being subject to a Right of First Refusal. Of course, this option can be checked in addition to Option 1, above.

☐ **Option 2: Transfers to relatives can be made without restriction or approval notwithstanding any other provision in this agreement.**

Section III: Providing the Right to Force Buyouts

Scenario 1. When an Active Owner Retires or Quits the Company's Employ
You may check Option 1 and/or Option 2 (or neither) below.

Check Option 1 below if you want the company and continuing owners to have the option to buy a retiring owner's interest.

☐ **Option 1: Option of Company and Continuing Owners to Purchase a Retiring Owner's Interest**

(a) When an owner voluntarily retires or quits the company's employ, he or she is deemed to have offered his or her ownership interest to the company and the continuing owners for sale. The company and the continuing owners shall then have an option, but not an obligation (unless otherwise stated in this agreement), to purchase all or part of the ownership interest within the time and according to the procedure in Section IV, Provision 1 of this agreement. The price to be paid, the manner of payments and other terms of the purchase shall be according to Sections VI and VII of this agreement. An owner who stops working for the company is referred to as a "retiring owner" below.

Check Option 2 below if you want a retiring owner to be able to force the company to buy his or her interest. This right can be in addition to Option 1 (company and continuing owners' option to purchase) above.

☐ **Option 2: Right of Retiring Owner to Force a Sale**

(a) When an owner voluntarily retires or quits the company's employ, he or she can require the company and the continuing owners to buy all, but not less than all, of his or her ownership interest by delivering to the company at least 60 days before his or her departure a notice of intention to force a sale ("Notice of Intent to Force a Sale"). The notice shall include the date of departure, the name and address of the owner, a description and amount of the owner's interest in the company and a statement that the owner wishes to force a sale due to the owner's retirement as provided in this provision. The procedure for purchase of the ownership interest shall be according to Section IV, Provision 2 of this agreement. The price to be paid, the manner of payments and other terms of the purchase shall be according to this section and Sections VI and VII of this agreement. An owner who requests that his interest be purchased is referred to as a "retiring owner" below.

(b) Disincentive option
If you checked Option 2, "Right of Retiring Owner to Force a Sale," above, you may check Option 2a or 2b, below, if you want to discount the Agreement Price if an owner retires or quits within a certain period of time. If you check Option 2a or 2b, also insert the time period required for payment of the full Agreement Price and the penalty that will be taken off the Agreement Price for retirement within that time period.

☐ Option 2a: Disincentive period, with illness/injury exception

If a retiring owner gives notice that he or she wishes his or her ownership interest to be bought before the end of _____ months of ownership of the company, he or she is entitled to receive only _____ % of the Agreement Price for the sale of ownership interests in this company under this agreement, unless he or she is required to leave because of serious personal illness or injury or the serious illness or injury of a spouse, parent or child, in which case he or she is entitled to 100% of the Agreement Price.

☐ Option 2b: Disincentive period, without illness/injury exception

If a retiring owner gives notice that he or she wishes his or her ownership interest to be bought before the end of _____ months of ownership of the company, he or she is entitled to receive only _____ % of the Agreement Price for the sale of ownership interests in this company under this agreement.

Scenario 2. When an Owner Becomes Disabled

You may check Option 1 and/or Option 2 (or neither) below.

Check Option 1 below if you want the company and continuing owners to have the option to buy a disabled owner's interest. If you check Option 1, also insert the amount of time an owner must be disabled before the company or the continuing owners can purchase his interest.

☐ Option 1: Option of Company and Continuing Owners to Purchase a Disabled Owner's Interest

(a) When an owner becomes permanently and totally disabled, and such disability lasts at least _____ months (the "waiting period"), either consecutively or cumulatively, he or she is deemed to have offered his or her ownership interest to the company and the continuing owners for sale. The company and the continuing owners shall then have an option, but not an obligation (unless otherwise stated in this agreement), to purchase all or part of the ownership interest within the time and according to the procedure in Section IV, Provision 1 of this agreement. The price to be paid, the manner of payments and other terms of the purchase shall be according to this section and Sections V and VI of this agreement.

An owner is considered disabled when he or she is unable to perform his or her regular duties. If disability insurance is used to fund a buyout under this provision, the insurance company shall establish whether an owner is disabled; without disability insurance, the owner's doctor will establish whether an owner is disabled. An owner who becomes disabled according to this section is referred to as a "disabled owner" below.

(b) Price

You must check either Option 1a or Option 1b below if you checked Option 1 above.

☐ Option 1a: Date disabled owner stops working

The Agreement Price as selected in Section VI of this agreement shall be established as of the date the disabled owner first stopped working.

☐ Option 1b: Date of buyout

The Agreement Price as selected in Section VI of this agreement shall be established as of the date of the proposed buyout of the disabled owner's interest.

Check Option 2 below if you want a disabled owner to be able to force the company to buy his or her interest. This right can be in addition to Option 1 (company and continuing owners' option to purchase) above. If you check Option 2, also insert the amount of time an owner must be disabled before he can force the company to purchase his interest.

☐ **Option 2: Right of Disabled Owner to Force a Sale**

(a) When an owner becomes permanently and totally disabled, and such disability lasts at least _____ months (the "waiting period"), either consecutively or cumulatively, he or she can require the company and the continuing owners to buy all, but not less than all, of his or her ownership interest by delivering to the company, within 30 days of the expiration of the waiting period, a notice of intention to force a sale ("Notice of Intent to Force a Sale") in writing. The notice shall include the name and address of the owner, a description and amount of the owner's interest in the company and a statement that the owner wishes to force a sale due to disability as provided in this provision. The procedure for purchase of the ownership interest shall be according to Section IV, Provision 2 of this agreement. The price to be paid, the manner of payments and other terms of the purchase shall be according to this section and Sections VI and VII of this agreement.

An owner is considered disabled when he or she is unable to perform his or her regular duties. If disability insurance is used to fund a buyout under this provision, the insurance company shall establish whether an owner is disabled; without disability insurance, the owner's doctor will establish whether an owner is disabled. An owner who becomes disabled according to this section is referred to as a "disabled owner" below.

(b) Price

You must check either Option 2a or Option 2b below if you checked Option 2 above.

☐ **Option 2a: Date disabled owner stops working**

The Agreement Price as selected in Section VI of this agreement shall be established as of the date the disabled owner first stopped working.

☐ **Option 2b: Date of buyout**

The Agreement Price as selected in Section VI of this agreement shall be established as of the date of the proposed buyout of the disabled owner's interest.

Scenario 3. When an Owner Dies
You may check Option 1 and/or Option 2 (or neither) below.

Check Option 1 below if you want the company and continuing owners to have the right to buy a deceased owner's interest.

☐ **Option 1: Option of Company and Continuing Owners to Purchase a Deceased Owner's Interest**

(a) When an owner dies, he or she, and the executor or administrator of his or her estate or the trustee of a trust holding his or her ownership interest, are deemed to have offered the deceased owner's ownership interest to the company and the continuing owners for sale as of the date of the notice of death received orally or in writing by the company. The company and the continuing owners shall then have an option, but not an obligation (unless otherwise stated in this agreement), to purchase all or part of the ownership

interest within the time and according to the procedure in Section IV, Provision 1 of this agreement. The price to be paid, the manner of payments and other terms of the purchase shall be according to Sections VI and VII of this agreement. An owner who has died is referred to as a "deceased owner" below.

Check Option 2 below if you want the estate, trust or inheritors of a deceased owner to be able to force the company to buy his or her interest. This right can be in addition to Option 1 (company and continuing owners' right to purchase) above.

☐ **Option 2: Right of Estate, Trust or Inheritors to Force a Sale**

    (a) When an owner dies, the executor or administrator of the deceased owner's estate, or the trustee of a trust holding the deceased owner's ownership interest, or the deceased owner's inheritors can require the company and the continuing owners to buy all, but not less than all, of the deceased owner's ownership interest by delivering to the company within 60 days a notice of intention to force a sale ("Notice of Intent to Force a Sale") in writing. The notice shall include the name and address of the deceased owner, the date of death, a description and amount of the owner's interest in the company, the name and address of the person exercising the right to force the sale and a statement that this person wishes to force a sale of the interest due to the owner's death as provided in this provision. The procedure for purchase of the ownership interest shall be according to Section IV, Provision 2 of this agreement. The price to be paid, the manner of payments and other terms of the purchase shall be according to Sections VI and VII of this agreement. An owner who has died is referred to as a "deceased owner" below.

Scenario 4. When an Owner's Interest Is Transferred to His or Her Former Spouse

You may check Option 1 below if you want the company and owners to have the right to buy a divorced owner's interest from his or her former spouse.

☐ **Option 1: Option of Company and Continuing Owners to Purchase Former Spouse's Interest**

    (a) If, in connection with the divorce or dissolution of the marriage of an owner, a court issues a decree or order that transfers, confirms or awards part or all of an ownership interest to a divorced owner's former spouse, the former spouse is deemed to have offered his or her newly acquired ownership interest to the divorced owner for purchase on the date of the court award or settlement, according to the terms of this agreement. If the divorced owner does not elect to make such purchase within 30 days of the date of the court award or settlement, the former spouse of the divorced owner is deemed to have offered his or her newly acquired ownership interest to the company and the co-owners (including the divorced owner) for purchase, according to the terms of this agreement. The divorced owner must send notice to the company, in writing, that his or her former spouse now owns an ownership interest in the company. The notice shall state the name and address of the owner, the name and address of the divorced owner's former spouse, a description and amount of the interest awarded to the former spouse and the date of the court award. If no notice is received by the company from the divorced owner, an offer to the company and the co-owners is deemed to have occurred when the company actually receives notice orally or in writing of the court award or settlement transferring the

divorced owner's interest to the owner's former spouse. The company and the co-owners (including the divorced owner) shall then have an option, but not an obligation (unless otherwise stated in this agreement), to purchase all or part of the ownership interest within the time and according to the procedure in Section IV, Provision 1 of this agreement. The price to be paid, the manner of payments and other terms of the purchase shall be according to Sections VI and VII of this agreement.

(b) A former spouse who sells his or her ownership interest back to the company or continuing owners agrees to be responsible for any taxes owed on his or her sales proceeds.

Scenario 5. When an Owner Loses His or Her Professional License

You may check Option 1 below if you want the company and owners to have the right to buy an owner's interest when he or she has lost his professional or vocational license. If you check Option 1, also check and/or fill in Options 1a through 1c.

☐ **Option 1: Option of Company and Continuing Owners to Purchase Interest of an Owner Who Has Lost His or Her Professional License**

(a) If an owner suffers the surrender, revocation or suspension, which will stand for at least three months, of his or her license to perform services essential to the business purposes of the company, that surrender, revocation or suspension of the license shall be deemed to constitute an offer by the owner to sell his or her interest to the company or the other owners. The owner shall notify the company in writing of such surrender, revocation or suspension. The notice shall include the name and address of the owner, a description and amount of the owner's interest in the company and a description and effective date of the decision that resulted in the surrender, revocation or suspension of the owner's license. If no notice is received by the company, an offer is deemed to have occurred when the company actually learns of the decision to surrender, revoke or suspend the owner's license. The company and the continuing owners shall then have an option, but not an obligation (unless otherwise stated in this agreement), to purchase all or part of the ownership interest within the time and according to the procedure in Section IV, Provision 1 of this agreement. The price to be paid shall be as specified in this section; if not so specified, then according to Section VI of this agreement. The manner of payments and other terms of the purchase shall be according to Section VII of this agreement.

(b) If an owner's license is surrendered, revoked or suspended, the price that the company and/or the continuing owners will pay for the expelled owner's ownership interest will be:

☐ **Option 1a: The full Agreement Price according to Section VI of this agreement**

☐ **Option 1b: Decided by an independent appraisal, according to the Appraised Value Method in Section VI of this agreement**

☐ **Option 1c: The Agreement Price as established in Section VI of this agreement, decreased by _____.**

Scenario 6. When an Owner Files for Personal Bankruptcy

You may check Option 1 below if you want the company and owners to have the right to buy an owner's interest when he or she has lost filed for personal bankruptcy. If you check Option 1, also insert the number of days' notice that the owner must give to the company before filing for bankruptcy.

☐ **Option 1: Option of Company and Continuing Owners to Purchase Interest of an Owner Who Has Filed for Bankruptcy**

    (a) When an owner is planning to file for bankruptcy, he or she must give notice to the company, in writing, _____ days before he or she files for bankruptcy. The notice shall state the name and address of the owner, a description and amount of the owner's interest and the expected date of filing by the owner for bankruptcy. This notice shall be deemed to constitute an offer by the owner to sell his or her interest to the company or the other owners. If an owner files for bankruptcy without giving notice, the date when the company learns of the filing for bankruptcy will be deemed to be the date of this notice. The company and the continuing owners shall then have an option, but not an obligation (unless otherwise stated in this agreement), to purchase all or part of the ownership interest within the time and according to the procedure in Section IV, Provision 1 of this agreement. The price to be paid, the manner of payments and other terms of the purchase shall be according to Sections VI and VII of this agreement. An owner who has filed for bankruptcy is referred to as a "bankrupt owner" below.

Scenario 7. Encumbrance of Interest

You must check either Option 1 or Option 2 below.

Check Option 1 below if you want to allow owners to use their ownership interest as collateral for personal loans or encumber their interest in other ways, subject to the option of the company and the continuing owners to purchase that interest in case of default.

☐ **Option 1: Encumbrances Allowed Subject to Option of Company and Continuing Owners to Purchase Encumbered Interest**

    (a) Any owner may encumber any or all of his or her ownership interest in the company in connection with any debt, but any such encumbrance is subject to the following condition:

    (b) If an owner defaults on a debt secured by his or her ownership interest, he or she must promptly give notice in writing to the company. The notice shall include the name and address of the owner, a description and amount of the owner's interest in the company, the date and description of the encumbrance on the owner's interest and the date and description of any action taken by creditors as a result of the default. If no notice is provided by the owner, notice shall be considered given to the company on the date the company learns of the owner's default or of any action by a creditor as a result of the default. (An owner who defaults on a debt secured by his or her ownership interest is referred to as a "defaulting owner" below.) The company and the continuing owners shall then have an option, but not an obligation (unless otherwise stated in this agreement), to pay off the debt and to take title to the interest.

    (c) If the amount paid to the creditor (debt plus any interest) is less than the Agreement Price selected in Section VI of this agreement, the remainder of the Agreement Price shall be

paid to the defaulting owner by the buyer of his or her ownership interest. If the amount paid to the creditor (debt plus any interest) is more than the Agreement Price selected in Section VI of this agreement, the defaulting owner shall owe the difference to the buyer of his or her ownership interest.

(d) If the company and/or the other owners do not cure the default as provided in subsection (b) above, the creditor may pursue any and all legal and equitable remedies.

Check Option 2 below if you want to prohibit owners from using their ownership interest as collateral for personal loans or encumbering their interest in any other way.

☐ **Option 2: No Encumbrance Allowed**
No owner may encumber any or all of his or her ownership interest in the company in connection with any debt, guarantee or other personal undertaking.

Scenario 8. Expulsion of Owner

Check Option 1 below if you want to give the company and the continuing owners the option to purchase an expelled owner's interest. If you check Option 1, also check and/or fill in Options 1a through 1f.

☐ **Option 1: Option of Company and Continuing Owners to Purchase an Expelled Owner's Interest**

(a) At a time when the company has three or more owners, situations may arise in which a group of owners wish to expel another owner. An owner may be expelled upon a unanimous vote of all other owners for adequate cause. Upon such expulsion, the expelled owner is deemed to have offered to sell all of his or her interest to the company and the continuing owners. The company and the continuing owners shall then have an option, but not an obligation (unless otherwise stated in this agreement), to purchase all or part of the ownership interest within the time and according to the procedure in Section IV, Provision 1 of this agreement. The price to be paid shall be as specified in this section; if not so specified, then according to Section VI of this agreement. The manner of payments and other terms of the purchase shall be according to Section VII of this agreement. An owner who has been expelled is referred to as an "expelled owner" below.

(b) Adequate cause includes, but is not limited to:

☐ **Option 1a: Any criminal conduct against the company (such as embezzlement)**

☐ **Option 1b: A serious breach of the owner's duties or of any written policy of the company, or**

☐ **Option 1c** _____

(c) If an owner is expelled for a reason listed in subsection (b), the price that the company and/or the continuing owners will pay for the expelled owner's ownership interest will be:

☐ **Option 1d: The full Agreement Price according to Section VI of this agreement**

☐ **Option 1e: Decided by an independent appraisal, according to the Appraised Value Method in Section VI of this agreement**

☐ **Option 1f: The Agreement Price as established in Section VI of this agreement, decreased by** _____%

Section IV: Buyout Procedure

Fill in the blanks in subsections (b) and (c) below, if you checked Option 1 anywhere in Sections II or III of this agreement.

(1) Option of Company and Continuing Owners to Purchase an Interest

(a) This provision is triggered upon receipt of notice by the company according to Section II or the notification of any of the events checked in Section III where the company and/or the continuing owners have an option, but not an obligation (unless otherwise stated in this agreement), to purchase the interest that is the subject of the notice (called the "available interest").

(b) The company shall have an option to purchase any or all of the available interest within _____ days after the date on which the company receives notice or becomes aware of the event triggering the Option to Purchase.

(c) If the company does not decide to purchase all of the available interest within the time allowed, it shall immediately, and, in all cases, no later than the date of expiration of the company's right to exercise its purchase option of the available interest, notify the continuing owners of their right to purchase the available interest not purchased by the company. This notice by the company to the continuing owners shall state:
   1) the amount and description of the interest available for purchase by the continuing owners
   2) the date by which the continuing owner must respond in writing to the company that he or she wishes to purchase any or all of the available interest, which date shall be _____ days after the date of the expiration of the company's purchase option, and
   3) that any purchase by a continuing owner must be according to the terms of this buy-sell agreement.

   A copy of this buy-sell agreement shall be immediately furnished to any continuing owner who requests a copy.

(d) Each continuing owner may exercise his or her option to purchase any or all of the available interest in writing by delivering or mailing to the company an individual Notice of Intent to Purchase. This notice shall be sent to the secretary or equivalent officer of the company, and shall show the name and address of the continuing owner who wishes to purchase part or all of the available interest and the amount and a description of the interest that the continuing owner wishes to purchase.

(e) If the total amount of interest specified in the notices by the continuing owners to the company exceeds the amount of the interest available for purchase by them, each continuing owner shall be entitled, up to the amount of interest specified in his or her individual Notice of Intent to Purchase, to purchase a fraction of the available interest, in the same proportion that the amount of the interest he or she currently owns bears to the total amount of the company's interest owned by all continuing owners electing to purchase.

(f) If the company or any continuing owner exercises their option to purchase a part or all of the available interest, the company shall deliver or mail to the current owner or, if different, the current holder of the available interest, no later than five business days after

the expiration of the period to exercise their option to purchase the available interest, a Notice of Intent to Purchase, that includes the following information:
- the name and address of the company, and the name and title of the officer or employee who can be contacted at the company
- a description and the amount of ownership interest to be purchased by the company and/or each of the continuing owners, and the name and address of each such continuing owner
- the total amount of the interest to be purchased by the company and the continuing owners
- the terms of the purchase according to Section VII of this agreement
- a copy of the buy-sell agreement, and
- if the interest to be purchased is represented by certificates, such as share certificates, a request for the surrender of the share certificates to the company.

(g) The company and the continuing owners shall purchase the portion or all of the available interest each has exercised an option to purchase in the Notice of Intent to Purchase, according to the terms specified in Section VII of this agreement, each making payment for the interest to be purchased and complying with other terms as appropriate. The sale shall be considered final when the company and the continuing owners make payment to the owner or holder of the interest or, if payment is made over time, when all paperwork necessary to the sale has been executed by the company, the continuing owners and the owner or holder of the interest to be purchased.

(2) Right to Force a Sale

If you checked Option 2 in Scenarios 1, 2 or 3 in Section III of this agreement, fill in the blanks in subsections (b) and (c) below.

(a) This provision is triggered upon receipt by the company of a Notice of Intent to Force a Sale according to Section III, where the company and the continuing owners have an obligation to purchase the interest that is the subject of the notice (called the "available interest").

(b) The company shall have an option to purchase any or all of the available interest within _____ days after the date on which the company receives the Notice of Intent to Force a Sale.

(c) If the company does not decide to purchase all of the available interest within the time allowed, it shall immediately, and, in all cases, no later than the date of expiration of the company's right to exercise its purchase option of the available interest, notify the continuing owners of their right to purchase the available interest not purchased by the company. This notice by the company to the continuing owners shall state:
   1) the amount and description of the interest available for purchase by the continuing owners
   2) the date by which the continuing owner must respond in writing to the company that he or she wishes to purchase any or all of the available interest, which date shall be _____ days after the date of the expiration of the company's purchase option, and
   3) that any purchase by a continuing owner must be according to the terms of this buy-sell agreement.

   A copy of this buy-sell agreement shall be immediately furnished to any continuing owner who requests a copy.

(d) Each continuing owner may individually exercise his or her option to purchase any or all of the available interest in writing by delivering or mailing to the company a Notice of Intent to Purchase. This notice shall be sent to the secretary or equivalent officer of the company, and shall show the name and address of the continuing owner who wishes to purchase part or all of the available interest and the amount and a description of the interest that the continuing owner wishes to purchase.

(e) If the total amount of interest specified in the continuing owners' notices exceeds the amount of the available interest, each continuing owner shall be entitled to purchase a fraction of the available interest, up to the amount of interest specified in his or her Notice of Intent to Purchase, in the same proportion that the amount of the interest he or she holds bears to the total amount of the company's interest held by all owners electing to purchase.

(f) If the continuing owners decline to purchase all of the available interest that remains, the company *shall* purchase the amount of available interest not purchased by the continuing owners.

(g) The company shall deliver or mail to the current owner or, if different, current holder of the available interest, no later than five business days after the expiration of the continuing owner's period to exercise their option to purchase the available interest, a Notice of Intent to Purchase, that includes the following information:
- the name and address of the company, and the name and title of the officer or employee who can be contacted at the company
- a description and the amount of ownership interest to be purchased by the company and/or each of the continuing owners, and the name and address of each such continuing owner
- the total amount of the interest to be purchased by the company and the continuing owners
- the terms of the purchase according to Section VII of this agreement
- a copy of the buy-sell agreement, and
- if the interest to be purchased is represented by certificates, such as share certificates, the notice should request their surrender to the company.

(h) The company and the continuing owners shall purchase the available interest each has exercised an option to purchase according to the terms specified in Section VII of this agreement, each making payment for the interest to be purchased and complying with other terms as appropriate. The sale shall be considered final when the company and the continuing owners make payment to the owner or holder of the interest or, if payment is made over time, when all paperwork necessary to the sale has been executed by the company, the continuing owners and the owner or holder of the interest to be purchased.

Section V: Funding

(1) Life Insurance
You may check Option 1 or Option 2 (or neither) below if you checked Option 1 or Option 2 under Section III, Scenario 3, Death, above. Check Option 1 for company-purchased life insurance, Option 2 for owner-purchased life insurance.

☐ **Option 1: Company-purchased life insurance**
The company will apply for, own and be the beneficiary of life insurance policies on the life of each owner. The company will take any actions necessary to maintain in force all of the insurance policies it is required to maintain under this section, including paying all premiums, and will not cancel them or allow them to lapse. The policy benefits shall be applied to the purchase price in a buyout of a deceased owner.

☐ **Option 2: Owner-purchased life insurance**
Each owner will apply for, own and be the beneficiary of life insurance policies on the life of each other owner. Each owner will take any actions necessary to maintain in force all of the insurance policies it is required to maintain under this section, including paying all premiums, and will not cancel them or allow them to lapse. The policy benefits shall be applied to the purchase price in a buyout of a deceased owner.

(2) Disability Insurance
You may check Option 1 or Option 2 (or neither) below if you checked Option 1 or Option 2 under Section III, Scenario 2, Disability, above. Check Option 1 for company-purchased disability insurance, Option 2 for owner-purchased disability insurance.

☐ **Option 1: Company-purchased disability insurance**
The company will apply for, own and be the beneficiary of disability insurance policies for each owner. The company will take any actions necessary to maintain in force all of the insurance policies it is required to maintain under this section, including paying all premiums, and will not cancel them or allow them to lapse. The policy benefits shall be applied to the purchase price in a buyout of a disabled owner.

☐ **Option 2: Owner-purchased disability insurance**
Each owner will apply for, own and be the beneficiary of disability insurance policies for each other owner. Each owner will take any actions necessary to maintain in force all of the insurance policies it is required to maintain under this section, including paying all premiums, and will not cancel them or allow them to lapse. The policy benefits shall be applied to the purchase price in a buyout of a disabled owner.

Section VI: Agreement Price

Unless otherwise provided in this agreement, the undersigned agree that the method checker, below for valuing the company shall be used to determine a price for ownership interests u⸱der this agreement.

You must check one and only one of the valuation methods below:

☐ **Valuation Method 1: Agreed Value**
The agreed value of the company shall be $_____, or such other am⸱unt as fixed by all owners of the company after the date of adoption of this agreement as sⱼecified in a written statement signed by each owner of the company. If more than one such statement is signed by the owners after the date of adoption of this agreement, the statement with the latest date shall control for purposes of fixing a price for the purchase of ownership interests under this agreement. The value of an individual owner's interest shall be the entire value for the company as determined under this paragraph, multiplied by his or her ownership percentage.

☐ **Valuation Method 2: Book Value**

The value of the company shall be its book value (its assets minus its liabilities as shown on the balance sheet of the company) as of the end of the most recent fiscal year prior to the purchase of an ownership interest under this agreement. The value of an individual owner's interest shall be the entire value for the company as determined under this paragraph, multiplied by his or her ownership percentage.

☐ **Valuation Method 3: Multiple of Book Value**

The value of the company shall be _____ times its book value (its assets minus its liabilities as shown on the balance sheet of the company) as of the end of the most recent fiscal year prior to the purchase of an ownership interest under this agreement. The value of an individual owner's interest shall be the entire value for the company as determined under this paragraph, multiplied by his or her ownership percentage.

☐ **Valuation Method 4: Capitalization of Earnings (Adjusted for Income Taxes)**

The value of the company shall be determined on the basis of _____ times the average net earnings (annual gross revenues of the company minus annual expenses and minus any annual federal, state and local income taxes payable by the company) for the _____ fiscal years of the company (or the number of fiscal years the company has been in existence, if fewer) that have occurred prior to the purchase of an ownership interest under this agreement. The value of an individual owner's interest shall be the entire value for the company as determined under this paragraph, multiplied by his or her ownership percentage.

☐ **Valuation Method 5: Appraised Value**

The value of the company shall be its fair market value as determined by an independent appraiser mutually selected by Buyer(s) and Seller of the ownership interest subject to purchase under this agreement. If Buyer(s) and Seller are unable to agree upon an independent appraiser within 30 days, Buyer(s) and Seller, within the next 10 days, shall each select an independent appraiser. If the two selected appraisers are unable, within 60 days, to agree on the fair market value of the company, then the two appraisers shall select a third independent appraiser within the next 10 days, who shall, within 30 days, determine the fair market value of the company. All costs of an appraiser mutually selected by Buyer(s) and Seller or of a third appraiser selected by two appraisers shall be shared equally by Buyer(s) and Seller. All costs of an individually selected appraiser shall be paid by the party selecting the appraiser. The value of an individual owner's interest shall be the entire value for the company as determined under this paragraph, multiplied by his or her ownership percentage.

Section VII: Payment Terms

Unless otherwise provided in this agreement, the undersigned agree that the payment terms checked below shall be used for the purchase of ownership interests under this agreement.

You must check one and only one of the payment terms alternatives below:

☐ **Payment Terms Alternative 1: Full Cash Payment**

Cash payment for the Seller's ownership interest shall be made by Buyer(s) to Seller within _____ days of the date the company provides a Notice of Intent to Purchase to the Seller under this agreement.

☐ **Payment Terms Alternative 2: Monthly Installments of Principal and Interest**

Buyer(s) shall pay Seller the purchase price for an ownership interest in equal installments over a term of _____ months, with interest added to the amount of each installment computed at an annual rate of _____ and compounded annually on the unpaid continuing balance of the purchase price of the ownership interest. The first installment payment shall be made to Seller by Buyer(s) on _____, and the continuing payments shall be made to Seller by Buyer(s) on the _____ of every month, until the full purchase price, together with any interest owed, is paid in full.

☐ **Payment Terms Alternative 3: Partial Cash Payment, Followed by Monthly Installments of Principal and Interest**

The purchase of an ownership interest shall be accomplished as follows: An initial cash payment of _____ shall be paid by Buyer(s) to Seller within _____ days of the date the company provides a Notice of Intent to Purchase to Seller. The remainder of the purchase price shall be paid by Buyer(s) to Seller in equal installments over a term of _____ months, with interest added to the amount of each installment computed at an annual rate of _____ % and compounded annually on the unpaid continuing balance of the purchase price of the ownership interest. The first installment payment shall be made by Buyer(s) on _____, and the continuing payments shall be made by Buyer(s) on the _____ of every month, until the full balance of the purchase price, together with any interest owed, is paid in full.

☐ **Payment Terms Alternative 4: Monthly Installments of Interest Only, With a Final Payment for the Full Purchase Price**

Buyer(s) shall pay Seller the purchase price for an ownership interest on _____ _____. Until such date, Buyer(s) shall pay Seller monthly payments of interest, computed at an annual rate of _____% on the purchase price for the ownership interest. The first installment payment of interest shall be made by Buyer(s) on _____, and the continuing installment payments of interest shall be made by Buyer(s) on the _____ of every month, until payment of the full amount of the purchase price by Buyer(s) as specified above. On the date for full payment of the purchase price by Buyer(s), interest owed on the purchase price from the date of the last payment of interest by Buyer(s) to the date of payment of the purchase price shall be added to and included with the payment of the purchase price by Buyer(s).

☐ **Payment Terms Alternative 5: Customized Schedule for Payment for Ownership Interest**

Buyer(s) shall pay Seller the purchase price for the ownership interest according to the schedule and other terms included below:

_____

_____

_____

_____

_____

_____

_____

_____

_____

Section VIII: Resolution of Disputes

Mediation Followed by Arbitration

Except as may otherwise be provided in this agreement or a later one dated and signed by all owners, any dispute concerning the contents of this agreement, if it cannot be settled through direct negotiation, shall first be submitted to mediation according to the terms specified below. All parties agree to try in good faith to settle the dispute by mediation before resorting to arbitration or litigation.

(a) An owner, an owner's legal representative, the spouse or ex-spouse of an owner, the executor or administrator of a deceased owner's estate or any other party with an interest in this company who wishes to have a dispute mediated shall submit a written request for mediation to each of the other owners of the company. Mediation shall commence within 15 days after the date of the written request for mediation.

(b) Any decision reached by mediation shall be reduced to writing, signed by all parties, and shall be binding on each party. The costs of mediation shall be shared equally by all parties to the dispute.

(c) Each party to the mediation process shall cooperate fully and fairly with the mediator in any attempt to reach a mutually satisfactory compromise to a dispute. If the dispute is not resolved within 30 days after it is referred to the mediator, the dispute shall be submitted for arbitration according to the terms specified below or on terms agreeable to all parties at the time the dispute is submitted to arbitration.

(d) Within 15 days of the delivery of the notice of intention to proceed to arbitration to all parties, each party shall reply in writing to the arbitrator, stating his or her views of the nature and appropriate outcome of the dispute.

(e) The arbitrator shall hold a hearing on the dispute within 15 days after replies have been received from all parties, or, if all replies have not been received, no later than 30 days after the giving of notice of intention to proceed to arbitration.

(f) At the arbitration hearing, each party shall be entitled to present any oral or written statements he or she wishes and may present witnesses. The arbitrator shall make his or her decision in writing, and his or her decision shall be conclusive and binding on all parties to the dispute.

(g) The cost of arbitration, including any lawyer's fees, shall be borne by the parties to the dispute equally unless the arbitrator directs otherwise.

Section IX: Placement of Notice of Transfer Restrictions on Certificates

(a) The following statement must appear conspicuously on each ownership certificate issued by the company:
THE INTERESTS REPRESENTED BY THIS CERTIFICATE ARE SUBJECT TO RESTRICTIONS UPON TRANSFER AND ARE REDEEMABLE PURSUANT TO PROVISIONS CONTAINED IN AN AGREEMENT AMONG THE OWNERS OF THE COMPANY. FOR A COPY OF THIS AGREEMENT, CONTACT THE SECRETARY OR EQUIVALENT OFFICER OF THE COMPANY AT THE PRINCIPAL OFFICE OF THE COMPANY AT _____
_____ .

(b) The secretary or other equivalent officer of the company shall provide to any owner or third person upon written request and without charge a copy of this agreement.

Section X: Continuation of Restrictions

All heirs, successors and assigns to an ownership interest in the company will be bound by the terms of this agreement.

Before receiving a purchased, donated or otherwise transferred interest from an owner or an owner's legal representative, the owner or the owner's legal representative will require any purchaser, donee or transferee, and his or her spouse, to sign this buy-sell agreement, agreeing to be bound by its terms.

Section XI: Signatures

1) Signatures of Owners

Each undersigned owner of the company acknowledges that he or she has read and understands the restrictions, limitations, conditions and other terms and provisions contained in the above agreement. Each has had the opportunity to consult with independent counsel. Each hereby expressly agrees to be bound by these restrictions, limitations, conditions and other terms and provisions, including terms for the valuation and sale of shares of the company.

Signature of Owner:_____ Date:_____

Printed Name of Owner_____

Signature of Owner:_____ Date:_____

Printed Name of Owner_____

Signature of Owner:_____ Date:_____

Printed Name of Owner_____

Signature of Owner:_____ Date:_____

Printed Name of Owner_____

2) Signatures of Spouses

Each undersigned spouse of an owner of the company acknowledges that he or she has read and understands the restrictions, limitations, conditions and other terms and provisions contained in the above agreement. Each has had the opportunity to consult with independent counsel. Each hereby expressly agrees to be bound by these restrictions, limitations, conditions and other terms and provisions, including terms for the valuation and sale of shares of the company.

Signature of Spouse:_____ Date:_____

Printed Name of Spouse_____

Signature of Spouse:_____ Date:_____

Printed Name of Spouse_____

Signature of Spouse:_____ Date:_____

Printed Name of Spouse_____

Signature of Spouse:_____ Date:_____

Printed Name of Spouse_____

Index

CATALOG

...more from Nolo Press

CALL 800-992-6656 OR USE THE ORDER FORM IN THE BACK OF THE BOOK

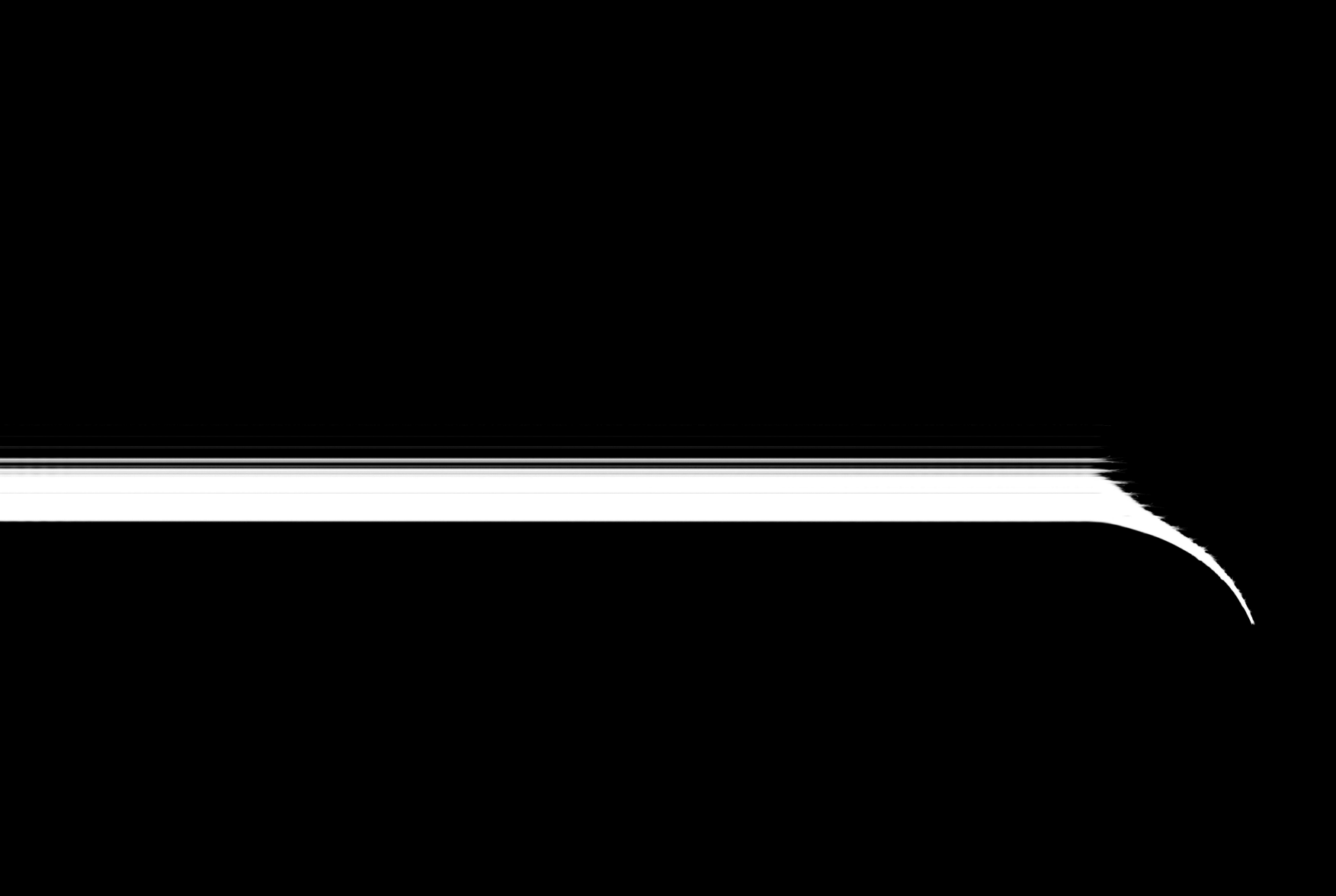

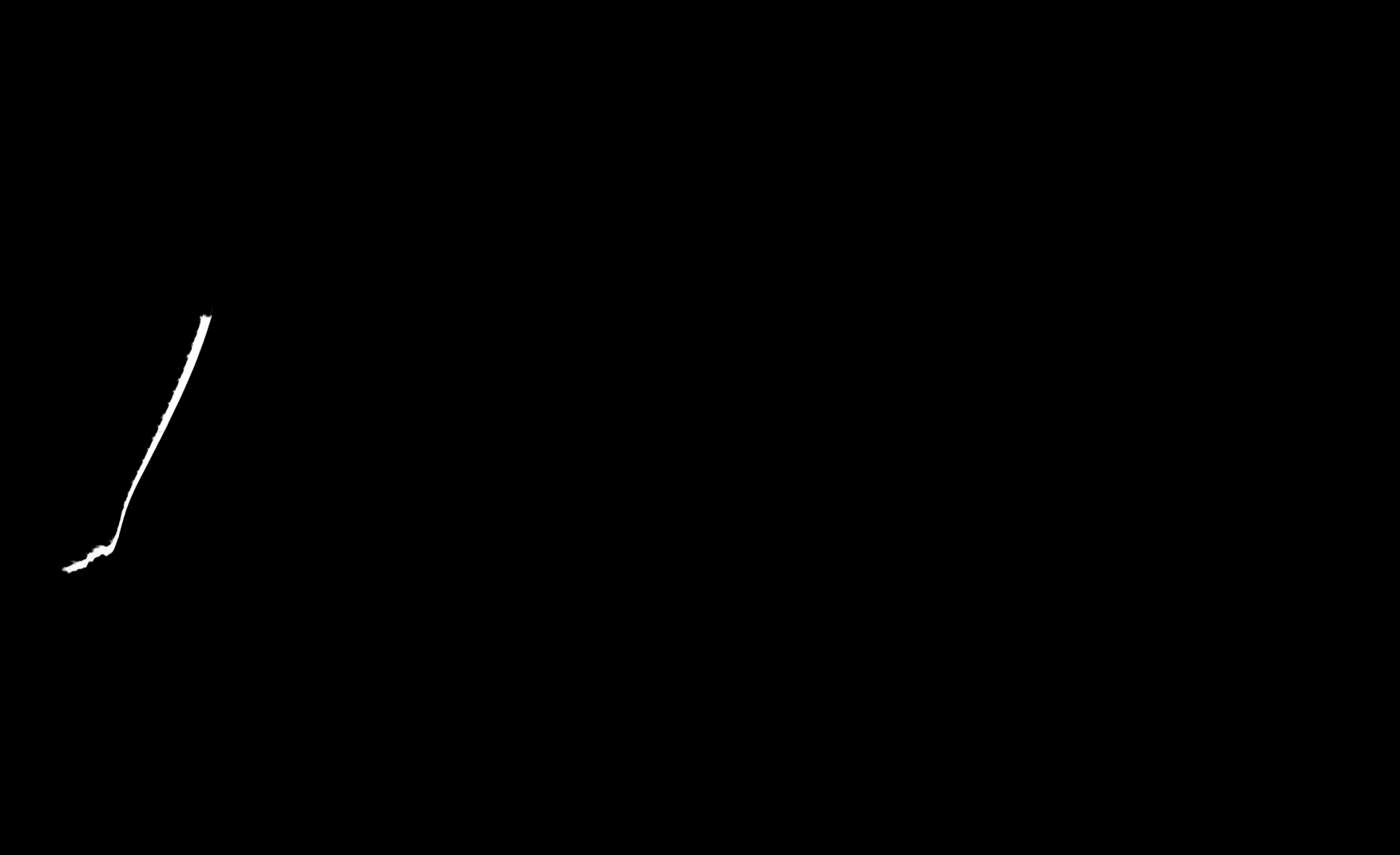

	PRICE	CODE

ESTATE PLANNING & PROBATE

8 Ways to Avoid Probate (Quick & Legal Series)	$15.95	PRO8
9 Ways to Avoid Estate Taxes (Quick & Legal Series)	$22.95	ESTX
How to Probate an Estate (California Edition)	$39.95	PAE
Make Your Own Living Trust	$24.95	LITR
Nolo's Law Form Kit: Wills	$14.95	KWL
Nolo's Will Book (Book w/Disk—PC)	$29.95	SWIL
Plan Your Estate	$24.95	NEST
Quick & Legal Will Book (Quick & Legal Series)	$15.95	QUIC

FAMILY MATTERS

Child Custody: Building Parenting Agreements That Work	$26.95	CUST
The Complete IEP Guide	$24.95	IEP
Divorce & Money: How to Make the Best Financial Decisions During Divorce	$26.95	DIMO
Do Your Own Divorce in Oregon	$19.95	ODIV
Get a Life: You Don't Need a Million to Retire Well	$18.95	LIFE
The Guardianship Book (California Edition)	$39.95	GB
How to Adopt Your Stepchild in California	$34.95	ADOP
How to Raise or Lower Child Support in California (Quick & Legal Series)	$19.95	CHLD
A Legal Guide for Lesbian and Gay Couples	$25.95	LG
The Living Together Kit	$29.95	LTK
Nolo's Pocket Guide to Family Law	$14.95	FLD
Using Divorce Mediation: Save Your Money & Your Sanity	$21.95	UDMD

GOING TO COURT

Beta Your Ticket: Go To Court and Win! (National Edition)	$19.95	BEYT
Collect Your Court Judgment (California Edition)	$29.95	JUDG
The Criminal Law Handbook: Know Your Rights, Survive the System	$24.95	KYR
Everybody's Guide to Small Claims Court (National Edition)	$18.95	NSCC
Everybody's Guide to Small Claims Court in California	$18.95	CSCC
Fight Your Ticket ... and Win! (California Edition)	$19.95	FYT
How to Change Your Name in California	$34.95	NAME
How to Mediate Your Dispute	$18.95	MEDI
How to Seal Your Juvenile & Criminal Records (California Edition)	$24.95	CRIM
How to Sue For Up to $25,000...and Win!	$29.95	MUNI
Mad at Your Lawyer	$21.95	MAD
Represent Yourself in Court: How to Prepare & Try a Winning Case	$29.95	RYC

HOMEOWNERS, LANDLORDS & TENANTS

Contractors' and Homeowners' Guide to Mechanics' Liens (Book w/Disk—PC)	$39.95	MIEN
The Deeds Book (California Edition)	$24.95	DEED
Dog Law	$14.95	DOG
Every Landlord's Legal Guide (National Edition, Book w/Disk—PC)	$34.95	ELLI
Every Tenant's Legal Guide	$26.95	EVTEN
For Sale by Owner in California	$24.95	FSBO
How to Buy a House in California	$24.95	BHCA
The Landlord's Law Book, Vol. 1: Rights & Responsibilities (California Edition)	$34.95	LBRT
The Landlord's Law Book, Vol. 2: Evictions (California Edition)	$34.95	LBEV
Leases & Rental Agreements (Quick & Legal Series)	$18.95	LEAR
Neighbor Law: Fences, Trees, Boundaries & Noise	$17.95	NEI
Renters' Rights (National Edition—Quick & Legal Series))	$15.95	RENT
Stop Foreclosure Now in California	$29.95	CLOS
Tenants' Rights (California Edition)	$21.95	CTEN

HUMOR

29 Reasons Not to Go to Law School	$9.95	29R
Poetic Justice	$9.95	PJ

Book with disk

Book with CD-ROM

CALL 800-992-6656 OR USE THE ORDER FORM IN THE BACK OF THE BOOK

		PRICE	CODE

IMMIGRATION

How to Get a Green Card: Legal Ways to Stay in the U.S.A.	$24.95	GRN
U.S. Immigration Made Easy	$44.95	IMEZ

MONEY MATTERS

101 Law Forms for Personal Use (Quick & Legal Series, Book w/disk—PC)	$24.95	SPOT
Bankruptcy: Is It the Right Solution to Your Debt Problems? (Quick & Legal Series)	$15.95	BRS
Chapter 13 Bankruptcy: Repay Your Debts	$29.95	CH13
Credit Repair (Quick & Legal Series)	$15.95	CREP
The Financial Power of Attorney Workbook (Book w/disk—PC)	$24.95	FINPOA
How to File for Chapter 7 Bankruptcy	$26.95	HFB
IRAs, 401(k)s & Other Retirement Plans: Taking Your Money Out	$21.95	RET
Money Troubles: Legal Strategies to Cope With Your Debts	$19.95	MT
Nolo's Law Form Kit: Personal Bankruptcy	$16.95	KBNK
Stand Up to the IRS	$24.95	SIRS
Take Control of Your Student Loans	$19.95	SLOAN

PATENTS AND COPYRIGHTS

The Copyright Handbook: How to Protect and Use Written Works (Book w/disk—PC)	$29.95	COHA
Copyright Your Software	$24.95	CYS
How to Make Patent Drawings Yourself	$29.95	DRAW
The Inventor's Notebook	$19.95	INOT
License Your Invention (Book w/Disk—PC)	$39.95	LICE
Patent, Copyright & Trademark	$24.95	PCTM
Patent It Yourself	$46.95	PAT
Patent Searching Made Easy	$24.95	PATSE
Software Development: A Legal Guide (Book with CD-ROM)	$44.95	SFT

RESEARCH & REFERENCE

Government on the Net (Book w/CD-ROM—Windows/Macintosh)	$39.95	GONE
Law on the Net (Book w/CD-ROM—Windows/Macintosh)	$39.95	LAWN
Legal Research: How to Find & Understand the Law	$24.95	LRES
Legal Research Made Easy (Video)	$89.95	LRME
Legal Research Online & in the Library (Book w/CD-ROM—Windows/Macintosh)	$39.95	LRO

SENIORS

Beat the Nursing Home Trap	$21.95	ELD
The Conservatorship Book (California Edition)	$44.95	CNSV
Social Security, Medicare & Pensions	$21.95	SOA

SOFTWARE

Call or check our website at www.nolo.com for special discounts on Software!

LeaseWriter CD—Windows/Macintosh	$99.95	LWD1
Living Trust Maker CD—Windows/Macintosh	$79.95	LTD2
Small Business Legal Pro 3 CD—Windows/Macintosh	$79.95	SBCD3
Personal RecordKeeper 5.0 CD—Windows/Macintosh	$59.95	RKD5
Patent It Yourself CD—Windows	$229.95	PPC12
WillMaker 7.0 CD—Windows/Macintosh	$69.95	WMD7

Special Upgrade Offer
Get 25% off the latest edition of your Nolo book

It's important to have the most current legal information. Because laws and legal procedures change often, we update our books regularly. To help keep you up-to-date we are extending this special upgrade offer. Cut out and mail the title portion of the cover of your old Nolo book and we'll give you 25% off the retail price of the NEW EDITION of that book when you purchase directly from us. For more information call us at 1-800-992-6656. This offer is to individuals only.

◨ Book with disk

◉ Book with CD-ROM

ORDER FORM

Code	Quantity	Title	Unit price	Total
		Subtotal		
		California residents add Sales Tax		
		Basic Shipping ($6.50)		
		UPS RUSH delivery $8.00–any size order*		
		TOTAL		

Name

Address

(UPS to street address, Priority Mail to P.O. boxes)   * Delivered in 3 business days from receipt of order.
S.F. Bay Area use regular shipping.

FOR FASTER SERVICE, USE YOUR CREDIT CARD AND OUR TOLL-FREE NUMBERS

Order 24 hours a day   1-800-992-6656

Fax your order   1-800-645-0895

Online   www.nolo.com

METHOD OF PAYMENT

☐ Check enclosed

☐ VISA   ☐ MasterCard   ☐ Discover Card   ☐ American Express

Account #   Expiration Date

Authorizing Signature

Daytime Phone

PRICES SUBJECT TO CHANGE.

VISIT OUR OUTLET STORES!   VISIT US ONLINE!

You'll find our complete line of books and software, all at a discount.

BERKELEY
950 Parker Street
Berkeley, CA 94710
1-510-704-2248

on the Internet
www.nolo.com

NOLO PRESS 950 PARKER ST., BERKELEY, CA 94710

more from
NOLO PRESS

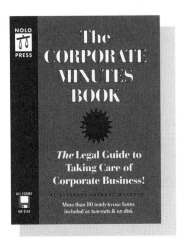

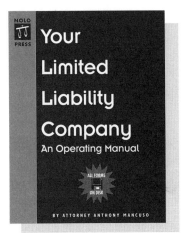

The Corporate Minutes Book

The Legal Guide to Taking Care of Corporate Business

Attorney Anthony Mancuso

If you've taken the time to turn your business into a corporation, chances are you'd like to see it stay that way. Your business card may say "incorporated," but if the courts and the IRS think differently, it's closing time.

Because meeting minutes are the primary paper trail of a corporation's legal life, it's important to know when and how to prepare these minutes. *The Corporate Minutes Book* provides all the answers, instructions and forms you need to get the job done. Tear-out and disk minutes forms include:

- Call of Meeting
- Meeting Participant List
- Shareholder Proxy
- Meeting Summary Sheet
- Minutes of Annual Shareholders' Meeting
- Approval of Corporate Minutes By Directors of Shareholders
- Cover Letter for Approval of Minutes of Paper Meeting
- Written Consent to Action Without Meeting.

$69.95/CORMI

Your Limited Liability Company

An Operating Manual

by Attorney Anthony Mancuso

Your Limited Liability Company gives you the necessary tools to maintain the legal validity of your LLC before the courts and the IRS. It helps you approve and document important legal, tax and business decisions to create a paper trail that avoids disputes among LLC owners later. Learn how to:

- prepare minutes of manager and membership meetings
- record important legal, tax and business decisions
- handle formal recordkeeping
- fill out an LLC Records Book.

Written by corporations expert Attorney Anthony Mancuso, *Your Limited Liability Company* provides checklists, minute forms, written consents, and more than 80, ready-to-use resolutions forms—both as tear-outs and on disk.

$49.95/LOP

800-992-6656 or www.nolo.com